Just The facts101

Textbook Key Facts

Kuwait Country Study Guide

by Cram101
Textbook NOT Included

Table of Contents

Just The Facts101

Exam Prep for

Kuwait Country Study Guide

Just The Facts101 Exam Prep is your link from
the texbook and lecture to your exams.

**Just The Facts101 Exam Preps are unauthorized and comprehensive reviews
of your textbooks.**

Just The Facts101 Exam Prep

eAIN 442387

Foundations of Business

A business, also known as an enterprise, agency or a firm, is an entity involved in the provision of goods and/or services to consumers. Businesses are prevalent in capitalist economies, where most of them are privately owned and provide goods and services to customers in exchange for other goods, services, or money.

:: Euthenics ::

_____ is an ethical framework and suggests that an entity, be it an organization or individual, has an obligation to act for the benefit of society at large. _____ is a duty every individual has to perform so as to maintain a balance between the economy and the ecosystems. A trade-off may exist between economic development, in the material sense, and the welfare of the society and environment, though this has been challenged by many reports over the past decade. _____ means sustaining the equilibrium between the two. It pertains not only to business organizations but also to everyone whose any action impacts the environment. This responsibility can be passive, by avoiding engaging in socially harmful acts, or active, by performing activities that directly advance social goals. _____ must be intergenerational since the actions of one generation have consequences on those following.

Exam Probability: **High**

1. *Answer choices:*

(see index for correct answer)

- a. Family and consumer science
- b. Home economics
- c. Minnie Cumnock Blodgett
- d. Euthenics

Guidance: level 1

:: Production and manufacturing ::

_____ is a set of techniques and tools for process improvement. Though as a shortened form it may be found written as 6S, it should not be confused with the methodology known as 6S .

Exam Probability: **Medium**

2. *Answer choices:*

(see index for correct answer)

- a. Nesting
- b. International MTM Directorate
- c. Bill of materials
- d. Six Sigma

Guidance: level 1

:: Information science ::

A _____ is a written, drawn, presented, or memorialized representation of thought. a _____ is a form, or written piece that trains a line of thought or as in history, a significant event. The word originates from the Latin _____ um, which denotes a "teaching" or "lesson": the verb doceo denotes "to teach". In the past, the word was usually used to denote a written proof useful as evidence of a truth or fact. In the computer age, " _____ " usually denotes a primarily textual computer file, including its structure and format, e.g. fonts, colors, and images. Contemporarily, " _____ " is not defined by its transmission medium, e.g., paper, given the existence of electronic _____ s. " _____ ation" is distinct because it has more denotations than " _____ ". _____ s are also distinguished from "realia", which are three-dimensional objects that would otherwise satisfy the definition of " _____ " because they memorialize or represent thought; _____ s are considered more as 2 dimensional representations. While _____ s are able to have large varieties of customization, all _____ s are able to be shared freely, and have the right to do so, creativity can be represented by _____ s, also. History, events, examples, opinion, etc. all can be expressed in _____ s.

Exam Probability: **Low**

3. *Answer choices:*

(see index for correct answer)

- a. Actionable information logistics
- b. Document
- c. Information architecture
- d. Source criticism

Guidance: level 1

:: Generally Accepted Accounting Principles ::

In business and accounting, _____ is an entity's income minus cost of goods sold, expenses and taxes for an accounting period. It is computed as the residual of all revenues and gains over all expenses and losses for the period, and has also been defined as the net increase in shareholders' equity that results from a company's operations. In the context of the presentation of financial statements, the IFRS Foundation defines _____ as synonymous with profit and loss. The difference between revenue and the cost of making a product or providing a service, before deducting overheads, payroll, taxation, and interest payments. This is different from operating income .

Exam Probability: **Medium**

4. *Answer choices:*

(see index for correct answer)

- a. Net income
- b. Treasury stock
- c. Standard Business Reporting
- d. Profit

Guidance: level 1

:: ::

Business is the activity of making one's living or making money by producing or buying and selling products . Simply put, it is "any activity or enterprise entered into for profit. It does not mean it is a company, a corporation, partnership, or have any such formal organization, but it can range from a street peddler to General Motors."

Exam Probability: **Low**

5. *Answer choices:*

(see index for correct answer)

- a. co-culture
- b. cultural
- c. Firm
- d. empathy

Guidance: level 1

:: International trade ::

The law or principle of _____ holds that under free trade, an agent will produce more of and consume less of a good for which they have a _____ . _____ is the economic reality describing the work gains from trade for individuals, firms, or nations, which arise from differences in their factor endowments or technological progress. In an economic model, agents have a _____ over others in producing a particular good if they can produce that good at a lower relative opportunity cost or autarky price, i.e. at a lower relative marginal cost prior to trade. One shouldn`t compare the monetary costs of production or even the resource costs of production. Instead, one must compare the opportunity costs of producing goods across countries.

Exam Probability: **High**

6. *Answer choices:*

(see index for correct answer)

- a. Comparative advantage
- b. Neomercantilism
- c. Intervention stocks
- d. Portuguese India Armadas

Guidance: level 1

:: Marketing ::

A _____ is an overall experience of a customer that distinguishes an organization or product from its rivals in the eyes of the customer. _____ s are used in business, marketing, and advertising. Name _____ s are sometimes distinguished from generic or store _____ s.

7. *Answer choices:*

(see index for correct answer)

- a. City marketing
- b. Brand
- c. Medical science liaison
- d. Predatory pricing

Guidance: level 1

:: Telecommunication theory ::

In reliability theory and reliability engineering, the term _____ has the following meanings.

Exam Probability: **Low**

8. *Answer choices:*

(see index for correct answer)

- a. Propagation constant
- b. Asynchronous operation
- c. Pulse duration
- d. Intersymbol interference

:: Environmental economics ::

_____ is the process of people maintaining change in a balanced environment, in which the exploitation of resources, the direction of investments, the orientation of technological development and institutional change are all in harmony and enhance both current and future potential to meet human needs and aspirations. For many in the field, _____ is defined through the following interconnected domains or pillars: environment, economic and social, which according to Fritjof Capra is based on the principles of Systems Thinking. Sub-domains of sustainable development have been considered also: cultural, technological and political. While sustainable development may be the organizing principle for _____ for some, for others, the two terms are paradoxical . Sustainable development is the development that meets the needs of the present without compromising the ability of future generations to meet their own needs. Brundtland Report for the World Commission on Environment and Development introduced the term of sustainable development.

Exam Probability: **Medium**

9. *Answer choices:*
(see index for correct answer)

- a. Sustainability
- b. Peak water
- c. World3
- d. Centre for Water Economics, Environment and Policy

:: Financial statements ::

In financial accounting, a _____ or statement of financial position or statement of financial condition is a summary of the financial balances of an individual or organization, whether it be a sole proprietorship, a business partnership, a corporation, private limited company or other organization such as Government or not-for-profit entity. Assets, liabilities and ownership equity are listed as of a specific date, such as the end of its financial year. A _____ is often described as a "snapshot of a company's financial condition". Of the four basic financial statements, the _____ is the only statement which applies to a single point in time of a business' calendar year.

Exam Probability: **Low**

10. *Answer choices:*

(see index for correct answer)

- a. Consolidated financial statement
- b. Financial statement
- c. Statement on Auditing Standards No. 55
- d. Statements on auditing standards

Guidance: level 1

:: Business planning ::

_____ is an organization's process of defining its strategy, or direction, and making decisions on allocating its resources to pursue this strategy. It may also extend to control mechanisms for guiding the implementation of the strategy. _____ became prominent in corporations during the 1960s and remains an important aspect of strategic management. It is executed by strategic planners or strategists, who involve many parties and research sources in their analysis of the organization and its relationship to the environment in which it competes.

Exam Probability: **Low**

11. *Answer choices:*

(see index for correct answer)

- a. Gap analysis
- b. Open Options Corporation
- c. Customer Demand Planning
- d. Strategic planning

Guidance: level 1

:: Business terms ::

A _____ is a short statement of why an organization exists, what its overall goal is, identifying the goal of its operations: what kind of product or service it provides, its primary customers or market, and its geographical region of operation. It may include a short statement of such fundamental matters as the organization's values or philosophies, a business's main competitive advantages, or a desired future state—the "vision".

12. *Answer choices:*

(see index for correct answer)

- a. churn rate
- b. Owner Controlled Insurance Program
- c. Personal selling
- d. operating cost

Guidance: level 1

:: Treaties ::

An _____ is a relationship among people, groups, or states that have joined together for mutual benefit or to achieve some common purpose, whether or not explicit agreement has been worked out among them. Members of an _____ are called allies. _____ s form in many settings, including political _____ s, military _____ s, and business _____ s. When the term is used in the context of war or armed struggle, such associations may also be called allied powers, especially when discussing World War I or World War II.

Exam Probability: **Low**

13. *Answer choices:*

(see index for correct answer)

- a. Full Powers
- b. Alliance
- c. Multilateral treaty
- d. Investor state dispute settlement

Guidance: level 1

:: Strategic management ::

_____ is a strategic planning technique used to help a person or organization identify strengths, weaknesses, opportunities, and threats related to business competition or project planning. It is intended to specify the objectives of the business venture or project and identify the internal and external factors that are favorable and unfavorable to achieving those objectives. Users of a _____ often ask and answer questions to generate meaningful information for each category to make the tool useful and identify their competitive advantage. SWOT has been described as the tried-and-true tool of strategic analysis.

Exam Probability: **Low**

14. *Answer choices:*
(see index for correct answer)

- a. SWOT analysis
- b. Strategic delegation
- c. Outsights
- d. Delta model

:: Marketing ::

_____ or stock is the goods and materials that a business holds for the ultimate goal of resale .

Exam Probability: **Medium**

15. *Answer choices:*

(see index for correct answer)

- a. Product category volume
- b. Gladvertising
- c. Interactive marketing
- d. Masstige

:: Currency ::

A _____ , in the most specific sense is money in any form when in use or circulation as a medium of exchange, especially circulating banknotes and coins. A more general definition is that a _____ is a system of money in common use, especially for people in a nation. Under this definition, US dollars , pounds sterling , Australian dollars , European euros , Russian rubles and Indian Rupees are examples of currencies. These various currencies are recognized as stores of value and are traded between nations in foreign exchange markets, which determine the relative values of the different currencies. Currencies in this sense are defined by governments, and each type has limited boundaries of acceptance.

Exam Probability: **High**

16. *Answer choices:*

(see index for correct answer)

- a. York rating
- b. Donationcoin
- c. Mutilated currency
- d. Remonetisation

Guidance: level 1

:: ::

_____ is the collection of mechanisms, processes and relations by which corporations are controlled and operated. Governance structures and principles identify the distribution of rights and responsibilities among different participants in the corporation and include the rules and procedures for making decisions in corporate affairs. _____ is necessary because of the possibility of conflicts of interests between stakeholders, primarily between shareholders and upper management or among shareholders.

Exam Probability: **High**

17. *Answer choices:*

(see index for correct answer)

- a. cultural
- b. deep-level diversity
- c. hierarchical perspective
- d. surface-level diversity

Guidance: level 1

:: Management ::

A _____ is a formal written document containing business goals, the methods on how these goals can be attained, and the time frame within which these goals need to be achieved. It also describes the nature of the business, background information on the organization, the organization's financial projections, and the strategies it intends to implement to achieve the stated targets. In its entirety, this document serves as a road map that provides direction to the business.

18. *Answer choices:*

(see index for correct answer)

- a. IT performance management
- b. Business value
- c. Business plan
- d. Peer pressure

Guidance: level 1

:: Systems theory ::

A _____ is a set of policies, processes and procedures used by an organization to ensure that it can fulfill the tasks required to achieve its objectives. These objectives cover many aspects of the organization's operations . For instance, an environmental _____ enables organizations to improve their environmental performance and an occupational health and safety _____ enables an organization to control its occupational health and safety risks, etc.

Exam Probability: **Medium**

19. *Answer choices:*

(see index for correct answer)

- a. steady state

- b. process system
- c. equifinality
- d. co-design

Guidance: level 1

:: International trade ::

In finance, an _____ is the rate at which one currency will be exchanged for another. It is also regarded as the value of one country's currency in relation to another currency. For example, an interbank _____ of 114 Japanese yen to the United States dollar means that ¥114 will be exchanged for each US$1 or that US$1 will be exchanged for each ¥114. In this case it is said that the price of a dollar in relation to yen is ¥114, or equivalently that the price of a yen in relation to dollars is $1/114.

Exam Probability: **High**

20. *Answer choices:*
(see index for correct answer)

- a. SinoLatin Capital
- b. Trade in Services Agreement
- c. Northwest Cattle Project
- d. Exchange rate

Guidance: level 1

:: Supply chain management ::

_____ is the process of finding and agreeing to terms, and acquiring goods, services, or works from an external source, often via a tendering or competitive bidding process. _____ is used to ensure the buyer receives goods, services, or works at the best possible price when aspects such as quality, quantity, time, and location are compared. Corporations and public bodies often define processes intended to promote fair and open competition for their business while minimizing risks such as exposure to fraud and collusion.

Exam Probability: **Low**

21. *Answer choices:*

(see index for correct answer)

- a. Keith Oliver
- b. Procurement
- c. Calculating demand forecast accuracy
- d. LLamasoft

Guidance: level 1

:: Business ::

The seller, or the provider of the goods or services, completes a sale in response to an acquisition, appropriation, requisition or a direct interaction with the buyer at the point of sale. There is a passing of title of the item, and the settlement of a price, in which agreement is reached on a price for which transfer of ownership of the item will occur. The seller, not the purchaser typically executes the sale and it may be completed prior to the obligation of payment. In the case of indirect interaction, a person who sells goods or service on behalf of the owner is known as a _____ man or _____ woman or _____ person, but this often refers to someone selling goods in a store/shop, in which case other terms are also common, including _____ clerk, shop assistant, and retail clerk.

Exam Probability: **Medium**

22. *Answer choices:*
(see index for correct answer)

- a. Sales
- b. Open-book contract
- c. Street marketing
- d. Equality impact assessment

Guidance: level 1

:: Management ::

_____ is a process by which entities review the quality of all factors involved in production. ISO 9000 defines _____ as "A part of quality management focused on fulfilling quality requirements".

23. *Answer choices:*

(see index for correct answer)

- a. Court of Assistants
- b. Total Worker Health
- c. Cynefin
- d. Quality control

Guidance: level 1

:: Management ::

A _____ is when two or more people come together to discuss one or more topics, often in a formal or business setting, but _____ s also occur in a variety of other environments. Many various types of _____ s exist.

Exam Probability: **High**

24. *Answer choices:*

(see index for correct answer)

- a. Meeting
- b. Swarm Development Group
- c. I-VMS
- d. Duality

Guidance: level 1

:: Analysis ::

_____ is the process of breaking a complex topic or substance into smaller parts in order to gain a better understanding of it. The technique has been applied in the study of mathematics and logic since before Aristotle , though _____ as a formal concept is a relatively recent development.

Exam Probability: **High**

25. *Answer choices:*

(see index for correct answer)

- a. Proximity analysis
- b. Dialogical analysis
- c. Psychopolitical validity
- d. Hydrogen pinch

Guidance: level 1

:: Rhetoric ::

_____ is the pattern of narrative development that aims to make vivid a place, object, character, or group. _____ is one of four rhetorical modes , along with exposition, argumentation, and narration. In practice it would be difficult to write literature that drew on just one of the four basic modes.

Exam Probability: **High**

26. *Answer choices:*

(see index for correct answer)

- a. Description
- b. Panegyrici Latini
- c. Sardonicism
- d. Facilitas

Guidance: level 1

:: Debt ::

_____ , in finance and economics, is payment from a borrower or deposit-taking financial institution to a lender or depositor of an amount above repayment of the principal sum , at a particular rate. It is distinct from a fee which the borrower may pay the lender or some third party. It is also distinct from dividend which is paid by a company to its shareholders from its profit or reserve, but not at a particular rate decided beforehand, rather on a pro rata basis as a share in the reward gained by risk taking entrepreneurs when the revenue earned exceeds the total costs.

Exam Probability: **Low**

27. *Answer choices:*

(see index for correct answer)

- a. gearing
- b. Borrowing base
- c. Interest
- d. Terminal debt

Guidance: level 1

:: Business law ::

A _____ is a group of people who jointly supervise the activities of an organization, which can be either a for-profit business, nonprofit organization, or a government agency. Such a board's powers, duties, and responsibilities are determined by government regulations and the organization's own constitution and bylaws. These authorities may specify the number of members of the board, how they are to be chosen, and how often they are to meet.

Exam Probability: **High**

28. *Answer choices:*

(see index for correct answer)

- a. Companies law

- b. Undervalue transaction
- c. Board of directors
- d. Business.gov

Guidance: level 1

:: Income ::

_____ is a ratio between the net profit and cost of investment resulting from an investment of some resources. A high ROI means the investment's gains favorably to its cost. As a performance measure, ROI is used to evaluate the efficiency of an investment or to compare the efficiencies of several different investments. In purely economic terms, it is one way of relating profits to capital invested. _____ is a performance measure used by businesses to identify the efficiency of an investment or number of different investments.

Exam Probability: **Medium**

29. *Answer choices:*

(see index for correct answer)

- a. Gratuity
- b. Passive income
- c. Aggregate expenditure
- d. Family income

Guidance: level 1

:: Management accounting ::

In economics, _____ s, indirect costs or overheads are business expenses that are not dependent on the level of goods or services produced by the business. They tend to be time-related, such as interest or rents being paid per month, and are often referred to as overhead costs. This is in contrast to variable costs, which are volume-related and unknown at the beginning of the accounting year. For a simple example, such as a bakery, the monthly rent for the baking facilities, and the monthly payments for the security system and basic phone line are _____ s, as they do not change according to how much bread the bakery produces and sells. On the other hand, the wage costs of the bakery are variable, as the bakery will have to hire more workers if the production of bread increases. Economists reckon _____ as a entry barrier for new entrepreneurs.

Exam Probability: **Medium**

30. *Answer choices:*

(see index for correct answer)

- a. Fixed cost
- b. Institute of Certified Management Accountants
- c. Resource consumption accounting
- d. Double counting

Guidance: level 1

:: Reputation management ::

_____ or image of a social entity is an opinion about that entity, typically as a result of social evaluation on a set of criteria.

Exam Probability: **Medium**

31. *Answer choices:*

(see index for correct answer)

- a. Trust metric
- b. TrustRank
- c. Reputation
- d. Raph Levien

Guidance: level 1

:: Marketing ::

A _____ is a group of customers within a business's serviceable available market at which a business aims its marketing efforts and resources. A _____ is a subset of the total market for a product or service. The _____ typically consists of consumers who exhibit similar characteristics and are considered most likely to buy a business's market offerings or are likely to be the most profitable segments for the business to service.

Exam Probability: **Low**

32. *Answer choices:*

(see index for correct answer)

- a. Carrying cost
- b. Product lining
- c. Target market
- d. Masstige

Guidance: level 1

:: Mereology ::

_____ , in the abstract, is what belongs to or with something, whether as an attribute or as a component of said thing. In the context of this article, it is one or more components , whether physical or incorporeal, of a person's estate; or so belonging to, as in being owned by, a person or jointly a group of people or a legal entity like a corporation or even a society. Depending on the nature of the _____ , an owner of _____ has the right to consume, alter, share, redefine, rent, mortgage, pawn, sell, exchange, transfer, give away or destroy it, or to exclude others from doing these things, as well as to perhaps abandon it; whereas regardless of the nature of the _____ , the owner thereof has the right to properly use it , or at the very least exclusively keep it.

Exam Probability: **High**

33. *Answer choices:*
(see index for correct answer)

- a. Mereology

- b. Simple
- c. Mereological essentialism
- d. Property

Guidance: level 1

:: E-commerce ::

_____ is the activity of buying or selling of products on online services or over the Internet. Electronic commerce draws on technologies such as mobile commerce, electronic funds transfer, supply chain management, Internet marketing, online transaction processing, electronic data interchange , inventory management systems, and automated data collection systems.

Exam Probability: **High**

34. *Answer choices:*

(see index for correct answer)

- a. PaySafe
- b. Maritime E-Commerce Association
- c. Alternative currency
- d. Triton

Guidance: level 1

:: ::

Some scenarios associate "this kind of planning" with learning "life skills".Schedules are necessary, or at least useful, in situations where individuals need to know what time they must be at a specific location to receive a specific service, and where people need to accomplish a set of goals within a set time period.

Exam Probability: **Low**

35. *Answer choices:*

(see index for correct answer)

- a. Scheduling
- b. deep-level diversity
- c. information systems assessment
- d. corporate values

Guidance: level 1

:: ::

A _____ is any person who contracts to acquire an asset in return for some form of consideration.

Exam Probability: **Low**

36. *Answer choices:*

(see index for correct answer)

- a. interpersonal communication
- b. open system
- c. Buyer
- d. empathy

Guidance: level 1

:: Corporate crime ::

_____ LLP, based in Chicago, was an American holding company. Formerly one of the "Big Five" accounting firms , the firm had provided auditing, tax, and consulting services to large corporations. By 2001, it had become one of the world`s largest multinational companies.

Exam Probability: **Low**

37. *Answer choices:*

(see index for correct answer)

- a. Equity Funding
- b. Arthur Andersen
- c. Corporate manslaughter
- d. FirstEnergy

:: Financial accounting ::

_____ is a financial metric which represents operating liquidity available to a business, organisation or other entity, including governmental entities. Along with fixed assets such as plant and equipment, _____ is considered a part of operating capital. Gross _____ is equal to current assets. _____ is calculated as current assets minus current liabilities. If current assets are less than current liabilities, an entity has a _____ deficiency, also called a _____ deficit.

Exam Probability: **Medium**

38. *Answer choices:*

(see index for correct answer)

- a. Valuation
- b. Carry
- c. Working capital
- d. Advance payment

Guidance: level 1

:: Office administration ::

An _____ is generally a room or other area where an organization's employees perform administrative work in order to support and realize objects and goals of the organization. The word " _____ " may also denote a position within an organization with specific duties attached to it ; the latter is in fact an earlier usage, _____ as place originally referring to the location of one's duty. When used as an adjective, the term " _____ " may refer to business-related tasks. In law, a company or organization has _____ s in any place where it has an official presence, even if that presence consists of a storage silo rather than an establishment with desk-and-chair. An _____ is also an architectural and design phenomenon: ranging from a small _____ such as a bench in the corner of a small business of extremely small size , through entire floors of buildings, up to and including massive buildings dedicated entirely to one company. In modern terms an _____ is usually the location where white-collar workers carry out their functions. As per James Stephenson, " _____ is that part of business enterprise which is devoted to the direction and co-ordination of its various activities."

Exam Probability: **High**

39. *Answer choices:*

(see index for correct answer)

- a. Inter departmental communication
- b. Office
- c. Fish! Philosophy
- d. Office administration

Guidance: level 1

:: Information science ::

_____ is the resolution of uncertainty; it is that which answers the question of "what an entity is" and thus defines both its essence and nature of its characteristics. _____ relates to both data and knowledge, as data is meaningful _____ representing values attributed to parameters, and knowledge signifies understanding of a concept. _____ is uncoupled from an observer, which is an entity that can access _____ and thus discern what it specifies; _____ exists beyond an event horizon for example. In the case of knowledge, the _____ itself requires a cognitive observer to be obtained.

Exam Probability: **Medium**

40. *Answer choices:*

(see index for correct answer)

- a. Integrated Operations in the High North
- b. Computational informatics
- c. Information
- d. Bibliometrician

Guidance: level 1

:: ::

_____ is the collection of techniques, skills, methods, and processes used in the production of goods or services or in the accomplishment of objectives, such as scientific investigation. _____ can be the knowledge of techniques, processes, and the like, or it can be embedded in machines to allow for operation without detailed knowledge of their workings. Systems applying _____ by taking an input, changing it according to the system's use, and then producing an outcome are referred to as _____ systems or technological systems.

Exam Probability: **Low**

41. *Answer choices:*

(see index for correct answer)

- a. surface-level diversity
- b. hierarchical
- c. corporate values
- d. cultural

Guidance: level 1

:: Majority–minority relations ::

_____ , also known as reservation in India and Nepal, positive discrimination / action in the United Kingdom, and employment equity in Canada and South Africa, is the policy of promoting the education and employment of members of groups that are known to have previously suffered from discrimination. Historically and internationally, support for _____ has sought to achieve goals such as bridging inequalities in employment and pay, increasing access to education, promoting diversity, and redressing apparent past wrongs, harms, or hindrances.

Exam Probability: **Medium**

42. *Answer choices:*

(see index for correct answer)

- a. Affirmative action
- b. positive discrimination
- c. cultural dissonance

Guidance: level 1

:: ::

An _____ is the production of goods or related services within an economy. The major source of revenue of a group or company is the indicator of its relevant _____ . When a large group has multiple sources of revenue generation, it is considered to be working in different industries. Manufacturing _____ became a key sector of production and labour in European and North American countries during the Industrial Revolution, upsetting previous mercantile and feudal economies. This came through many successive rapid advances in technology, such as the production of steel and coal.

Exam Probability: **High**

43. *Answer choices:*

(see index for correct answer)

- a. levels of analysis
- b. hierarchical perspective
- c. Industry
- d. interpersonal communication

Guidance: level 1

:: Stock market ::

A _____ , securities exchange or bourse, is a facility where stock brokers and traders can buy and sell securities, such as shares of stock and bonds and other financial instruments. _____ s may also provide for facilities the issue and redemption of such securities and instruments and capital events including the payment of income and dividends. Securities traded on a _____ include stock issued by listed companies, unit trusts, derivatives, pooled investment products and bonds. _____ s often function as "continuous auction" markets with buyers and sellers consummating transactions via open outcry at a central location such as the floor of the exchange or by using an electronic trading platform.

Exam Probability: **High**

44. *Answer choices:*

(see index for correct answer)

- a. Stock market data systems
- b. Stock exchange
- c. stock price
- d. Secondary market offering

Guidance: level 1

:: ::

_____ is a means of protection from financial loss. It is a form of risk management, primarily used to hedge against the risk of a contingent or uncertain loss

Exam Probability: **High**

45. *Answer choices:*

(see index for correct answer)

- a. empathy
- b. information systems assessment
- c. hierarchical perspective
- d. Insurance

Guidance: level 1

:: ::

A _____ is an organization, usually a group of people or a company, authorized to act as a single entity and recognized as such in law. Early incorporated entities were established by charter . Most jurisdictions now allow the creation of new _____ s through registration.

Exam Probability: **Medium**

46. *Answer choices:*

(see index for correct answer)

- a. functional perspective
- b. Sarbanes-Oxley act of 2002
- c. Corporation

- d. imperative

Guidance: level 1

:: Credit cards ::

The _____ Company, also known as Amex, is an American multinational financial services corporation headquartered in Three World Financial Center in New York City. The company was founded in 1850 and is one of the 30 components of the Dow Jones Industrial Average. The company is best known for its charge card, credit card, and traveler's cheque businesses.

Exam Probability: **Medium**

47. *Answer choices:*
(see index for correct answer)

- a. Netbanx
- b. Barclaycard
- c. American Express
- d. North American Bancard

Guidance: level 1

:: Project management ::

A _____ is a source or supply from which a benefit is produced and it has some utility. _____ s can broadly be classified upon their availability—they are classified into renewable and non-renewable _____ s.Examples of non renewable _____ s are coal ,crude oil natural gas nuclear energy etc. Examples of renewable _____ s are air,water,wind,solar energy etc. They can also be classified as actual and potential on the basis of level of development and use, on the basis of origin they can be classified as biotic and abiotic, and on the basis of their distribution, as ubiquitous and localized . An item becomes a _____ with time and developing technology. Typically, _____ s are materials, energy, services, staff, knowledge, or other assets that are transformed to produce benefit and in the process may be consumed or made unavailable. Benefits of _____ utilization may include increased wealth, proper functioning of a system, or enhanced well-being. From a human perspective a natural _____ is anything obtained from the environment to satisfy human needs and wants. From a broader biological or ecological perspective a _____ satisfies the needs of a living organism .

Exam Probability: **Low**

48. *Answer choices:*

(see index for correct answer)

- a. Resource
- b. Theory X
- c. PM Declaration of Interdependence
- d. Project cycle management

Guidance: level 1

:: Interest rates ::

An _____ is the amount of interest due per period, as a proportion of the amount lent, deposited or borrowed . The total interest on an amount lent or borrowed depends on the principal sum, the _____ , the compounding frequency, and the length of time over which it is lent, deposited or borrowed.

Exam Probability: **Low**

49. *Answer choices:*

(see index for correct answer)

- a. Nominal interest rate
- b. London Interbank Bid Rate
- c. Interest rate
- d. Qualified residence interest

Guidance: level 1

:: International trade ::

_____ involves the transfer of goods or services from one person or entity to another, often in exchange for money. A system or network that allows _____ is called a market.

Exam Probability: **Medium**

50. *Answer choices:*

(see index for correct answer)

- a. Trade
- b. International Organisation of Employers
- c. International Association for Technology Trade
- d. Trade diversion

Guidance: level 1

:: Public relations ::

_____ is the public visibility or awareness for any product, service or company. It may also refer to the movement of information from its source to the general public, often but not always via the media. The subjects of _____ include people , goods and services, organizations, and works of art or entertainment.

Exam Probability: **Low**

51. *Answer choices:*
(see index for correct answer)

- a. Mobile Public Affairs Detachment
- b. Zakazukha
- c. Publicity
- d. Kompromat

Guidance: level 1

:: Project management ::

_____ is the right to exercise power, which can be formalized by a state and exercised by way of judges, appointed executives of government, or the ecclesiastical or priestly appointed representatives of a God or other deities.

Exam Probability: **High**

52. *Answer choices:*

(see index for correct answer)

- a. Authority
- b. Task
- c. Punch list
- d. Time to completion

Guidance: level 1

:: Employment ::

The _____ is an individual`s metaphorical "journey" through learning, work and other aspects of life. There are a number of ways to define _____ and the term is used in a variety of ways.

53. *Answer choices:*

(see index for correct answer)

- a. Career Development Practitioner
- b. Career
- c. Paradox of toil
- d. Pennsylvania CareerLink

Guidance: level 1

:: Health promotion ::

_____ , as defined by the World _____ Organization , is "a state of complete physical, mental and social well-being and not merely the absence of disease or infirmity." This definition has been subject to controversy, as it may have limited value for implementation. _____ may be defined as the ability to adapt and manage physical, mental and social challenges throughout life.

Exam Probability: **High**

54. *Answer choices:*

(see index for correct answer)

- a. Healthy community design
- b. Health

- c. Carers rights movement
- d. Jakarta Declaration

Guidance: level 1

:: Marketing ::

The _____ is a foundation model for businesses. The _____ has been defined as the "set of marketing tools that the firm uses to pursue its marketing objectives in the target market". Thus the _____ refers to four broad levels of marketing decision, namely: product, price, place, and promotion. Marketing practice has been occurring for millennia, but marketing theory emerged in the early twentieth century. The contemporary _____ , or the 4 Ps, which has become the dominant framework for marketing management decisions, was first published in 1960. In services marketing, an extended _____ is used, typically comprising 7 Ps, made up of the original 4 Ps extended by process, people, and physical evidence. Occasionally service marketers will refer to 8 Ps, comprising these 7 Ps plus performance.

Exam Probability: **Medium**

55. *Answer choices:*

(see index for correct answer)

- a. Audience development
- b. Hakan Okay
- c. Marketing mix
- d. Mystery shopping

:: Management accounting ::

_____ s are costs that change as the quantity of the good or service that a business produces changes. _____ s are the sum of marginal costs over all units produced. They can also be considered normal costs. Fixed costs and _____ s make up the two components of total cost. Direct costs are costs that can easily be associated with a particular cost object. However, not all _____ s are direct costs. For example, variable manufacturing overhead costs are _____ s that are indirect costs, not direct costs. _____ s are sometimes called unit-level costs as they vary with the number of units produced.

Exam Probability: **High**

56. *Answer choices:*

(see index for correct answer)

- a. Direct material total variance
- b. Revenue center
- c. Fixed cost
- d. Variable cost

:: Macroeconomics ::

A foreign _____ is an investment in the form of a controlling ownership in a business in one country by an entity based in another country. It is thus distinguished from a foreign portfolio investment by a notion of direct control.

Exam Probability: **Low**

57. *Answer choices:*

(see index for correct answer)

- a. Direct investment
- b. SIMIC
- c. General disequilibrium
- d. Price level

Guidance: level 1

:: Globalization-related theories ::

_____ is the process in which a nation is being improved in the sector of the economic, political, and social well-being of its people. The term has been used frequently by economists, politicians, and others in the 20th and 21st centuries. The concept, however, has been in existence in the West for centuries. "Modernization, "westernization", and especially "industrialization" are other terms often used while discussing _____ . _____ has a direct relationship with the environment and environmental issues. _____ is very often confused with industrial development, even in some academic sources.

58. *Answer choices:*

(see index for correct answer)

- a. Economic Development
- b. postmodernism
- c. post-industrial

Guidance: level 1

:: ::

_____ is a marketing communication that employs an openly sponsored, non-personal message to promote or sell a product, service or idea. Sponsors of _____ are typically businesses wishing to promote their products or services. _____ is differentiated from public relations in that an advertiser pays for and has control over the message. It differs from personal selling in that the message is non-personal, i.e., not directed to a particular individual. _____ is communicated through various mass media, including traditional media such as newspapers, magazines, television, radio, outdoor _____ or direct mail; and new media such as search results, blogs, social media, websites or text messages. The actual presentation of the message in a medium is referred to as an advertisement, or "ad" or advert for short.

59. *Answer choices:*

(see index for correct answer)

- a. process perspective
- b. imperative
- c. surface-level diversity
- d. deep-level diversity

Guidance: level 1

Management

Management is the administration of an organization, whether it is a business, a not-for-profit organization, or government body. Management includes the activities of setting the strategy of an organization and coordinating the efforts of its employees (or of volunteers) to accomplish its objectives through the application of available resources, such as financial, natural, technological, and human resources.

:: Project management ::

A _____ is a source or supply from which a benefit is produced and it has some utility. _____ s can broadly be classified upon their availability—they are classified into renewable and non-renewable _____ s.Examples of non renewable _____ s are coal ,crude oil natural gas nuclear energy etc. Examples of renewable _____ s are air,water,wind,solar energy etc. They can also be classified as actual and potential on the basis of level of development and use, on the basis of origin they can be classified as biotic and abiotic, and on the basis of their distribution, as ubiquitous and localized . An item becomes a _____ with time and developing technology. Typically, _____ s are materials, energy, services, staff, knowledge, or other assets that are transformed to produce benefit and in the process may be consumed or made unavailable. Benefits of _____ utilization may include increased wealth, proper functioning of a system, or enhanced well-being. From a human perspective a natural _____ is anything obtained from the environment to satisfy human needs and wants. From a broader biological or ecological perspective a _____ satisfies the needs of a living organism .

Exam Probability: **High**

1. *Answer choices:*

(see index for correct answer)

- a. Problem domain analysis
- b. Bottleneck
- c. Graphical Evaluation and Review Technique
- d. Resource

Guidance: level 1

:: Project management ::

_____ is a process of setting goals, planning and/or controlling the organizing and leading the execution of any type of activity, such as.

2. *Answer choices:*

(see index for correct answer)

- a. Small-scale project management
- b. Goodwerp
- c. Iteration
- d. Expected commercial value

Guidance: level 1

:: ::

A _____ is a fund into which a sum of money is added during an employee's employment years, and from which payments are drawn to support the person's retirement from work in the form of periodic payments. A _____ may be a "defined benefit plan" where a fixed sum is paid regularly to a person, or a "defined contribution plan" under which a fixed sum is invested and then becomes available at retirement age. _____ s should not be confused with severance pay; the former is usually paid in regular installments for life after retirement, while the latter is typically paid as a fixed amount after involuntary termination of employment prior to retirement.

3. *Answer choices:*

(see index for correct answer)

- a. interpersonal communication
- b. Pension
- c. deep-level diversity
- d. personal values

Guidance: level 1

:: ::

The _____ is a political and economic union of 28 member states that are located primarily in Europe. It has an area of 4,475,757 km2 and an estimated population of about 513 million. The EU has developed an internal single market through a standardised system of laws that apply in all member states in those matters, and only those matters, where members have agreed to act as one. EU policies aim to ensure the free movement of people, goods, services and capital within the internal market, enact legislation in justice and home affairs and maintain common policies on trade, agriculture, fisheries and regional development. For travel within the Schengen Area, passport controls have been abolished. A monetary union was established in 1999 and came into full force in 2002 and is composed of 19 EU member states which use the euro currency.

Exam Probability: **Medium**

4. *Answer choices:*

(see index for correct answer)

- a. cultural
- b. surface-level diversity
- c. process perspective
- d. empathy

Guidance: level 1

:: Project management ::

A _____ is a type of bar chart that illustrates a project schedule, named after its inventor, Henry Gantt , who designed such a chart around the years 1910–1915. Modern _____ s also show the dependency relationships between activities and current schedule status.

Exam Probability: **Low**

5. *Answer choices:*

(see index for correct answer)

- a. Effort management
- b. Task
- c. Gantt chart
- d. Logical framework approach

Guidance: level 1

:: ::

_____ refers to a business or organization attempting to acquire goods or services to accomplish its goals. Although there are several organizations that attempt to set standards in the _____ process, processes can vary greatly between organizations. Typically the word " _____ " is not used interchangeably with the word "procurement", since procurement typically includes expediting, supplier quality, and transportation and logistics in addition to _____ .

Exam Probability: **High**

6. *Answer choices:*

(see index for correct answer)

- a. information systems assessment
- b. hierarchical
- c. Purchasing
- d. corporate values

Guidance: level 1

:: Employee relations ::

_____ ownership, or employee share ownership, is an ownership interest in a company held by the company's workforce. The ownership interest may be facilitated by the company as part of employees' remuneration or incentive compensation for work performed, or the company itself may be employee owned.

7. *Answer choices:*

(see index for correct answer)

- a. Employee stock
- b. Employee engagement
- c. Employee morale
- d. Employee handbook

Guidance: level 1

:: Discrimination ::

In social psychology, a _____ is an over-generalized belief about a particular category of people. _____ s are generalized because one assumes that the _____ is true for each individual person in the category. While such generalizations may be useful when making quick decisions, they may be erroneous when applied to particular individuals. _____ s encourage prejudice and may arise for a number of reasons.

8. *Answer choices:*

(see index for correct answer)

- a. Elitism
- b. Economic discrimination

- c. Stereotype

Guidance: level 1

:: Management ::

_____ is the practice of initiating, planning, executing, controlling, and closing the work of a team to achieve specific goals and meet specific success criteria at the specified time.

Exam Probability: **Low**

9. *Answer choices:*
(see index for correct answer)

- a. Project management
- b. Business process improvement
- c. Empowerment
- d. Middle management

Guidance: level 1

:: Human resource management ::

_____ , also known as management by results , was first popularized by Peter Drucker in his 1954 book The Practice of Management. _____ is the process of defining specific objectives within an organization that management can convey to organization members, then deciding on how to achieve each objective in sequence. This process allows managers to take work that needs to be done one step at a time to allow for a calm, yet productive work environment. This process also helps organization members to see their accomplishments as they achieve each objective, which reinforces a positive work environment and a sense of achievement. An important part of MBO is the measurement and comparison of an employee's actual performance with the standards set. Ideally, when employees themselves have been involved with the goal-setting and choosing the course of action to be followed by them, they are more likely to fulfill their responsibilities.According to George S. Odiorne, the system of _____ can be described as a process whereby the superior and subordinate jointly identify common goals, define each individual's major areas of responsibility in terms of the results expected of him or her, and use these measures as guides for operating the unit and assessing the contribution of each of its members.

Exam Probability: **Low**

10. *Answer choices:*

(see index for correct answer)

- a. Recruitment process outsourcing
- b. Inclusive business
- c. Potential analysis
- d. Management due diligence

Guidance: level 1

:: Legal terms ::

_____ is a type of meaning in which a phrase, statement or resolution is not explicitly defined, making several interpretations plausible. A common aspect of _____ is uncertainty. It is thus an attribute of any idea or statement whose intended meaning cannot be definitively resolved according to a rule or process with a finite number of steps.

Exam Probability: **Medium**

11. *Answer choices:*

(see index for correct answer)

- a. Legal age
- b. Further and better particulars
- c. Form of action
- d. Advisory jury

Guidance: level 1

:: Packaging ::

In work place, _____ or job _____ means good ranking with the hypothesized conception of requirements of a role. There are two types of job _____ s: contextual and task. Task _____ is related to cognitive ability while contextual _____ is dependent upon personality. Task _____ are behavioral roles that are recognized in job descriptions and by remuneration systems, they are directly related to organizational _____ , whereas, contextual _____ are value based and additional behavioral roles that are not recognized in job descriptions and covered by compensation; they are extra roles that are indirectly related to organizational _____ . Citizenship _____ like contextual _____ means a set of individual activity/contribution that supports the organizational culture.

Exam Probability: **Low**

12. *Answer choices:*

(see index for correct answer)

- a. Record sleeve
- b. Performance
- c. Tamper-evident
- d. Dangerous Substances Directive

Guidance: level 1

:: ::

In mathematics, a _____ is a relationship between two numbers indicating how many times the first number contains the second. For example, if a bowl of fruit contains eight oranges and six lemons, then the _____ of oranges to lemons is eight to six . Similarly, the _____ of lemons to oranges is 6:8 and the _____ of oranges to the total amount of fruit is 8:14 .

Exam Probability: **Low**

13. *Answer choices:*

(see index for correct answer)

- a. similarity-attraction theory
- b. cultural
- c. levels of analysis
- d. empathy

Guidance: level 1

:: Credit cards ::

The _____ Company, also known as Amex, is an American multinational financial services corporation headquartered in Three World Financial Center in New York City. The company was founded in 1850 and is one of the 30 components of the Dow Jones Industrial Average. The company is best known for its charge card, credit card, and traveler's cheque businesses.

Exam Probability: **Low**

14. *Answer choices:*

(see index for correct answer)

- a. China UnionPay
- b. Payoneer
- c. Credit card debt
- d. American Express

Guidance: level 1

:: Information technology management ::

_____ is a collective term for all approaches to prepare , support and help individuals, teams, and organizations in making organizational change. The most common change drivers include: technological evolution, process reviews, crisis, and consumer habit changes; pressure from new business entrants, acquisitions, mergers, and organizational restructuring. It includes methods that redirect or redefine the use of resources, business process, budget allocations, or other modes of operation that significantly change a company or organization. Organizational _____ considers the full organization and what needs to change, while _____ may be used solely to refer to how people and teams are affected by such organizational transition. It deals with many different disciplines, from behavioral and social sciences to information technology and business solutions.

Exam Probability: **Low**

15. *Answer choices:*

(see index for correct answer)

- a. Change management
- b. Service desk
- c. FORTRAS
- d. IT Service Management Forum

Guidance: level 1

:: Marketing ::

A _____ is an overall experience of a customer that distinguishes an organization or product from its rivals in the eyes of the customer. _____ s are used in business, marketing, and advertising. Name _____ s are sometimes distinguished from generic or store _____ s.

Exam Probability: **Low**

16. *Answer choices:*
(see index for correct answer)

- a. Buyer decision process
- b. Postmodern branding
- c. Franchise fee
- d. Mass affluent

Guidance: level 1

:: Statistical terminology ::

_____ is the magnitude or dimensions of a thing. _____ can be measured as length, width, height, diameter, perimeter, area, volume, or mass.

Exam Probability: **Medium**

17. *Answer choices:*

(see index for correct answer)

- a. Drift rate
- b. Covariate
- c. Contrast
- d. Size

Guidance: level 1

:: Information systems ::

_____ is the process of creating, sharing, using and managing the knowledge and information of an organisation. It refers to a multidisciplinary approach to achieving organisational objectives by making the best use of knowledge.

Exam Probability: **High**

18. *Answer choices:*

(see index for correct answer)

- a. Knowledge management
- b. CountrySTAT
- c. Data system
- d. EuResist

Guidance: level 1

:: ::

According to Torrington, a _____ is usually developed by conducting a job analysis, which includes examining the tasks and sequences of tasks necessary to perform the job. The analysis considers the areas of knowledge and skills needed for the job. A job usually includes several roles. According to Hall, the _____ might be broadened to form a person specification or may be known as "terms of reference". The person/job specification can be presented as a stand-alone document, but in practice it is usually included within the _____ . A _____ is often used by employers in the recruitment process.

Exam Probability: **Medium**

19. *Answer choices:*

(see index for correct answer)

- a. corporate values
- b. functional perspective

- c. Job description
- d. Character

Guidance: level 1

:: ::

_____ refers to the confirmation of certain characteristics of an object, person, or organization. This confirmation is often, but not always, provided by some form of external review, education, assessment, or audit. Accreditation is a specific organization's process of _____ . According to the National Council on Measurement in Education, a _____ test is a credentialing test used to determine whether individuals are knowledgeable enough in a given occupational area to be labeled "competent to practice" in that area.

Exam Probability: **High**

20. *Answer choices:*

(see index for correct answer)

- a. similarity-attraction theory
- b. information systems assessment
- c. deep-level diversity
- d. Certification

Guidance: level 1

_____ is the capacity of consciously making sense of things, establishing and verifying facts, applying logic, and changing or justifying practices, institutions, and beliefs based on new or existing information. It is closely associated with such characteristically human activities as philosophy, science, language, mathematics and art, and is normally considered to be a distinguishing ability possessed by humans. _____ , or an aspect of it, is sometimes referred to as rationality.

Exam Probability: **High**

21. *Answer choices:*

(see index for correct answer)

- a. Reason
- b. corporate values
- c. information systems assessment
- d. interpersonal communication

Guidance: level 1

:: Business ::

_____ is a trade policy that does not restrict imports or exports; it can also be understood as the free market idea applied to international trade. In government, _____ is predominantly advocated by political parties that hold liberal economic positions while economically left-wing and nationalist political parties generally support protectionism, the opposite of _____ .

Exam Probability: **Medium**

22. *Answer choices:*

(see index for correct answer)

- a. Free trade
- b. Growth platform
- c. Business agility
- d. Business idea

Guidance: level 1

:: Production and manufacturing ::

_____ consists of organization-wide efforts to "install and make permanent climate where employees continuously improve their ability to provide on demand products and services that customers will find of particular value." "Total" emphasizes that departments in addition to production are obligated to improve their operations; "management" emphasizes that executives are obligated to actively manage quality through funding, training, staffing, and goal setting. While there is no widely agreed-upon approach, TQM efforts typically draw heavily on the previously developed tools and techniques of quality control. TQM enjoyed widespread attention during the late 1980s and early 1990s before being overshadowed by ISO 9000, Lean manufacturing, and Six Sigma.

Exam Probability: **Low**

23. *Answer choices:*

(see index for correct answer)

- a. SERCOS III
- b. Production engineering
- c. Total quality management
- d. Highly accelerated life test

Guidance: level 1

:: ::

An _____ is the production of goods or related services within an economy. The major source of revenue of a group or company is the indicator of its relevant _____ . When a large group has multiple sources of revenue generation, it is considered to be working in different industries.
Manufacturing _____ became a key sector of production and labour in European and North American countries during the Industrial Revolution, upsetting previous mercantile and feudal economies. This came through many successive rapid advances in technology, such as the production of steel and coal.

Exam Probability: **High**

24. *Answer choices:*

(see index for correct answer)

- a. Industry
- b. hierarchical perspective
- c. interpersonal communication
- d. Sarbanes-Oxley act of 2002

Guidance: level 1

:: International relations ::

A _____ is any event that is going to lead to an unstable and dangerous situation affecting an individual, group, community, or whole society. Crises are deemed to be negative changes in the security, economic, political, societal, or environmental affairs, especially when they occur abruptly, with little or no warning. More loosely, it is a term meaning "a testing time" or an "emergency event".

Exam Probability: **Medium**

25. *Answer choices:*
(see index for correct answer)

- a. Kellogg Foundation for Education in International Relations
- b. Crisis
- c. Periphery countries
- d. Oopali Operajita

Guidance: level 1

:: Market research ::

_____ is an organized effort to gather information about target markets or customers. It is a very important component of business strategy. The term is commonly interchanged with marketing research; however, expert practitioners may wish to draw a distinction, in that marketing research is concerned specifically about marketing processes, while _____ is concerned specifically with markets.

26. *Answer choices:*

(see index for correct answer)

- a. Market research
- b. Brand elections
- c. Multistage sampling
- d. BrandZ

Guidance: level 1

:: ::

The _____ or labour force is the labour pool in employment. It is generally used to describe those working for a single company or industry, but can also apply to a geographic region like a city, state, or country. Within a company, its value can be labelled as its " _____ in Place". The _____ of a country includes both the employed and the unemployed. The labour force participation rate, LFPR , is the ratio between the labour force and the overall size of their cohort . The term generally excludes the employers or management, and can imply those involved in manual labour. It may also mean all those who are available for work.

Exam Probability: **High**

27. *Answer choices:*

(see index for correct answer)

- a. Sarbanes-Oxley act of 2002
- b. cultural
- c. process perspective
- d. Workforce

Guidance: level 1

:: Management accounting ::

_____ s are costs that change as the quantity of the good or service that a business produces changes. _____ s are the sum of marginal costs over all units produced. They can also be considered normal costs. Fixed costs and _____ s make up the two components of total cost. Direct costs are costs that can easily be associated with a particular cost object. However, not all _____ s are direct costs. For example, variable manufacturing overhead costs are _____ s that are indirect costs, not direct costs. _____ s are sometimes called unit-level costs as they vary with the number of units produced.

Exam Probability: **High**

28. *Answer choices:*

(see index for correct answer)

- a. Pre-determined overhead rate
- b. Institute of Cost and Management Accountants of Bangladesh
- c. Chartered Institute of Management Accountants
- d. activity based costing

:: Problem solving ::

In other words, _____ is a situation where a group of people meet to generate new ideas and solutions around a specific domain of interest by removing inhibitions. People are able to think more freely and they suggest as many spontaneous new ideas as possible. All the ideas are noted down and those ideas are not criticized and after _____ session the ideas are evaluated. The term was popularized by Alex Faickney Osborn in the 1953 book Applied Imagination.

Exam Probability: **Low**

29. *Answer choices:*
(see index for correct answer)

- a. Creative problem-solving
- b. Brainstorming
- c. Problem statement
- d. Unified structured inventive thinking

:: Human resource management ::

_____ encompasses values and behaviors that contribute to the unique social and psychological environment of a business. The _____ influences the way people interact, the context within which knowledge is created, the resistance they will have towards certain changes, and ultimately the way they share knowledge. _____ represents the collective values, beliefs and principles of organizational members and is a product of factors such as history, product, market, technology, strategy, type of employees, management style, and national culture; culture includes the organization's vision, values, norms, systems, symbols, language, assumptions, environment, location, beliefs and habits.

Exam Probability: **Medium**

30. *Answer choices:*

(see index for correct answer)

- a. Appreciative inquiry
- b. Up or out
- c. Incentive program
- d. Talent management

Guidance: level 1

:: ::

In organizational behavior and industrial/organizational psychology, proactivity or _____ behavior by individuals refers to anticipatory, change-oriented and self-initiated behavior in situations. _____ behavior involves acting in advance of a future situation, rather than just reacting. It means taking control and making things happen rather than just adjusting to a situation or waiting for something to happen. _____ employees generally do not need to be asked to act, nor do they require detailed instructions.

Exam Probability: **High**

31. *Answer choices:*

(see index for correct answer)

- a. Character
- b. Proactive
- c. co-culture
- d. hierarchical

Guidance: level 1

:: Labor rights ::

A _____ is a wrong or hardship suffered, real or supposed, which forms legitimate grounds of complaint. In the past, the word meant the infliction or cause of hardship.

Exam Probability: **Medium**

32. *Answer choices:*

(see index for correct answer)

- a. Labor rights
- b. Grievance
- c. The Hyatt 100
- d. Right to work

Guidance: level 1

:: Meetings ::

A _____ is a body of one or more persons that is subordinate to a deliberative assembly. Usually, the assembly sends matters into a _____ as a way to explore them more fully than would be possible if the assembly itself were considering them. _____ s may have different functions and their type of work differ depending on the type of the organization and its needs.

Exam Probability: **High**

33. *Answer choices:*

(see index for correct answer)

- a. Committee
- b. Open town meeting
- c. Skeptics in the Pub
- d. Official function

:: Labor ::

The workforce or labour force is the labour pool in employment. It is generally used to describe those working for a single company or industry, but can also apply to a geographic region like a city, state, or country. Within a company, its value can be labelled as its "Workforce in Place". The workforce of a country includes both the employed and the unemployed. The labour force participation rate, LFPR , is the ratio between the labour force and the overall size of their cohort . The term generally excludes the employers or management, and can imply those involved in manual labour. It may also mean all those who are available for work.

Exam Probability: **Medium**

34. *Answer choices:*

(see index for correct answer)

- a. New Unionism
- b. Labour economics
- c. Union label
- d. Occupational safety and health

:: ::

A _____ is a problem offering two possibilities, neither of which is unambiguously acceptable or preferable. The possibilities are termed the horns of the _____ , a clichéd usage, but distinguishing the _____ from other kinds of predicament as a matter of usage.

Exam Probability: **Medium**

35. *Answer choices:*

(see index for correct answer)

- a. personal values
- b. Dilemma
- c. deep-level diversity
- d. functional perspective

Guidance: level 1

:: Management ::

A _____ is a formal written document containing business goals, the methods on how these goals can be attained, and the time frame within which these goals need to be achieved. It also describes the nature of the business, background information on the organization, the organization's financial projections, and the strategies it intends to implement to achieve the stated targets. In its entirety, this document serves as a road map that provides direction to the business.

Exam Probability: **High**

36. *Answer choices:*

(see index for correct answer)

- a. Economic order quantity
- b. Omnex
- c. Business plan
- d. Project management

Guidance: level 1

:: Management ::

A _____ describes the rationale of how an organization creates, delivers, and captures value, in economic, social, cultural or other contexts. The process of _____ construction and modification is also called _____ innovation and forms a part of business strategy.

Exam Probability: **High**

37. *Answer choices:*

(see index for correct answer)

- a. Plan
- b. Strategic lenses
- c. Business model
- d. Crisis plan

:: Autonomy ::

In developmental psychology and moral, political, and bioethical philosophy, _____ is the capacity to make an informed, uncoerced decision. Autonomous organizations or institutions are independent or self-governing. _____ can also be defined from a human resources perspective, where it denotes a level of discretion granted to an employee in his or her work. In such cases, _____ is known to generally increase job satisfaction. _____ is a term that is also widely used in the field of medicine — personal _____ is greatly recognized and valued in health care.

Exam Probability: **Low**

38. *Answer choices:*
(see index for correct answer)

- a. Autonomy
- b. Equality of autonomy
- c. Rhex
- d. Self-ownership

:: Regression analysis ::

A _____ often refers to a set of documented requirements to be satisfied by a material, design, product, or service. A _____ is often a type of technical standard.

Exam Probability: **High**

39. *Answer choices:*

(see index for correct answer)

- a. Specification
- b. Moving least squares
- c. Variable rules analysis
- d. Probit model

Guidance: level 1

:: ::

_____ is a kind of action that occur as two or more objects have an effect upon one another. The idea of a two-way effect is essential in the concept of _____ , as opposed to a one-way causal effect. A closely related term is interconnectivity, which deals with the _____ s of _____ s within systems: combinations of many simple _____ s can lead to surprising emergent phenomena. _____ has different tailored meanings in various sciences. Changes can also involve _____ .

Exam Probability: **Medium**

40. *Answer choices:*

(see index for correct answer)

- a. personal values
- b. imperative
- c. functional perspective
- d. Interaction

Guidance: level 1

:: Industrial relations ::

_____ or employee satisfaction is a measure of workers' contentedness with their job, whether or not they like the job or individual aspects or facets of jobs, such as nature of work or supervision. _____ can be measured in cognitive , affective , and behavioral components. Researchers have also noted that _____ measures vary in the extent to which they measure feelings about the job . or cognitions about the job .

Exam Probability: **Medium**

41. *Answer choices:*

(see index for correct answer)

- a. European Journal of Industrial Relations
- b. Job satisfaction
- c. Injury prevention
- d. Workforce Investment Board

:: ::

The _____ officer or just _____ , is the most senior corporate, executive, or administrative officer in charge of managing an organization especially an independent legal entity such as a company or nonprofit institution. CEOs lead a range of organizations, including public and private corporations, non-profit organizations and even some government organizations . The CEO of a corporation or company typically reports to the board of directors and is charged with maximizing the value of the entity, which may include maximizing the share price, market share, revenues or another element. In the non-profit and government sector, CEOs typically aim at achieving outcomes related to the organization`s mission, such as reducing poverty, increasing literacy, etc.

Exam Probability: **High**

42. *Answer choices:*

(see index for correct answer)

- a. information systems assessment
- b. Chief executive
- c. functional perspective
- d. cultural

:: Management occupations ::

_____ ship is the process of designing, launching and running a new business, which is often initially a small business. The people who create these businesses are called _____ s.

Exam Probability: **Medium**

43. *Answer choices:*

(see index for correct answer)

- a. Comptroller
- b. Hayward
- c. Comprador
- d. General counsel

Guidance: level 1

:: Critical thinking ::

An _____ is someone who has a prolonged or intense experience through practice and education in a particular field. Informally, an _____ is someone widely recognized as a reliable source of technique or skill whose faculty for judging or deciding rightly, justly, or wisely is accorded authority and status by peers or the public in a specific well-distinguished domain. An _____ , more generally, is a person with extensive knowledge or ability based on research, experience, or occupation and in a particular area of study. _____ s are called in for advice on their respective subject, but they do not always agree on the particulars of a field of study. An _____ can be believed, by virtue of credential, training, education, profession, publication or experience, to have special knowledge of a subject beyond that of the average person, sufficient that others may officially rely upon the individual's opinion. Historically, an _____ was referred to as a sage . The individual was usually a profound thinker distinguished for wisdom and sound judgment.

Exam Probability: **Low**

44. *Answer choices:*

(see index for correct answer)

- a. Expert
- b. Vagueness
- c. Socratic questioning
- d. Fallacy

Guidance: level 1

:: E-commerce ::

_____ is the activity of buying or selling of products on online services or over the Internet. Electronic commerce draws on technologies such as mobile commerce, electronic funds transfer, supply chain management, Internet marketing, online transaction processing, electronic data interchange , inventory management systems, and automated data collection systems.

Exam Probability: **Medium**

45. *Answer choices:*

(see index for correct answer)

- a. E-commerce
- b. Lyoness
- c. SwapSimple
- d. Online shopping

Guidance: level 1

:: Logistics ::

_____ is generally the detailed organization and implementation of a complex operation. In a general business sense, _____ is the management of the flow of things between the point of origin and the point of consumption in order to meet requirements of customers or corporations. The resources managed in _____ may include tangible goods such as materials, equipment, and supplies, as well as food and other consumable items. The _____ of physical items usually involves the integration of information flow, materials handling, production, packaging, inventory, transportation, warehousing, and often security.

46. *Answer choices:*

(see index for correct answer)

- a. Ground Parachute Extraction System
- b. Logistics Support System
- c. Spetstyazhavtotrans
- d. Logistics

Guidance: level 1

:: Management ::

The _____ is a strategy performance management tool – a semi-standard structured report, that can be used by managers to keep track of the execution of activities by the staff within their control and to monitor the consequences arising from these actions.

47. *Answer choices:*

(see index for correct answer)

- a. Event chain methodology
- b. Balanced scorecard
- c. Scenario planning

- d. Empowerment

Guidance: level 1

:: Strategic management ::

_____ is a strategic planning technique used to help a person or organization identify strengths, weaknesses, opportunities, and threats related to business competition or project planning. It is intended to specify the objectives of the business venture or project and identify the internal and external factors that are favorable and unfavorable to achieving those objectives. Users of a _____ often ask and answer questions to generate meaningful information for each category to make the tool useful and identify their competitive advantage. SWOT has been described as the tried-and-true tool of strategic analysis.

Exam Probability: **Low**

48. *Answer choices:*

(see index for correct answer)

- a. Critical success factor
- b. business unit
- c. SWOT analysis
- d. BSC SWOT

Guidance: level 1

:: Teams ::

A _____ usually refers to a group of individuals who work together from different geographic locations and rely on communication technology such as email, FAX, and video or voice conferencing services in order to collaborate. The term can also refer to groups or teams that work together asynchronously or across organizational levels. Powell, Piccoli and Ives define _____ s as "groups of geographically, organizationally and/or time dispersed workers brought together by information and telecommunication technologies to accomplish one or more organizational tasks." According to Ale Ebrahim et. al. , _____ s can also be defined as "small temporary groups of geographically, organizationally and/or time dispersed knowledge workers who coordinate their work predominantly with electronic information and communication technologies in order to accomplish one or more organization tasks."

Exam Probability: **Medium**

49. *Answer choices:*

(see index for correct answer)

- a. team composition
- b. Team-building

Guidance: level 1

:: ::

_____ is the amount of time someone works beyond normal working hours. The term is also used for the pay received for this time. Normal hours may be determined in several ways.

Exam Probability: **Low**

50. *Answer choices:*

(see index for correct answer)

- a. Character
- b. personal values
- c. Overtime
- d. interpersonal communication

Guidance: level 1

:: ::

_____ is the process of collecting, analyzing and/or reporting information regarding the performance of an individual, group, organization, system or component. _____ is not a new concept, some of the earliest records of human activity relate to the counting or recording of activities.

Exam Probability: **Medium**

51. *Answer choices:*

(see index for correct answer)

- a. corporate values
- b. process perspective
- c. deep-level diversity
- d. Performance measurement

Guidance: level 1

:: ::

An _____ is a contingent motivator. Traditional _____ s are extrinsic motivators which reward actions to yield a desired outcome. The effectiveness of traditional _____ s has changed as the needs of Western society have evolved. While the traditional _____ model is effective when there is a defined procedure and goal for a task, Western society started to require a higher volume of critical thinkers, so the traditional model became less effective. Institutions are now following a trend in implementing strategies that rely on intrinsic motivations rather than the extrinsic motivations that the traditional _____ s foster.

Exam Probability: **Medium**

52. *Answer choices:*

(see index for correct answer)

- a. functional perspective
- b. hierarchical
- c. surface-level diversity
- d. Incentive

:: Types of marketing ::

In microeconomics and management, _____ is an arrangement in which the supply chain of a company is owned by that company. Usually each member of the supply chain produces a different product or service, and the products combine to satisfy a common need. It is contrasted with horizontal integration, wherein a company produces several items which are related to one another. _____ has also described management styles that bring large portions of the supply chain not only under a common ownership, but also into one corporation .

Exam Probability: **Low**

53. *Answer choices:*

(see index for correct answer)

- a. Z-CARD
- b. Figure of merit
- c. Evangelism marketing
- d. Vertical integration

:: Production economics ::

_____ is the joint use of a resource or space. It is also the process of dividing and distributing. In its narrow sense, it refers to joint or alternating use of inherently finite goods, such as a common pasture or a shared residence. Still more loosely, "_____" can actually mean giving something as an outright gift: for example, to "share" one's food really means to give some of it as a gift. _____ is a basic component of human interaction, and is responsible for strengthening social ties and ensuring a person's well-being.

Exam Probability: **Medium**

54. *Answer choices:*

(see index for correct answer)

- a. Split-off point
- b. Choice of techniques
- c. Multifactor productivity
- d. Sharing

Guidance: level 1

:: Business process ::

A _____ or business method is a collection of related, structured activities or tasks by people or equipment which in a specific sequence produce a service or product for a particular customer or customers. _____ es occur at all organizational levels and may or may not be visible to the customers. A _____ may often be visualized as a flowchart of a sequence of activities with interleaving decision points or as a process matrix of a sequence of activities with relevance rules based on data in the process. The benefits of using _____ es include improved customer satisfaction and improved agility for reacting to rapid market change. Process-oriented organizations break down the barriers of structural departments and try to avoid functional silos.

Exam Probability: **Medium**

55. *Answer choices:*

(see index for correct answer)

- a. Business process
- b. Business communication
- c. ADONIS
- d. Process mining

Guidance: level 1

:: Social psychology ::

In social psychology, _____ is the phenomenon of a person exerting less effort to achieve a goal when he or she works in a group than when working alone. This is seen as one of the main reasons groups are sometimes less productive than the combined performance of their members working as individuals, but should be distinguished from the accidental coordination problems that groups sometimes experience.

Exam Probability: **Low**

56. *Answer choices:*

(see index for correct answer)

- a. post-feminism
- b. co-optation
- c. Social loafing
- d. coercive persuasion

Guidance: level 1

:: Survey methodology ::

An _____ is a conversation where questions are asked and answers are given. In common parlance, the word " _____ " refers to a one-on-one conversation between an _____ er and an _____ ee. The _____ er asks questions to which the _____ ee responds, usually so information may be transferred from _____ ee to _____ er . Sometimes, information can be transferred in both directions. It is a communication, unlike a speech, which produces a one-way flow of information.

57. *Answer choices:*
(see index for correct answer)

- a. Interview
- b. Survey sampling
- c. Coverage error
- d. National Health Interview Survey

Guidance: level 1

:: ::

An _____ is, most an organized examination or formal evaluation exercise. In engineering activities _____ involves the measurements, tests, and gauges applied to certain characteristics in regard to an object or activity. The results are usually compared to specified requirements and standards for determining whether the item or activity is in line with these targets, often with a Standard _____ Procedure in place to ensure consistent checking. _____ s are usually non-destructive.

58. *Answer choices:*
(see index for correct answer)

- a. information systems assessment

- b. co-culture
- c. hierarchical perspective
- d. Inspection

Guidance: level 1

:: Business law ::

A _____ is a business entity created by two or more parties, generally characterized by shared ownership, shared returns and risks, and shared governance. Companies typically pursue _____ s for one of four reasons: to access a new market, particularly emerging markets; to gain scale efficiencies by combining assets and operations; to share risk for major investments or projects; or to access skills and capabilities.

Exam Probability: **Low**

59. *Answer choices:*

(see index for correct answer)

- a. Copyright transfer agreement
- b. Double ticketing
- c. Lien
- d. Joint venture

Guidance: level 1

Business law

Corporate law (also known as business law) is the body of law governing the rights, relations, and conduct of persons, companies, organizations and businesses. It refers to the legal practice relating to, or the theory of corporations. Corporate law often describes the law relating to matters which derive directly from the life-cycle of a corporation. It thus encompasses the formation, funding, governance, and death of a corporation.

:: ::

_____ is the body of law that governs the activities of administrative agencies of government. Government agency action can include rule making, adjudication, or the enforcement of a specific regulatory agenda. _____ is considered a branch of public law. As a body of law, _____ deals with the decision-making of the administrative units of government that are part of a national regulatory scheme in such areas as police law, international trade, manufacturing, the environment, taxation, broadcasting, immigration and transport. _____ expanded greatly during the twentieth century, as legislative bodies worldwide created more government agencies to regulate the social, economic and political spheres of human interaction.

Exam Probability: **High**

1. *Answer choices:*

(see index for correct answer)

- a. Sarbanes-Oxley act of 2002
- b. imperative
- c. Administrative law
- d. Character

Guidance: level 1

:: ::

_____ is the production of products for use or sale using labour and machines, tools, chemical and biological processing, or formulation. The term may refer to a range of human activity, from handicraft to high tech, but is most commonly applied to industrial design, in which raw materials are transformed into finished goods on a large scale. Such finished goods may be sold to other manufacturers for the production of other, more complex products, such as aircraft, household appliances, furniture, sports equipment or automobiles, or sold to wholesalers, who in turn sell them to retailers, who then sell them to end users and consumers.

Exam Probability: **Low**

2. *Answer choices:*

(see index for correct answer)

- a. functional perspective
- b. Character
- c. personal values
- d. cultural

Guidance: level 1

:: Majority–minority relations ::

_____ , also known as reservation in India and Nepal, positive discrimination / action in the United Kingdom, and employment equity in Canada and South Africa, is the policy of promoting the education and employment of members of groups that are known to have previously suffered from discrimination. Historically and internationally, support for _____ has sought to achieve goals such as bridging inequalities in employment and pay, increasing access to education, promoting diversity, and redressing apparent past wrongs, harms, or hindrances.

Exam Probability: **High**

3. *Answer choices:*

(see index for correct answer)

- a. Affirmative action
- b. cultural Relativism
- c. cultural dissonance

Guidance: level 1

:: ::

In legal terminology, a _____ is any formal legal document that sets out the facts and legal reasons that the filing party or parties believes are sufficient to support a claim against the party or parties against whom the claim is brought that entitles the plaintiff to a remedy . For example, the Federal Rules of Civil Procedure that govern civil litigation in United States courts provide that a civil action is commenced with the filing or service of a pleading called a _____ . Civil court rules in states that have incorporated the Federal Rules of Civil Procedure use the same term for the same pleading.

Exam Probability: **Medium**

4. *Answer choices:*

(see index for correct answer)

- a. similarity-attraction theory
- b. Complaint
- c. hierarchical perspective
- d. process perspective

Guidance: level 1

:: Film production ::

_____ is a legal term more comprehensive and of higher import than either warranty or "security". It most commonly designates a private transaction by means of which one person, to obtain some trust, confidence or credit for another, engages to be answerable for him. It may also designate a treaty through which claims, rights or possessions are secured. It is to be differentiated from the colloquial "personal _____" in that a _____ is a legal concept which produces an economic effect. A personal _____ by contrast is often used to refer to a promise made by an individual which is supported by, or assured through, the word of the individual. In the same way, a _____ produces a legal effect wherein one party affirms the promise of another by promising to themselves pay if default occurs.

Exam Probability: **High**

5. *Answer choices:*

(see index for correct answer)

- a. Artistic control
- b. Mafer
- c. Craft service
- d. Martini Shot

Guidance: level 1

:: Shareholders ::

A _____ is a payment made by a corporation to its shareholders, usually as a distribution of profits. When a corporation earns a profit or surplus, the corporation is able to re-invest the profit in the business and pay a proportion of the profit as a _____ to shareholders. Distribution to shareholders may be in cash or, if the corporation has a _____ reinvestment plan, the amount can be paid by the issue of further shares or share repurchase. When _____ s are paid, shareholders typically must pay income taxes, and the corporation does not receive a corporate income tax deduction for the _____ payments.

Exam Probability: **Medium**

6. *Answer choices:*

(see index for correct answer)

- a. Poison pill
- b. Shareholder oppression
- c. Say on pay
- d. Dividend

Guidance: level 1

:: Stock market ::

The _____ of a corporation is all of the shares into which ownership of the corporation is divided. In American English, the shares are commonly known as " _____ s". A single share of the _____ represents fractional ownership of the corporation in proportion to the total number of shares. This typically entitles the _____ holder to that fraction of the company's earnings, proceeds from liquidation of assets , or voting power, often dividing these up in proportion to the amount of money each _____ holder has invested. Not all _____ is necessarily equal, as certain classes of _____ may be issued for example without voting rights, with enhanced voting rights, or with a certain priority to receive profits or liquidation proceeds before or after other classes of shareholders.

Exam Probability: **Medium**

7. *Answer choices:*

(see index for correct answer)

- a. Extended hours trading
- b. Program trading
- c. Stock
- d. Participating preferred stock

Guidance: level 1

:: Chemical industry ::

The _____ for the Protection of Literary and Artistic Works, usually known as the _____ , is an international agreement governing copyright, which was first accepted in Berne, Switzerland, in 1886.

8. *Answer choices:*

(see index for correct answer)

- a. Berne Convention
- b. Blue colour works
- c. Chemical leasing
- d. Regulation of chemicals

Guidance: level 1

:: Manufactured goods ::

A _____ or final good is any commodity that is produced or consumed by the consumer to satisfy current wants or needs. _____ s are ultimately consumed, rather than used in the production of another good. For example, a microwave oven or a bicycle that is sold to a consumer is a final good or _____ , but the components that are sold to be used in those goods are intermediate goods. For example, textiles or transistors can be used to make some further goods.

Exam Probability: **Low**

9. *Answer choices:*

(see index for correct answer)

- a. Tarpaulin

- b. Product ecosystem theory
- c. Consumer Good
- d. Final good

Guidance: level 1

:: Arbitration law ::

The United States Arbitration Act , more commonly referred to as the
_____ or FAA, is an act of Congress that provides for judicial
facilitation of private dispute resolution through arbitration. It applies in
both state courts and federal courts, as was held constitutional in Southland
Corp. v. Keating. It applies where the transaction contemplated by the parties
"involves" interstate commerce and is predicated on an exercise of the Commerce
Clause powers granted to Congress in the U.S. Constitution.

Exam Probability: **Low**

10. *Answer choices:*

(see index for correct answer)

- a. Convention on the Recognition and Enforcement of Foreign Arbitral Awards
- b. Title 9 of the United States Code
- c. Uniform Arbitration Act
- d. UNCITRAL Model Law on International Commercial Arbitration

Guidance: level 1

:: Contract law ::

A _____ is a contract in which one party agrees to supply as much of a good or service as is required by the other party, and in exchange the other party expressly or implicitly promises that it will obtain its goods or services exclusively from the first party. For example, a grocery store might enter into a contract with the farmer who grows oranges under which the farmer would supply the grocery store with as many oranges as the store could sell. The farmer could sue for breach of contract if the store were thereafter to purchase oranges for this purpose from any other party. The converse of this situation is an output contract, in which one buyer agrees to purchase however much of a good or service the seller is able to produce.

Exam Probability: **Medium**

11. *Answer choices:*
(see index for correct answer)

- a. Third-party beneficiary
- b. Synallagmatic contract
- c. Requirements contract
- d. Void contract

Guidance: level 1

:: ::

A concept of English law, a _____ is an untrue or misleading statement of fact made during negotiations by one party to another, the statement then inducing that other party into the contract. The misled party may normally rescind the contract, and sometimes may be awarded damages as well

.

Exam Probability: **Low**

12. *Answer choices:*

(see index for correct answer)

- a. Misrepresentation
- b. Character
- c. deep-level diversity
- d. functional perspective

Guidance: level 1

:: Debt ::

_____ is the trust which allows one party to provide money or resources to another party wherein the second party does not reimburse the first party immediately , but promises either to repay or return those resources at a later date. In other words, _____ is a method of making reciprocity formal, legally enforceable, and extensible to a large group of unrelated people.

Exam Probability: **Medium**

13. *Answer choices:*

(see index for correct answer)

- a. Arrears
- b. Asset protection
- c. Troubled Debt Restructuring
- d. Crown debt

Guidance: level 1

:: ::

The _____ is one of the several United States Uniform Acts proposed by the National Conference of Commissioners on Uniform State Laws . Forty-seven states, the District of Columbia, and the U.S. Virgin Islands have adopted the UETA. Its purpose is to harmonize state laws concerning retention of paper records and the validity of electronic signatures.

Exam Probability: **High**

14. *Answer choices:*

(see index for correct answer)

- a. open system
- b. interpersonal communication
- c. Uniform Electronic Transactions Act
- d. deep-level diversity

:: Contract law ::

_____ of Contract is a legal term. In contract law, it is the implied ability of an individual to make a legally binding contract on behalf of an organization, by way of uniform or interaction with the public on behalf of that organization. When a person is wearing a uniform or nametag bearing the logo or trademark of a business or organization; or if that person is functioning in an obviously authorized capacity on behalf of a business or organization, that person carries an _____ of Contract. _____ is authority that is not express or written into the contract, but which the agent is assumed to have in order to transact the business of insurance for the principal. _____ is incidental to express authority since not every single detail of an agent`s authority can be spelled out in the written contract.

Exam Probability: **Low**

15. *Answer choices:*

(see index for correct answer)

- a. Implied authority
- b. Synallagmatic contract
- c. Requirements contract
- d. Recording contract

:: Contract law ::

Offer and acceptance analysis is a traditional approach in contract law. The offer and acceptance formula, developed in the 19th century, identifies a moment of formation when the parties are of one mind. This classical approach to contract formation has been modified by developments in the law of estoppel, misleading conduct, misrepresentation and unjust enrichment.

Exam Probability: **Low**

16. *Answer choices:*

(see index for correct answer)

- a. Four corners
- b. Forum selection clause
- c. Offeree
- d. Choice of law clause

Guidance: level 1

:: ::

A _____ is a person who trades in commodities produced by other people. Historically, a _____ is anyone who is involved in business or trade. _____ s have operated for as long as industry, commerce, and trade have existed. During the 16th-century, in Europe, two different terms for _____ s emerged: One term, meerseniers, described local traders such as bakers, grocers, etc.; while a new term, koopman (Dutch: koopman, described _____ s who operated on a global stage, importing and exporting goods over vast distances, and offering added-value services such as credit and finance.

Exam Probability: **High**

17. *Answer choices:*

(see index for correct answer)

- a. Merchant
- b. empathy
- c. Character
- d. open system

Guidance: level 1

:: ::

_____ is the collection of techniques, skills, methods, and processes used in the production of goods or services or in the accomplishment of objectives, such as scientific investigation. _____ can be the knowledge of techniques, processes, and the like, or it can be embedded in machines to allow for operation without detailed knowledge of their workings. Systems applying _____ by taking an input, changing it according to the system`s use, and then producing an outcome are referred to as _____ systems or technological systems.

Exam Probability: **Low**

18. *Answer choices:*

(see index for correct answer)

- a. deep-level diversity
- b. Technology
- c. Sarbanes-Oxley act of 2002
- d. information systems assessment

Guidance: level 1

:: Contract law ::

_____ is a legal cause of action and a type of civil wrong, in which a binding agreement or bargained-for exchange is not honored by one or more of the parties to the contract by non-performance or interference with the other party's performance. Breach occurs when a party to a contract fails to fulfill its obligation as described in the contract, or communicates an intent to fail the obligation or otherwise appears not to be able to perform its obligation under the contract. Where there is _____ , the resulting damages will have to be paid by the party breaching the contract to the aggrieved party.

Exam Probability: **Low**

19. *Answer choices:*

(see index for correct answer)

- a. Breach of contract
- b. Flexible contracts
- c. Pre-existing duty rule
- d. Penal damages

Guidance: level 1

:: ::

Punishment is the imposition of an undesirable or unpleasant outcome upon a group or individual, meted out by an authority—in contexts ranging from child discipline to criminal law—as a response and deterrent to a particular action or behaviour that is deemed undesirable or unacceptable. The reasoning may be to condition a child to avoid self-endangerment, to impose social conformity , to defend norms, to protect against future harms , and to maintain the law—and respect for rule of law—under which the social group is governed. Punishment may be self-inflicted as with self-flagellation and mortification of the flesh in the religious setting, but is most often a form of social coercion.

Exam Probability: **Medium**

20. *Answer choices:*

(see index for correct answer)

- a. levels of analysis
- b. process perspective
- c. personal values
- d. information systems assessment

Guidance: level 1

:: ::

In contract law, rescission is an equitable remedy which allows a contractual party to cancel the contract. Parties may _____ if they are the victims of a vitiating factor, such as misrepresentation, mistake, duress, or undue influence. Rescission is the unwinding of a transaction. This is done to bring the parties, as far as possible, back to the position in which they were before they entered into a contract .

Exam Probability: **Low**

21. *Answer choices:*

(see index for correct answer)

- a. deep-level diversity
- b. functional perspective
- c. hierarchical
- d. Rescind

Guidance: level 1

:: ::

At common law, _____ are a remedy in the form of a monetary award to be paid to a claimant as compensation for loss or injury. To warrant the award, the claimant must show that a breach of duty has caused foreseeable loss. To be recognised at law, the loss must involve damage to property, or mental or physical injury; pure economic loss is rarely recognised for the award of

_____ .

22. *Answer choices:*

(see index for correct answer)

- a. functional perspective
- b. hierarchical
- c. personal values
- d. Damages

Guidance: level 1

:: Statutory law ::

_____ is a principal's approval of an act of its agent that lacked the authority to bind the principal legally. _____ defines the international act in which a state indicates its consent to be bound to a treaty if the parties intended to show their consent by such an act. In the case of bilateral treaties, _____ is usually accomplished by exchanging the requisite instruments, and in the case of multilateral treaties, the usual procedure is for the depositary to collect the _____ s of all states, keeping all parties informed of the situation.

Exam Probability: **Medium**

23. *Answer choices:*

(see index for correct answer)

- a. incorporation by reference
- b. Statutory law
- c. Statute of repose
- d. Ratification

Guidance: level 1

:: Contract law ::

An _____, or simply option, is defined as "a promise which meets the requirements for the formation of a contract and limits the promisor`s power to revoke an offer."

Exam Probability: **High**

24. *Answer choices:*
(see index for correct answer)

- a. Offeror
- b. Option contract
- c. Personal contract purchase
- d. Bonus clause

Guidance: level 1

:: ::

_____ is a concept of English common law and is a necessity for simple contracts but not for special contracts. The concept has been adopted by other common law jurisdictions, including the US.

Exam Probability: **Low**

25. *Answer choices:*

(see index for correct answer)

- a. co-culture
- b. surface-level diversity
- c. functional perspective
- d. interpersonal communication

Guidance: level 1

:: ::

_____ s and acquisitions are transactions in which the ownership of companies, other business organizations, or their operating units are transferred or consolidated with other entities. As an aspect of strategic management, M&A can allow enterprises to grow or downsize, and change the nature of their business or competitive position.

Exam Probability: **Low**

26. *Answer choices:*

(see index for correct answer)

- a. co-culture
- b. deep-level diversity
- c. cultural
- d. Merger

Guidance: level 1

:: Services management and marketing ::

A _____ or servicemark is a trademark used in the United States and several other countries to identify a service rather than a product.

Exam Probability: **Low**

27. *Answer choices:*
(see index for correct answer)

- a. Service mark
- b. Services marketing
- c. Internet hosting service
- d. Backend as a service

Guidance: level 1

_____ is the study and management of exchange relationships. _____ is the business process of creating relationships with and satisfying customers. With its focus on the customer, _____ is one of the premier components of business management.

Exam Probability: **Medium**

28. *Answer choices:*

(see index for correct answer)

- a. Marketing
- b. Character
- c. imperative
- d. personal values

Guidance: level 1

:: Legal doctrines and principles ::

In the common law of torts, _____ loquitur is a doctrine that infers negligence from the very nature of an accident or injury in the absence of direct evidence on how any defendant behaved. Although modern formulations differ by jurisdiction, common law originally stated that the accident must satisfy the necessary elements of negligence: duty, breach of duty, causation, and injury. In _____ loquitur, the elements of duty of care, breach, and causation are inferred from an injury that does not ordinarily occur without negligence.

Exam Probability: **Medium**

29. *Answer choices:*

(see index for correct answer)

- a. Exclusionary rule
- b. Res ipsa
- c. Duty to rescue
- d. Mutual assent

Guidance: level 1

:: Legal terms ::

_____ , a form of alternative dispute resolution , is a way to resolve disputes outside the courts. The dispute will be decided by one or more persons , which renders the " _____ award". An _____ award is legally binding on both sides and enforceable in the courts.

30. *Answer choices:*

(see index for correct answer)

- a. Arbitration
- b. Medical advice
- c. Plain meaning rule
- d. Abandonment

Guidance: level 1

:: Sexual harassment in the United States ::

In law, a _____ , reasonable man, or the man on the Clapham omnibus is a hypothetical person of legal fiction crafted by the courts and communicated through case law and jury instructions.

Exam Probability: **Medium**

31. *Answer choices:*

(see index for correct answer)

- a. Sandy Gallin
- b. Reasonable person
- c. Blakey v. Continental Airlines
- d. North Country

:: ::

_____ is the act or practice of forbidding something by law; more particularly the term refers to the banning of the manufacture, storage , transportation, sale, possession, and consumption of alcoholic beverages. The word is also used to refer to a period of time during which such bans are enforced.

Exam Probability: **Medium**

32. *Answer choices:*

(see index for correct answer)

- a. Prohibition
- b. cultural
- c. personal values
- d. deep-level diversity

:: ::

According to the philosopher Piyush Mathur , "Tangibility is the property that a phenomenon exhibits if it has and/or transports mass and/or energy and/or momentum".

Exam Probability: **Medium**

33. *Answer choices:*

(see index for correct answer)

- a. personal values
- b. surface-level diversity
- c. Tangible
- d. hierarchical perspective

Guidance: level 1

:: ::

A _____ is monetary compensation paid by an employer to an employee in exchange for work done. Payment may be calculated as a fixed amount for each task completed , or at an hourly or daily rate , or based on an easily measured quantity of work done.

Exam Probability: **High**

34. *Answer choices:*

(see index for correct answer)

- a. personal values
- b. hierarchical
- c. Wage
- d. empathy

Guidance: level 1

:: Contract law ::

In contract law, a _____ is a promise which is not a condition of the contract or an innominate term: it is a term "not going to the root of the contract", and which only entitles the innocent party to damages if it is breached: i.e. the _____ is not true or the defaulting party does not perform the contract in accordance with the terms of the _____ . A _____ is not guarantee. It is a mere promise. It may be enforced if it is breached by an award for the legal remedy of damages.

Exam Probability: **Low**

35. *Answer choices:*
(see index for correct answer)

- a. Warranty
- b. Contingent contracts
- c. Standard form contract
- d. Fundamental breach

:: Business law ::

A _____ is an arrangement where parties, known as partners, agree to cooperate to advance their mutual interests. The partners in a _____ may be individuals, businesses, interest-based organizations, schools, governments or combinations. Organizations may partner to increase the likelihood of each achieving their mission and to amplify their reach. A _____ may result in issuing and holding equity or may be only governed by a contract.

Exam Probability: **Medium**

36. *Answer choices:*

(see index for correct answer)

- a. Business courts
- b. Lessor
- c. Business license
- d. Rules of origin

:: ::

The _____ to the United States Constitution prevents the government from making laws which respect an establishment of religion, prohibit the free exercise of religion, or abridge the freedom of speech, the freedom of the press, the right to peaceably assemble, or the right to petition the government for redress of grievances. It was adopted on December 15, 1791, as one of the ten amendments that constitute the Bill of Rights.

Exam Probability: **Medium**

37. *Answer choices:*

(see index for correct answer)

- a. hierarchical perspective
- b. imperative
- c. First Amendment
- d. corporate values

Guidance: level 1

:: Business law ::

In the United States, the United Kingdom, Australia, Canada and South Africa, _____ relates to the doctrines of the law of agency. It is relevant particularly in corporate law and constitutional law. _____ refers to a situation where a reasonable third party would understand that an agent had authority to act. This means a principal is bound by the agent's actions, even if the agent had no actual authority, whether express or implied. It raises an estoppel because the third party is given an assurance, which he relies on and would be inequitable for the principal to deny the authority given. _____ can legally be found, even if actual authority has not been given.

Exam Probability: **Medium**

38. *Answer choices:*

(see index for correct answer)

- a. Ease of doing business index
- b. Duty of fair representation
- c. Apparent authority
- d. Financial Security Law of France

Guidance: level 1

:: ::

_____ is the administration of an organization, whether it is a business, a not-for-profit organization, or government body. _____ includes the activities of setting the strategy of an organization and coordinating the efforts of its employees to accomplish its objectives through the application of available resources, such as financial, natural, technological, and human resources. The term "_____" may also refer to those people who manage an organization.

Exam Probability: **Low**

39. *Answer choices:*

(see index for correct answer)

- a. corporate values
- b. cultural
- c. Sarbanes-Oxley act of 2002
- d. hierarchical

Guidance: level 1

:: ::

A contract is a legally-binding agreement which recognises and governs the rights and duties of the parties to the agreement. A contract is legally enforceable because it meets the requirements and approval of the law. An agreement typically involves the exchange of goods, services, money, or promises of any of those. In the event of breach of contract, the law awards the injured party access to legal remedies such as damages and cancellation.

40. *Answer choices:*

(see index for correct answer)

- a. hierarchical
- b. Contract law
- c. functional perspective
- d. open system

Guidance: level 1

:: United States corporate law ::

In tort law, a _____ is a legal obligation which is imposed on an individual requiring adherence to a standard of reasonable care while performing any acts that could foreseeably harm others. It is the first element that must be established to proceed with an action in negligence. The claimant must be able to show a _____ imposed by law which the defendant has breached. In turn, breaching a duty may subject an individual to liability. The _____ may be imposed by operation of law between individuals who have no current direct relationship but eventually become related in some manner, as defined by common law .

Exam Probability: **Medium**

41. *Answer choices:*

(see index for correct answer)

- a. Duty of care
- b. New York Business Corporation Law
- c. NYSE Listed Company Manual
- d. Dunlop Commission on the Future of Worker-Management Relations: Final Report

Guidance: level 1

:: Criminal procedure ::

_____ is the adjudication process of the criminal law. While _____ differs dramatically by jurisdiction, the process generally begins with a formal criminal charge with the person on trial either being free on bail or incarcerated, and results in the conviction or acquittal of the defendant. _____ can be either in form of inquisitorial or adversarial _____ .

Exam Probability: **High**

42. *Answer choices:*

(see index for correct answer)

- a. Criminal procedure
- b. directed verdict

Guidance: level 1

:: ::

A _____ is a request to do something, most commonly addressed to a government official or public entity. _____ s to a deity are a form of prayer called supplication.

Exam Probability: **Low**

43. *Answer choices:*

(see index for correct answer)

- a. personal values
- b. levels of analysis
- c. co-culture
- d. similarity-attraction theory

Guidance: level 1

:: ::

An _____ is the production of goods or related services within an economy. The major source of revenue of a group or company is the indicator of its relevant _____ . When a large group has multiple sources of revenue generation, it is considered to be working in different industries. Manufacturing _____ became a key sector of production and labour in European and North American countries during the Industrial Revolution, upsetting previous mercantile and feudal economies. This came through many successive rapid advances in technology, such as the production of steel and coal.

Exam Probability: **Low**

44. *Answer choices:*

(see index for correct answer)

- a. Industry
- b. interpersonal communication
- c. surface-level diversity
- d. empathy

Guidance: level 1

:: Equity (law) ::

An assignment is a legal term used in the context of the law of contract and of property. In both instances, assignment is the process whereby a person, the assignor, transfers rights or benefits to another, the _____ . An assignment may not transfer a duty, burden or detriment without the express agreement of the _____ . The right or benefit being assigned may be a gift or it may be paid for with a contractual consideration such as money.

Exam Probability: **High**

45. *Answer choices:*

(see index for correct answer)

- a. Assignee
- b. Equitable conversion

Guidance: level 1

:: American legal terms ::

The phrase "by _____ " is a legal term that indicates that a right or liability has been created for a party, irrespective of the intent of that party, because it is dictated by existing legal principles. For example, if a person dies without a will, his or her heirs are determined by _____ . Similarly, if a person marries or has a child after his or her will has been executed, the law writes this pretermitted spouse or pretermitted heir into the will if no provision for this situation was specifically included. Adverse possession, in which title to land passes because non-owners have occupied it for a certain period of time, is another important right that vests by _____ .

46. *Answer choices:*

(see index for correct answer)

- a. Operation of law
- b. Chilling effect

Guidance: level 1

:: Sureties ::

In finance, a _____ , _____ bond or guaranty involves a promise by one party to assume responsibility for the debt obligation of a borrower if that borrower defaults. The person or company providing the promise is also known as a " _____ " or as a "guarantor".

Exam Probability: **Low**

47. *Answer choices:*

(see index for correct answer)

- a. Payment bond
- b. Miller Act
- c. Little Miller Act
- d. Surety

:: Real property law ::

A _____ is the grant of authority or rights, stating that the granter formally recognizes the prerogative of the recipient to exercise the rights specified. It is implicit that the granter retains superiority , and that the recipient admits a limited status within the relationship, and it is within that sense that _____ s were historically granted, and that sense is retained in modern usage of the term.

Exam Probability: **Medium**

48. *Answer choices:*

(see index for correct answer)

- a. Loss factor
- b. Infectious invalidity
- c. Purveyance
- d. Charter

:: Project management ::

A _____ is a source or supply from which a benefit is produced and it has some utility. _____ s can broadly be classified upon their availability—they are classified into renewable and non-renewable _____ s. Examples of non renewable _____ s are coal ,crude oil natural gas nuclear energy etc. Examples of renewable _____ s are air,water,wind,solar energy etc. They can also be classified as actual and potential on the basis of level of development and use, on the basis of origin they can be classified as biotic and abiotic, and on the basis of their distribution, as ubiquitous and localized . An item becomes a _____ with time and developing technology. Typically, _____ s are materials, energy, services, staff, knowledge, or other assets that are transformed to produce benefit and in the process may be consumed or made unavailable. Benefits of _____ utilization may include increased wealth, proper functioning of a system, or enhanced well-being. From a human perspective a natural _____ is anything obtained from the environment to satisfy human needs and wants. From a broader biological or ecological perspective a _____ satisfies the needs of a living organism .

Exam Probability: **Low**

49. *Answer choices:*
(see index for correct answer)

- a. Resource
- b. Project anatomy
- c. Theory X and Theory Y
- d. Changes clause

Guidance: level 1

:: Business ::

An _____ is a key document used by limited liability companies to outline the business' financial and functional decisions including rules, regulations and provisions. The purpose of the document is to govern the internal operations of the business in a way that suits the specific needs of the business owners. Once the document is signed by the members of the limited liability company, it acts as an official contract binding them to its terms. _____ is mandatory as per laws only in 5 states - California, Delaware, Maine, Missouri, and New York LLCs operating without an _____ are governed by the state's default rules contained in the relevant statute and developed through state court decisions. An _____ is similar in function to corporate by-laws, or analogous to a partnership agreement in multi-member LLCs. In single-member LLCs, an _____ is a declaration of the structure that the member has chosen for the company and sometimes used to prove in court that the LLC structure is separate from that of the individual owner and thus necessary so that the owner has documentation to prove that he or she is indeed separate from the entity itself.

Exam Probability: **Low**

50. *Answer choices:*

(see index for correct answer)

- a. Business as usual
- b. Number
- c. Operating agreement
- d. Closure

Guidance: level 1

:: International relations ::

_____ is double mindedness or double heartedness in duplicity, fraud, or deception. It may involve intentional deceit of others, or self-deception.

Exam Probability: **Medium**

51. *Answer choices:*

(see index for correct answer)

- a. Democracy promotion
- b. Great power
- c. Democracy building
- d. Bad faith

Guidance: level 1

:: Intention ::

_____ is the mental element of a person's intention to commit a crime; or knowledge that one's action or lack of action would cause a crime to be committed. It is a necessary element of many crimes.

Exam Probability: **High**

52. *Answer choices:*

(see index for correct answer)

- a. Letter of Intent
- b. bona fide

Guidance: level 1

:: Business models ::

A _____ , _____ company or daughter company is a company that is owned or controlled by another company, which is called the parent company, parent, or holding company. The _____ can be a company, corporation, or limited liability company. In some cases it is a government or state-owned enterprise. In some cases, particularly in the music and book publishing industries, subsidiaries are referred to as imprints.

Exam Probability: **Medium**

53. *Answer choices:*

(see index for correct answer)

- a. Subsidiary
- b. Business-agile enterprise
- c. Interactive contract manufacturing
- d. Organizational architecture

Guidance: level 1

:: Debt ::

A _____ is a party that has a claim on the services of a second party. It is a person or institution to whom money is owed. The first party, in general, has provided some property or service to the second party under the assumption that the second party will return an equivalent property and service. The second party is frequently called a debtor or borrower. The first party is called the _____ , which is the lender of property, service, or money.

Exam Probability: **High**

54. *Answer choices:*
(see index for correct answer)

- a. Paid outside closing
- b. Tax benefits of debt
- c. Debt crisis
- d. Creditor

Guidance: level 1

:: Contract Clause case law ::

The _____ appears in the United States Constitution, Article I, section 10, clause 1. The clause prohibits a State from passing any law that "impairs the obligation of contracts" or "makes any thing but gold and silver coin a tender in payment of debts". It states.

Exam Probability: **Low**

55. *Answer choices:*

(see index for correct answer)

- a. Fletcher v. Peck
- b. Smyth v. Ames
- c. Contract Clause

Guidance: level 1

:: Insurance law ::

_____ exists when an insured person derives a financial or other kind of benefit from the continuous existence, without repairment or damage, of the insured object . A person has an _____ in something when loss of or damage to that thing would cause the person to suffer a financial or other kind of loss.Normally, _____ is established by ownership, possession, or direct relationship. For example, people have _____ s in their own homes and vehicles, but not in their neighbors` homes and vehicles, and almost certainly not those of strangers.

Exam Probability: **High**

56. *Answer choices:*

(see index for correct answer)

- a. Bermuda Form
- b. Hangarter v. Provident
- c. Insurable interest

- d. Marine Insurance Act 1906

Guidance: level 1

:: ::

In law, a _____ is a coming together of parties to a dispute, to present information in a tribunal, a formal setting with the authority to adjudicate claims or disputes. One form of tribunal is a court. The tribunal, which may occur before a judge, jury, or other designated trier of fact, aims to achieve a resolution to their dispute.

Exam Probability: **Low**

57. *Answer choices:*

(see index for correct answer)

- a. Trial
- b. empathy
- c. hierarchical perspective
- d. surface-level diversity

Guidance: level 1

:: Promotion and marketing communications ::

In everyday language, _____ refers to exaggerated or false praise. In law, _____ is a promotional statement or claim that expresses subjective rather than objective views, which no "reasonable person" would take literally. _____ serves to "puff up" an exaggerated image of what is being described and is especially featured in testimonials.

Exam Probability: **High**

58. *Answer choices:*

(see index for correct answer)

- a. Target audience
- b. Open2save
- c. Helter Skelter
- d. Street team

Guidance: level 1

:: Business law ::

A _____ is a form of security interest granted over an item of property to secure the payment of a debt or performance of some other obligation. The owner of the property, who grants the _____ , is referred to as the _____ ee and the person who has the benefit of the _____ is referred to as the _____ or or _____ holder.

Exam Probability: **Medium**

59. *Answer choices:*

(see index for correct answer)

- a. Board of directors
- b. Lessor
- c. Lien
- d. Recharacterisation

Guidance: level 1

Finance

Finance is a field that is concerned with the allocation (investment) of assets and liabilities over space and time, often under conditions of risk or uncertainty. Finance can also be defined as the science of money management. Participants in the market aim to price assets based on their risk level, fundamental value, and their expected rate of return. Finance can be split into three sub-categories: public finance, corporate finance and personal finance.

:: ::

_____ is an eight-block-long street running roughly northwest to southeast from Broadway to South Street, at the East River, in the Financial District of Lower Manhattan in New York City. Over time, the term has become a metonym for the financial markets of the United States as a whole, the American financial services industry , or New York–based financial interests.

Exam Probability: **Medium**

1. *Answer choices:*

(see index for correct answer)

- a. personal values
- b. co-culture
- c. information systems assessment
- d. Wall Street

Guidance: level 1

:: Inventory ::

Costs are associated with particular goods using one of the several formulas, including specific identification, first-in first-out , or average cost. Costs include all costs of purchase, costs of conversion and other costs that are incurred in bringing the inventories to their present location and condition. Costs of goods made by the businesses include material, labor, and allocated overhead. The costs of those goods which are not yet sold are deferred as costs of inventory until the inventory is sold or written down in value.

2. *Answer choices:*

(see index for correct answer)

- a. Stock obsolescence
- b. New old stock
- c. Cost of goods sold
- d. Order fulfillment

Guidance: level 1

:: Leasing ::

A finance lease is a type of lease in which a finance company is typically the legal owner of the asset for the duration of the lease, while the lessee not only has operating control over the asset, but also has a some share of the economic risks and returns from the change in the valuation of the underlying asset.

Exam Probability: **Low**

3. *Answer choices:*

(see index for correct answer)

- a. Capital lease
- b. Synthetic lease

Guidance: level 1

:: ::

In the field of analysis of algorithms in computer science, the _____ is a method of amortized analysis based on accounting. The _____ often gives a more intuitive account of the amortized cost of an operation than either aggregate analysis or the potential method. Note, however, that this does not guarantee such analysis will be immediately obvious; often, choosing the correct parameters for the _____ requires as much knowledge of the problem and the complexity bounds one is attempting to prove as the other two methods.

Exam Probability: **Medium**

4. *Answer choices:*

(see index for correct answer)

- a. Character
- b. similarity-attraction theory
- c. Sarbanes-Oxley act of 2002
- d. Accounting method

Guidance: level 1

:: Derivatives (finance) ::

In finance, a _____ or simply a forward is a non-standardized contract between two parties to buy or to sell an asset at a specified future time at a price agreed upon today, making it a type of derivative instrument. The party agreeing to buy the underlying asset in the future assumes a long position, and the party agreeing to sell the asset in the future assumes a short position. The price agreed upon is called the delivery price, which is equal to the forward price at the time the contract is entered into.

Exam Probability: **Medium**

5. *Answer choices:*

(see index for correct answer)

- a. Interest rate option
- b. Calendar spread
- c. Forward contract
- d. Constant maturity swap

Guidance: level 1

:: Financial risk ::

_____ is any of various types of risk associated with financing, including financial transactions that include company loans in risk of default. Often it is understood to include only downside risk, meaning the potential for financial loss and uncertainty about its extent.

Exam Probability: **High**

6. *Answer choices:*

(see index for correct answer)

- a. Tail risk
- b. Financial risk
- c. Entropic risk measure
- d. Fixed bill

Guidance: level 1

:: Mathematical finance ::

In economics and finance, _____ , also known as present discounted value, is the value of an expected income stream determined as of the date of valuation. The _____ is always less than or equal to the future value because money has interest-earning potential, a characteristic referred to as the time value of money, except during times of negative interest rates, when the _____ will be more than the future value. Time value can be described with the simplified phrase, "A dollar today is worth more than a dollar tomorrow". Here, `worth more` means that its value is greater. A dollar today is worth more than a dollar tomorrow because the dollar can be invested and earn a day`s worth of interest, making the total accumulate to a value more than a dollar by tomorrow. Interest can be compared to rent. Just as rent is paid to a landlord by a tenant without the ownership of the asset being transferred, interest is paid to a lender by a borrower who gains access to the money for a time before paying it back. By letting the borrower have access to the money, the lender has sacrificed the exchange value of this money, and is compensated for it in the form of interest. The initial amount of the borrowed funds is less than the total amount of money paid to the lender.

Exam Probability: **Low**

7. *Answer choices:*

(see index for correct answer)

- a. Statistical arbitrage
- b. Snell envelope
- c. Modigliani risk-adjusted performance
- d. Admissible trading strategy

Guidance: level 1

:: Finance ::

_____ is a field that is concerned with the allocation of assets and liabilities over space and time, often under conditions of risk or uncertainty. _____ can also be defined as the art of money management. Participants in the market aim to price assets based on their risk level, fundamental value, and their expected rate of return. _____ can be split into three sub-categories: public _____, corporate _____ and personal _____ .

Exam Probability: **Medium**

8. *Answer choices:*

(see index for correct answer)

- a. Gage
- b. Lex monetae
- c. Universal default

- d. Target benefit plan

Guidance: level 1

:: Derivatives (finance) ::

A _____ or _____ row is a line of closely spaced shrubs and sometimes trees, planted and trained to form a barrier or to mark the boundary of an area, such as between neighbouring properties. _____ s used to separate a road from adjoining fields or one field from another, and of sufficient age to incorporate larger trees, are known as _____ rows. Often they serve as windbreaks to improve conditions for the adjacent crops, as in bocage country. When clipped and maintained, _____ s are also a simple form of topiary.

Exam Probability: **High**

9. *Answer choices:*

(see index for correct answer)

- a. Hedge
- b. John J. Ensminger
- c. Commodity tick
- d. Exotic derivative

Guidance: level 1

:: International trade ::

_____ involves the transfer of goods or services from one person or entity to another, often in exchange for money. A system or network that allows _____ is called a market.

Exam Probability: **Low**

10. *Answer choices:*

(see index for correct answer)

- a. Portable Sanitation Association International
- b. Trade
- c. Cross-border cooperation
- d. International commodity agreement

Guidance: level 1

:: Financial markets ::

For an individual, a _____ is the minimum amount of money by which the expected return on a risky asset must exceed the known return on a risk-free asset in order to induce an individual to hold the risky asset rather than the risk-free asset. It is positive if the person is risk averse. Thus it is the minimum willingness to accept compensation for the risk.

Exam Probability: **Low**

11. *Answer choices:*

(see index for correct answer)

- a. Virtual bidding
- b. Security analysis
- c. Hot equity periods
- d. Risk premium

Guidance: level 1

:: ::

_____ is a concept of English common law and is a necessity for simple contracts but not for special contracts . The concept has been adopted by other common law jurisdictions, including the US.

Exam Probability: **Low**

12. *Answer choices:*

(see index for correct answer)

- a. Consideration
- b. Sarbanes-Oxley act of 2002
- c. Character
- d. corporate values

Guidance: level 1

:: Consumer theory ::

A _____ is a technical term in psychology, economics and philosophy usually used in relation to choosing between alternatives. For example, someone prefers A over B if they would rather choose A than B.

Exam Probability: **Medium**

13. *Answer choices:*

(see index for correct answer)

- a. Preference
- b. Lexicographic preferences
- c. Marginal rate of substitution
- d. Demand vacuum

Guidance: level 1

:: ::

_____ is the production of products for use or sale using labour and machines, tools, chemical and biological processing, or formulation. The term may refer to a range of human activity, from handicraft to high tech, but is most commonly applied to industrial design, in which raw materials are transformed into finished goods on a large scale. Such finished goods may be sold to other manufacturers for the production of other, more complex products, such as aircraft, household appliances, furniture, sports equipment or automobiles, or sold to wholesalers, who in turn sell them to retailers, who then sell them to end users and consumers.

Exam Probability: **High**

14. *Answer choices:*
(see index for correct answer)

- a. Manufacturing
- b. functional perspective
- c. hierarchical
- d. similarity-attraction theory

Guidance: level 1

:: ::

_____ is the quantity of three-dimensional space enclosed by a closed surface, for example, the space that a substance or shape occupies or contains. _____ is often quantified numerically using the SI derived unit, the cubic metre. The _____ of a container is generally understood to be the capacity of the container; i. e., the amount of fluid that the container could hold, rather than the amount of space the container itself displaces. Three dimensional mathematical shapes are also assigned _____ s. _____ s of some simple shapes, such as regular, straight-edged, and circular shapes can be easily calculated using arithmetic formulas. _____ s of complicated shapes can be calculated with integral calculus if a formula exists for the shape`s boundary. One-dimensional figures and two-dimensional shapes are assigned zero _____ in the three-dimensional space.

Exam Probability: **High**

15. *Answer choices:*
(see index for correct answer)

- a. Sarbanes-Oxley act of 2002
- b. hierarchical perspective
- c. Volume
- d. cultural

Guidance: level 1

:: Inventory ::

_____ is a system of inventory in which updates are made on a periodic basis. This differs from perpetual inventory systems, where updates are made as seen fit.

Exam Probability: **Low**

16. *Answer choices:*

(see index for correct answer)

- a. Lower of cost or market
- b. Inventory optimization
- c. Stock demands
- d. Periodic inventory

Guidance: level 1

:: ::

A _____ is the period used by governments for accounting and budget purposes, which varies between countries. It is also used for financial reporting by business and other organizations. Laws in many jurisdictions require company financial reports to be prepared and published on an annual basis, but generally do not require the reporting period to align with the calendar year . Taxation laws generally require accounting records to be maintained and taxes calculated on an annual basis, which usually corresponds to the _____ used for government purposes. The calculation of tax on an annual basis is especially relevant for direct taxation, such as income tax. Many annual government fees—such as Council rates, licence fees, etc.—are also levied on a _____ basis, while others are charged on an anniversary basis.

Exam Probability: **High**

17. *Answer choices:*

(see index for correct answer)

- a. corporate values
- b. interpersonal communication
- c. information systems assessment
- d. empathy

Guidance: level 1

:: Decision theory ::

Within economics the concept of _____ is used to model worth or value, but its usage has evolved significantly over time. The term was introduced initially as a measure of pleasure or satisfaction within the theory of utilitarianism by moral philosophers such as Jeremy Bentham and John Stuart Mill. But the term has been adapted and reapplied within neoclassical economics, which dominates modern economic theory, as a _____ function that represents a consumer's preference ordering over a choice set. As such, it is devoid of its original interpretation as a measurement of the pleasure or satisfaction obtained by the consumer from that choice.

Exam Probability: **High**

18. *Answer choices:*

(see index for correct answer)

- a. Influence diagram
- b. Institutionalism
- c. Menu dependence
- d. Applied information economics

Guidance: level 1

:: Stock market ::

The _____ of a corporation is all of the shares into which ownership of the corporation is divided. In American English, the shares are commonly known as " _____ s". A single share of the _____ represents fractional ownership of the corporation in proportion to the total number of shares. This typically entitles the _____ holder to that fraction of the company's earnings, proceeds from liquidation of assets , or voting power, often dividing these up in proportion to the amount of money each _____ holder has invested. Not all _____ is necessarily equal, as certain classes of _____ may be issued for example without voting rights, with enhanced voting rights, or with a certain priority to receive profits or liquidation proceeds before or after other classes of shareholders.

Exam Probability: **Low**

19. *Answer choices:*

(see index for correct answer)

- a. Block premium
- b. PLUS Markets Group
- c. Stock
- d. Smaller reporting company

Guidance: level 1

:: Financial ratios ::

_____ is a measure of how revenue growth translates into growth in operating income. It is a measure of leverage, and of how risky, or volatile, a company's operating income is.

20. *Answer choices:*

(see index for correct answer)

- a. Cash flow return on investment
- b. Operating margin
- c. Operating leverage
- d. Capitalization rate

Guidance: level 1

:: Accounting terminology ::

In accounting/accountancy, _____ are journal entries usually made at the end of an accounting period to allocate income and expenditure to the period in which they actually occurred. The revenue recognition principle is the basis of making _____ that pertain to unearned and accrued revenues under accrual-basis accounting. They are sometimes called Balance Day adjustments because they are made on balance day.

Exam Probability: **Low**

21. *Answer choices:*

(see index for correct answer)

- a. profit and loss statement
- b. Capital appreciation

- c. Adjusting entries
- d. Capital surplus

Guidance: level 1

:: Financial risk ::

The _____ on a financial investment is the expected value of its return . It is a measure of the center of the distribution of the random variable that is the return.

Exam Probability: **Low**

22. *Answer choices:*

(see index for correct answer)

- a. Interest rate risk
- b. Acceptance set
- c. Over-the-counter
- d. Expected return

Guidance: level 1

:: Contract law ::

A _____ is a legally-binding agreement which recognises and governs the rights and duties of the parties to the agreement. A _____ is legally enforceable because it meets the requirements and approval of the law. An agreement typically involves the exchange of goods, services, money, or promises of any of those. In the event of breach of _____ , the law awards the injured party access to legal remedies such as damages and cancellation.

Exam Probability: **Medium**

23. *Answer choices:*

(see index for correct answer)

- a. Efficient breach
- b. Pact ink
- c. Implied warranty
- d. Unenforceable contract

Guidance: level 1

:: Asset ::

In financial accounting, an _____ is any resource owned by the business. Anything tangible or intangible that can be owned or controlled to produce value and that is held by a company to produce positive economic value is an _____ . Simply stated, _____ s represent value of ownership that can be converted into cash . The balance sheet of a firm records the monetary value of the _____ s owned by that firm. It covers money and other valuables belonging to an individual or to a business.

24. *Answer choices:*

(see index for correct answer)

- a. Current asset
- b. Fixed asset

Guidance: level 1

:: Financial risk ::

_____ is the risk that arises for bond owners from fluctuating interest rates. How much _____ a bond has depends on how sensitive its price is to interest rate changes in the market. The sensitivity depends on two things, the bond's time to maturity, and the coupon rate of the bond.

25. *Answer choices:*

(see index for correct answer)

- a. Trading room
- b. Modern portfolio theory
- c. Cascades in Financial Networks
- d. Consumer credit risk

Guidance: level 1

:: Data management ::

_____ is a form of intellectual property that grants the creator of an original creative work an exclusive legal right to determine whether and under what conditions this original work may be copied and used by others, usually for a limited term of years. The exclusive rights are not absolute but limited by limitations and exceptions to _____ law, including fair use. A major limitation on _____ on ideas is that _____ protects only the original expression of ideas, and not the underlying ideas themselves.

Exam Probability: **Medium**

26. *Answer choices:*

(see index for correct answer)

- a. Copyright
- b. Enterprise manufacturing intelligence
- c. SQL programming tool
- d. Open Compute Project

Guidance: level 1

:: Accounting terminology ::

In management accounting or _____ , managers use the provisions of accounting information in order to better inform themselves before they decide matters within their organizations, which aids their management and performance of control functions.

Exam Probability: **High**

27. *Answer choices:*

(see index for correct answer)

- a. Accrued liabilities
- b. Basis of accounting
- c. Managerial accounting
- d. double-entry bookkeeping

Guidance: level 1

:: Business law ::

A _____ is an arrangement where parties, known as partners, agree to cooperate to advance their mutual interests. The partners in a _____ may be individuals, businesses, interest-based organizations, schools, governments or combinations. Organizations may partner to increase the likelihood of each achieving their mission and to amplify their reach. A _____ may result in issuing and holding equity or may be only governed by a contract.

Exam Probability: **High**

28. *Answer choices:*

(see index for correct answer)

- a. Ordinary resolution
- b. Turnkey
- c. Business courts
- d. Financial Security Law of France

Guidance: level 1

:: Project management ::

Some scenarios associate "this kind of planning" with learning "life skills". _____ s are necessary, or at least useful, in situations where individuals need to know what time they must be at a specific location to receive a specific service, and where people need to accomplish a set of goals within a set time period.

Exam Probability: **High**

29. *Answer choices:*

(see index for correct answer)

- a. IPMA
- b. Schedule
- c. Project planning
- d. NetPoint

:: ::

In finance, return is a profit on an investment. It comprises any change in value of the investment, and/or cash flows which the investor receives from the investment, such as interest payments or dividends. It may be measured either in absolute terms or as a percentage of the amount invested. The latter is also called the holding period return.

Exam Probability: **High**

30. *Answer choices:*

(see index for correct answer)

- a. cultural
- b. Sarbanes-Oxley act of 2002
- c. open system
- d. hierarchical perspective

:: Cash flow ::

In corporate finance, _____ or _____ to firm is a way of looking at a business's cash flow to see what is available for distribution among all the securities holders of a corporate entity. This may be useful to parties such as equity holders, debt holders, preferred stock holders, and convertible security holders when they want to see how much cash can be extracted from a company without causing issues to its operations.

Exam Probability: **Low**

31. *Answer choices:*

(see index for correct answer)

- a. Free cash flow
- b. First Chicago Method
- c. Operating cash flow
- d. Factoring

Guidance: level 1

:: Legal terms ::

_____ s may be governments, corporations or investment trusts. _____ s are legally responsible for the obligations of the issue and for reporting financial conditions, material developments and any other operational activities as required by the regulations of their jurisdictions.

Exam Probability: **Medium**

32. *Answer choices:*

(see index for correct answer)

- a. Gross floor area
- b. Issuer
- c. Error
- d. Force

Guidance: level 1

:: Finance ::

A _____ , publicly-traded company, publicly-held company, publicly-listed company, or public limited company is a corporation whose ownership is dispersed among the general public in many shares of stock which are freely traded on a stock exchange or in over-the-counter markets. In some jurisdictions, public companies over a certain size must be listed on an exchange. A _____ can be listed or unlisted .

Exam Probability: **Medium**

33. *Answer choices:*

(see index for correct answer)

- a. Pet banks
- b. Portfolio margin
- c. Swisspartners Group
- d. ITR-2

:: ::

_____ is the process of making predictions of the future based on past and present data and most commonly by analysis of trends. A commonplace example might be estimation of some variable of interest at some specified future date. Prediction is a similar, but more general term. Both might refer to formal statistical methods employing time series, cross-sectional or longitudinal data, or alternatively to less formal judgmental methods. Usage can differ between areas of application: for example, in hydrology the terms "forecast" and "_____" are sometimes reserved for estimates of values at certain specific future times, while the term "prediction" is used for more general estimates, such as the number of times floods will occur over a long period.

Exam Probability: **Medium**

34. *Answer choices:*

(see index for correct answer)

- a. cultural
- b. Sarbanes-Oxley act of 2002
- c. personal values
- d. Forecasting

:: Financial ratios ::

The _____ or dividend-price ratio of a share is the dividend per share, divided by the price per share. It is also a company's total annual dividend payments divided by its market capitalization, assuming the number of shares is constant. It is often expressed as a percentage.

Exam Probability: **Medium**

35. *Answer choices:*

(see index for correct answer)

- a. Interest coverage ratio
- b. Dividend yield
- c. Accounting liquidity
- d. Retention rate

Guidance: level 1

:: Goods ::

In most contexts, the concept of _____ denotes the conduct that should be preferred when posed with a choice between possible actions. _____ is generally considered to be the opposite of evil, and is of interest in the study of morality, ethics, religion and philosophy. The specific meaning and etymology of the term and its associated translations among ancient and contemporary languages show substantial variation in its inflection and meaning depending on circumstances of place, history, religious, or philosophical context.

36. *Answer choices:*

(see index for correct answer)

- a. Case
- b. Global public good
- c. Credence good
- d. Good

Guidance: level 1

:: ::

In accounting, the _____ is a measure of the number of times inventory is sold or used in a time period such as a year. It is calculated to see if a business has an excessive inventory in comparison to its sales level. The equation for _____ equals the cost of goods sold divided by the average inventory. _____ is also known as inventory turns, merchandise turnover, stockturn, stock turns, turns, and stock turnover.

Exam Probability: **Medium**

37. *Answer choices:*

(see index for correct answer)

- a. open system
- b. functional perspective

- c. Character
- d. corporate values

Guidance: level 1

:: Management accounting ::

In economics, _____ s, indirect costs or overheads are business expenses
that are not dependent on the level of goods or services produced by the
business. They tend to be time-related, such as interest or rents being paid
per month, and are often referred to as overhead costs. This is in contrast to
variable costs, which are volume-related and unknown at the beginning of the
accounting year. For a simple example, such as a bakery, the monthly rent for
the baking facilities, and the monthly payments for the security system and
basic phone line are _____ s, as they do not change according to how much
bread the bakery produces and sells. On the other hand, the wage costs of the
bakery are variable, as the bakery will have to hire more workers if the
production of bread increases. Economists reckon _____ as a entry barrier
for new entrepreneurs.

Exam Probability: **Medium**

38. *Answer choices:*

(see index for correct answer)

- a. Fixed cost
- b. Chartered Cost Accountant
- c. Managerial risk accounting
- d. Contribution margin

:: Generally Accepted Accounting Principles ::

_____ , or non-current liabilities, are liabilities that are due beyond a year or the normal operation period of the company. The normal operation period is the amount of time it takes for a company to turn inventory into cash. On a classified balance sheet, liabilities are separated between current and _____ to help users assess the company's financial standing in short-term and long-term periods. _____ give users more information about the long-term prosperity of the company, while current liabilities inform the user of debt that the company owes in the current period. On a balance sheet, accounts are listed in order of liquidity, so _____ come after current liabilities. In addition, the specific long-term liability accounts are listed on the balance sheet in order of liquidity. Therefore, an account due within eighteen months would be listed before an account due within twenty-four months. Examples of _____ are bonds payable, long-term loans, capital leases, pension liabilities, post-retirement healthcare liabilities, deferred compensation, deferred revenues, deferred income taxes, and derivative liabilities.

Exam Probability: **Medium**

39. *Answer choices:*

(see index for correct answer)

- a. Engagement letter
- b. Historical cost
- c. Long-term liabilities
- d. Shares outstanding

:: Income ::

_____ is a ratio between the net profit and cost of investment resulting from an investment of some resources. A high ROI means the investment's gains favorably to its cost. As a performance measure, ROI is used to evaluate the efficiency of an investment or to compare the efficiencies of several different investments. In purely economic terms, it is one way of relating profits to capital invested. _____ is a performance measure used by businesses to identify the efficiency of an investment or number of different investments.

Exam Probability: **High**

40. *Answer choices:*
(see index for correct answer)

- a. Windfall gain
- b. Giganomics
- c. Return on investment
- d. Income earner

:: Inventory ::

_____ is the amount of inventory a company has in stock at the end of its fiscal year. It is closely related with _____ cost, which is the amount of money spent to get these goods in stock. It should be calculated at the lower of cost or market.

Exam Probability: **High**

41. *Answer choices:*

(see index for correct answer)

- a. Stock-taking
- b. just-in-time manufacturing
- c. Ending inventory
- d. Stock mix

Guidance: level 1

:: Banking ::

A _____ is a financial account maintained by a bank for a customer. A _____ can be a deposit account, a credit card account, a current account, or any other type of account offered by a financial institution, and represents the funds that a customer has entrusted to the financial institution and from which the customer can make withdrawals. Alternatively, accounts may be loan accounts in which case the customer owes money to the financial institution.

Exam Probability: **Medium**

42. *Answer choices:*

(see index for correct answer)

- a. Direct bank
- b. Bank account
- c. Christmas club
- d. Mount of piety

Guidance: level 1

:: Funds ::

_____ value is the value of an entity's assets minus the value of its liabilities, often in relation to open-end or mutual funds, since shares of such funds registered with the U.S. Securities and Exchange Commission are redeemed at their _____ value. It is also a key figure with regard to hedge funds and venture capital funds when calculating the value of the underlying investments in these funds by investors. This may also be the same as the book value or the equity value of a business. _____ value may represent the value of the total equity, or it may be divided by the number of shares outstanding held by investors, thereby representing the _____ value per share.

Exam Probability: **High**

43. *Answer choices:*

(see index for correct answer)

- a. Indie Fund

- b. Designation Scheme
- c. Net asset
- d. New Energy to Reinvent and Diversify Fund

Guidance: level 1

:: Fixed income analysis ::

The _____ , book yield or redemption yield of a bond or other fixed-interest security, such as gilts, is the internal rate of return earned by an investor who buys the bond today at the market price, assuming that the bond is held until maturity, and that all coupon and principal payments are made on schedule. _____ is the discount rate at which the sum of all future cash flows from the bond is equal to the current price of the bond. The YTM is often given in terms of Annual Percentage Rate , but more often market convention is followed. In a number of major markets the convention is to quote annualized yields with semi-annual compounding ; thus, for example, an annual effective yield of 10.25% would be quoted as 10.00%, because $1.05 \times 1.05 = 1.1025$ and $2 \times 5 = 10$.

Exam Probability: **Medium**

44. *Answer choices:*

(see index for correct answer)

- a. Mortgage yield
- b. Fisher equation
- c. Option-adjusted spread
- d. Bond duration closed-form formula

:: Stock market ::

A _____ , equity market or share market is the aggregation of buyers and sellers of stocks , which represent ownership claims on businesses; these may include securities listed on a public stock exchange, as well as stock that is only traded privately. Examples of the latter include shares of private companies which are sold to investors through equity crowdfunding platforms. Stock exchanges list shares of common equity as well as other security types, e.g. corporate bonds and convertible bonds.

Exam Probability: **Low**

45. *Answer choices:*

(see index for correct answer)

- a. Red herring prospectus
- b. Secondary market offering
- c. Tech Buzz
- d. Program trading

:: Elementary geometry ::

The _____ is the front of an animal's head that features three of the head's sense organs, the eyes, nose, and mouth, and through which animals express many of their emotions. The _____ is crucial for human identity, and damage such as scarring or developmental deformities affects the psyche adversely.

Exam Probability: **Medium**

46. *Answer choices:*

(see index for correct answer)

- a. Direction
- b. Parallel
- c. Face
- d. Face diagonal

Guidance: level 1

:: Management ::

_____ is the identification, evaluation, and prioritization of risks followed by coordinated and economical application of resources to minimize, monitor, and control the probability or impact of unfortunate events or to maximize the realization of opportunities.

Exam Probability: **Medium**

47. *Answer choices:*

(see index for correct answer)

- a. Enterprise planning system
- b. Risk management
- c. Facilitator
- d. Economic production quantity

Guidance: level 1

:: Generally Accepted Accounting Principles ::

The term _____ is most often used to describe a practice or document that is provided as a courtesy or satisfies minimum requirements, conforms to a norm or doctrine, tends to be performed perfunctorily or is considered a formality.

Exam Probability: **Medium**

48. *Answer choices:*

(see index for correct answer)

- a. Pro forma
- b. Consolidation
- c. net realisable value
- d. Historical cost

:: ::

MCI, Inc. was an American telecommunication corporation, currently a subsidiary of Verizon Communications, with its main office in Ashburn, Virginia. The corporation was formed originally as a result of the merger of _____ and MCI Communications corporations, and used the name MCI _____ , succeeded by _____ , before changing its name to the present version on April 12, 2003, as part of the corporation's ending of its bankruptcy status. The company traded on NASDAQ as WCOM and MCIP . The corporation was purchased by Verizon Communications with the deal finalizing on January 6, 2006, and is now identified as that company's Verizon Enterprise Solutions division with the local residential divisions being integrated slowly into local Verizon subsidiaries.

Exam Probability: **Low**

49. *Answer choices:*

(see index for correct answer)

- a. hierarchical perspective
- b. imperative
- c. surface-level diversity
- d. interpersonal communication

:: Money ::

Cash and _____ s are the most liquid current assets found on a business's balance sheet. _____ s are short-term commitments "with temporarily idle cash and easily convertible into a known cash amount". An investment normally counts to be a _____ when it has a short maturity period of 90 days or less, and can be included in the cash and _____ s balance from the date of acquisition when it carries an insignificant risk of changes in the asset value; with more than 90 days maturity, the asset is not considered as cash and _____ s. Equity investments mostly are excluded from _____ s, unless they are essentially _____ s, for instance, if the preferred shares acquired within a short maturity period and with specified recovery date.

Exam Probability: **Low**

50. *Answer choices:*

(see index for correct answer)

- a. The Death of Money
- b. Slang terms for money
- c. Cash equivalent
- d. Purse bid

Guidance: level 1

:: Bonds (finance) ::

A _____ is a fund established by an economic entity by setting aside revenue over a period of time to fund a future capital expense, or repayment of a long-term debt.

Exam Probability: **High**

51. *Answer choices:*

(see index for correct answer)

- a. Residential mortgage-backed security
- b. Sinking fund
- c. Nominal yield
- d. Formosa bond

Guidance: level 1

:: Management accounting ::

_____ is a managerial accounting cost concept. Under this method, manufacturing overhead is incurred in the period that a product is produced. This addresses the issue of absorption costing that allows income to rise as production rises. Under an absorption cost method, management can push forward costs to the next period when products are sold. This artificially inflates profits in the period of production by incurring less cost than would be incurred under a _____ system. _____ is generally not used for external reporting purposes. Under the Tax Reform Act of 1986, income statements must use absorption costing to comply with GAAP.

Exam Probability: **Low**

52. *Answer choices:*

(see index for correct answer)

- a. Target income sales
- b. Institute of Certified Management Accountants
- c. Variable Costing
- d. Variance

Guidance: level 1

:: Management accounting ::

_____ , or dollar contribution per unit, is the selling price per unit minus the variable cost per unit. "Contribution" represents the portion of sales revenue that is not consumed by variable costs and so contributes to the coverage of fixed costs. This concept is one of the key building blocks of break-even analysis.

Exam Probability: **Low**

53. *Answer choices:*

(see index for correct answer)

- a. Constraints accounting
- b. Contribution margin

- c. Accounting management
- d. Fixed assets management

Guidance: level 1

:: Generally Accepted Accounting Principles ::

_____ is a small amount of discretionary funds in the form of cash used for expenditures where it is not sensible to make any disbursement by cheque, because of the inconvenience and costs of writing, signing, and then cashing the cheque.

Exam Probability: **High**

54. *Answer choices:*

(see index for correct answer)

- a. Fixed investment
- b. Petty cash
- c. net realisable value
- d. Cost pool

Guidance: level 1

:: Investment ::

In finance, the benefit from an _____ is called a return. The return may consist of a gain realised from the sale of property or an _____, unrealised capital appreciation , or _____ income such as dividends, interest, rental income etc., or a combination of capital gain and income. The return may also include currency gains or losses due to changes in foreign currency exchange rates.

Exam Probability: **Low**

55. *Answer choices:*

(see index for correct answer)

- a. Greater fool
- b. Investment
- c. Bandon Capital Management
- d. Money management

Guidance: level 1

:: ::

_____ is a marketing communication that employs an openly sponsored, non-personal message to promote or sell a product, service or idea. Sponsors of _____ are typically businesses wishing to promote their products or services. _____ is differentiated from public relations in that an advertiser pays for and has control over the message. It differs from personal selling in that the message is non-personal, i.e., not directed to a particular individual. _____ is communicated through various mass media, including traditional media such as newspapers, magazines, television, radio, outdoor _____ or direct mail; and new media such as search results, blogs, social media, websites or text messages. The actual presentation of the message in a medium is referred to as an advertisement, or "ad" or advert for short.

Exam Probability: **High**

56. *Answer choices:*

(see index for correct answer)

- a. similarity-attraction theory
- b. process perspective
- c. open system
- d. empathy

Guidance: level 1

:: Loans ::

In corporate finance, a _____ is a medium- to long-term debt instrument used by large companies to borrow money, at a fixed rate of interest. The legal term "_____" originally referred to a document that either creates a debt or acknowledges it, but in some countries the term is now used interchangeably with bond, loan stock or note. A _____ is thus like a certificate of loan or a loan bond evidencing the fact that the company is liable to pay a specified amount with interest and although the money raised by the _____ s becomes a part of the company's capital structure, it does not become share capital. Senior _____ s get paid before subordinate _____ s, and there are varying rates of risk and payoff for these categories.

Exam Probability: **High**

57. *Answer choices:*

(see index for correct answer)

- a. Back-to-back loan
- b. Debenture
- c. Bridge loan
- d. Student Loan Guarantor

Guidance: level 1

:: Stock market ::

A _____ or stock divide increases the number of shares in a company. The price is adjusted such that the before and after market capitalization of the company remains the same and dilution does not occur. Options and warrants are included.

58. *Answer choices:*

(see index for correct answer)

- a. Stock split
- b. Reverse stock split
- c. Primary shares
- d. Stock promoter

Guidance: level 1

:: Financial ratios ::

The _____ shows the percentage of how profitable a company's assets are in generating revenue.

Exam Probability: **High**

59. *Answer choices:*

(see index for correct answer)

- a. price-to-cash flow ratio
- b. Savings ratio
- c. Capital employed
- d. Operating ratio

Human resource management

Human resource (HR) management is the strategic approach to the effective management of organization workers so that they help the business gain a competitive advantage. It is designed to maximize employee performance in service of an employer's strategic objectives. HR is primarily concerned with the management of people within organizations, focusing on policies and on systems. HR departments are responsible for overseeing employee-benefits design, employee recruitment, training and development, performance appraisal, and rewarding (e.g., managing pay and benefit systems). HR also concerns itself with organizational change and industrial relations, that is, the balancing of organizational practices with requirements arising from collective bargaining and from governmental laws.

:: United States employment discrimination case law ::

_____ , 524 U.S. 775 , is a US labor law case of the United States Supreme Court in which the Court identified the circumstances under which an employer may be held liable under Title VII of the Civil Rights Act of 1964 for the acts of a supervisory employee whose sexual harassment of subordinates has created a hostile work environment amounting to employment discrimination. The court held that "an employer is vicariously liable for actionable discrimination caused by a supervisor, but subject to an affirmative defense looking to the reasonableness of the employer's conduct as well as that of a plaintiff victim."

Exam Probability: **Low**

1. *Answer choices:*

(see index for correct answer)

- a. Glenn v. Brumby
- b. Faragher v. City of Boca Raton
- c. Griggs v. Duke Power Co.
- d. Gross v. FBL Financial Services, Inc.

Guidance: level 1

:: Human resource management ::

_____ involves improving the effectiveness of organizations and the individuals and teams within them. Training may be viewed as related to immediate changes in organizational effectiveness via organized instruction, while development is related to the progress of longer-term organizational and employee goals. While _____ technically have differing definitions, the two are oftentimes used interchangeably and/or together. _____ has historically been a topic within applied psychology but has within the last two decades become closely associated with human resources management, talent management, human resources development, instructional design, human factors, and knowledge management.

Exam Probability: **High**

2. *Answer choices:*

(see index for correct answer)

- a. Cross-training
- b. Workforce planning
- c. Employeeship
- d. Training and development

Guidance: level 1

:: ::

_____ are interactive computer-mediated technologies that facilitate the creation and sharing of information, ideas, career interests and other forms of expression via virtual communities and networks. The variety of stand-alone and built-in _____ services currently available introduces challenges of definition; however, there are some common features.

Exam Probability: **Low**

3. *Answer choices:*

(see index for correct answer)

- a. Social media
- b. information systems assessment
- c. hierarchical
- d. personal values

Guidance: level 1

:: Recruitment ::

_____ , also known as Recruitment communications and Recruitment agency, includes all communications used by an organization to attract talent to work within it. Recruitment advertisements may be the first impression of a company for many job seekers. In turn, the strength of employer branding in job postings can directly impact interest in job openings.

Exam Probability: **High**

4. *Answer choices:*

(see index for correct answer)

- a. Realistic job preview
- b. Induction
- c. Curriculum vitae
- d. ProClinical

Guidance: level 1

:: Offshoring ::

Outsourcing is an agreement in which one company hires another company to be responsible for a planned or existing activity that is or could be done internally,and sometimes involves transferring employees and assets from one firm to another.

Exam Probability: **Low**

5. *Answer choices:*

(see index for correct answer)

- a. Nearshoring
- b. Offshoring Research Network
- c. Flag of convenience
- d. Offshore company

:: Unemployment ::

_____ is the support service provided by responsible organizations, keen to support individuals who are exiting the business − to help former employees transition to new jobs and help them re-orient themselves in the job market. A consultancy firm usually provides the _____ services which are paid for by the former employer and are achieved usually through practical advice, training materials and workshops. Some companies may offer psychological support.

Exam Probability: **High**

6. *Answer choices:*

(see index for correct answer)

- a. Texas Workforce Commission
- b. Structural unemployment
- c. Functional finance
- d. Frictional unemployment

:: Organizational behavior ::

Greenberg introduced the concept of _____ with regard to how an employee judges the behaviour of the organization and the employee's resulting attitude and behaviour. .

Exam Probability: **High**

7. *Answer choices:*

(see index for correct answer)

- a. Organizational retaliatory behavior
- b. Burnout
- c. Collaborative partnerships
- d. History of contingency theories of leadership

Guidance: level 1

:: Job interview ::

An _____ is a survey conducted with an individual who is separating from an organization or relationship. Most commonly, this occurs between an employee and an organization, a student and an educational institution, or a member and an association. An organization can use the information gained from an _____ to assess what should be improved, changed, or remain intact. More so, an organization can use the results from _____ s to reduce employee, student, or member turnover and increase productivity and engagement, thus reducing the high costs associated with turnover. Some examples of the value of conducting _____ s include shortening the recruiting and hiring process, reducing absenteeism, improving innovation, sustaining performance, and reducing possible litigation if issues mentioned in the _____ are addressed. It is important for each organization to customize its own _____ in order to maintain the highest levels of survey validity and reliability.

Exam Probability: **Medium**

8. *Answer choices:*

(see index for correct answer)

- a. Mock interview
- b. Microsoft interview
- c. Exit interview
- d. Programming interview

Guidance: level 1

:: Employment compensation ::

A _____ , also known as a flexible spending arrangement, is one of a number of tax-advantaged financial accounts, resulting in payroll tax savings. Before the Patient Protection and Affordable Care Act, one significant disadvantage to using an FSA was that funds not used by the end of the plan year were forfeited to the employer, known as the "use it or lose it" rule. Under the terms of the Affordable Care Act, a plan may permit an employee to carry over up to $500 into the following year without losing the funds.

Exam Probability: **High**

9. *Answer choices:*

(see index for correct answer)

- a. Flexible spending account
- b. Federal Wage System
- c. Labour law
- d. Employee benefit

Guidance: level 1

:: Asset ::

In financial accounting, an _____ is any resource owned by the business. Anything tangible or intangible that can be owned or controlled to produce value and that is held by a company to produce positive economic value is an _____ . Simply stated, _____ s represent value of ownership that can be converted into cash . The balance sheet of a firm records the monetary value of the _____ s owned by that firm. It covers money and other valuables belonging to an individual or to a business.

10. *Answer choices:*

(see index for correct answer)

- a. Fixed asset
- b. Current asset

Guidance: level 1

:: Occupational safety and health ::

_____ is a set of six naturally occurring silicate minerals, which all have in common their asbestiform habit: i.e., long , thin fibrous crystals, with each visible fiber composed of millions of microscopic "fibrils" that can be released by abrasion and other processes. The minerals are chrysotile, amosite, crocidolite, tremolite, anthophyllite, and actinolite.

Exam Probability: **Low**

11. *Answer choices:*

(see index for correct answer)

- a. Occupational medicine
- b. CLP Regulation
- c. Certified safety professional
- d. ENVIRON

:: Management ::

A _____ is a method or technique that has been generally accepted as superior to any alternatives because it produces results that are superior to those achieved by other means or because it has become a standard way of doing things, e.g., a standard way of complying with legal or ethical requirements.

Exam Probability: **High**

12. *Answer choices:*

(see index for correct answer)

- a. Best practice
- b. Business rule mining
- c. Design management
- d. Commercial management

Guidance: level 1

:: Human resource management ::

_____ is a sub-discipline of human resources, focused on employee _____ policy-making. While _____ are tangible, there are intangible rewards such as recognition, work-life and development. Combined, these are referred to as total rewards . The term " _____ " refers to the discipline as well as the rewards themselves.

Exam Probability: **Low**

13. *Answer choices:*

(see index for correct answer)

- a. Bonus payment
- b. Workforce planning
- c. Recruitment process outsourcing
- d. Compensation and benefits

Guidance: level 1

:: Management ::

A _____ is when two or more people come together to discuss one or more topics, often in a formal or business setting, but _____ s also occur in a variety of other environments. Many various types of _____ s exist.

Exam Probability: **Medium**

14. *Answer choices:*

(see index for correct answer)

- a. Law practice management
- b. Discovery-driven planning
- c. Meeting
- d. Supplier performance management

Guidance: level 1

:: Production and manufacturing ::

_____ is a theory of management that analyzes and synthesizes workflows. Its main objective is improving economic efficiency, especially labor productivity. It was one of the earliest attempts to apply science to the engineering of processes and to management. _____ is sometimes known as Taylorism after its founder, Frederick Winslow Taylor.

Exam Probability: **Medium**

15. *Answer choices:*

(see index for correct answer)

- a. Scientific management
- b. Reverse engineering
- c. Equipment service management and rental
- d. PCR food testing

:: Termination of employment ::

The _____ of 1988 is a US labor law which protects employees, their families, and communities by requiring most employers with 100 or more employees to provide 60 calendar-day advance notification of plant closings and mass layoffs of employees, as defined in the Act. In 2001, there were about 2,000 mass layoffs and plant closures which were subject to WARN advance notice requirements and which affected about 660,000 employees.

Exam Probability: **Medium**

16. *Answer choices:*

(see index for correct answer)

- a. Luis Gabriel Aguilera
- b. Letter of resignation
- c. Worker Adjustment and Retraining Notification Act
- d. The Disposable American

:: United States employment discrimination case law ::

_____ , 411 U.S. 792 , is a US employment law case by the United States Supreme Court regarding the burdens and nature of proof in proving a Title VII case and the order in which plaintiffs and defendants present proof. It was the seminal case in the McDonnell Douglas burden-shifting framework.

Exam Probability: **Low**

17. *Answer choices:*

(see index for correct answer)

- a. McDonnell Douglas Corp. v. Green
- b. Reeves v. Sanderson Plumbing Products, Inc.
- c. Faragher v. City of Boca Raton
- d. Gross v. FBL Financial Services, Inc.

Guidance: level 1

:: Human resource management ::

_____ means increasing the scope of a job through extending the range of its job duties and responsibilities generally within the same level and periphery. _____ involves combining various activities at the same level in the organization and adding them to the existing job. It is also called the horizontal expansion of job activities. This contradicts the principles of specialisation and the division of labour whereby work is divided into small units, each of which is performed repetitively by an individual worker and the responsibilities are always clear. Some motivational theories suggest that the boredom and alienation caused by the division of labour can actually cause efficiency to fall. Thus, _____ seeks to motivate workers through reversing the process of specialisation. A typical approach might be to replace assembly lines with modular work; instead of an employee repeating the same step on each product, they perform several tasks on a single item. In order for employees to be provided with _____ they will need to be retrained in new fields to understand how each field works.

Exam Probability: **Medium**

18. *Answer choices:*
(see index for correct answer)

- a. On-ramping
- b. Job description management
- c. Job enlargement
- d. Appreciative inquiry

Guidance: level 1

:: Employment compensation ::

_____ refers to various incentive plans introduced by businesses that provide direct or indirect payments to employees that depend on company`s profitability in addition to employees` regular salary and bonuses. In publicly traded companies these plans typically amount to allocation of shares to employees. One of the earliest pioneers of _____ was Englishman Theodore Cooke Taylor, who is known to have introduced the practice in his woollen mills during the late 1800s .

Exam Probability: **High**

19. *Answer choices:*

(see index for correct answer)

- a. Explanation of benefits
- b. General Schedule
- c. Annual leave
- d. Golden parachute

Guidance: level 1

:: Industrial engineering ::

_____ is the formal process that sits alongside Requirements analysis and focuses on the human elements of the requirements.

Exam Probability: **Low**

20. *Answer choices:*

(see index for correct answer)

- a. Operations and technology management
- b. Systematic layout planning
- c. Standard time
- d. Needs analysis

Guidance: level 1

:: Human resource management ::

_____ , also known as organizational socialization, is management jargon first created in 1988 that refers to the mechanism through which new employees acquire the necessary knowledge, skills, and behaviors in order to become effective organizational members and insiders.

Exam Probability: **Low**

21. *Answer choices:*

(see index for correct answer)

- a. Cross-functional team
- b. Job enlargement
- c. Bradford Factor
- d. Onboarding

:: Production and manufacturing ::

_____ is a set of techniques and tools for process improvement. Though as a shortened form it may be found written as 6S, it should not be confused with the methodology known as 6S .

Exam Probability: **High**

22. *Answer choices:*

(see index for correct answer)

- a. Six Sigma
- b. Seweasy
- c. Managed services
- d. Fiberglass molding

:: Employment compensation ::

Generally PTO hours cover everything from planned vacations to sick days, and are becoming more prevalent in the field of human resource management. Unlike more traditional leave plans, PTO plans don't distinguish employee absences from personal days, vacation days, or sick days. Upon employment, the company determines how many PTO hours will be allotted per year and a "rollover" policy. Some companies let PTO hours accumulate for only a year, and unused hours disappear at year-end. Some PTO plans may also accommodate unexpected or unforeseeable circumstances such as jury duty, military duty, and bereavement leave. PTO bank plans typically do not include short-term or long-term disability leave, workers compensation, family and medical leave, sabbatical, or community service leave.

Exam Probability: **Medium**

23. *Answer choices:*

(see index for correct answer)

- a. Severance package
- b. Fringe benefits tax
- c. Lilly Ledbetter Fair Pay Act of 2009
- d. Paid time off

Guidance: level 1

:: ::

_____ is the formal act of giving up or quitting one's office or position. A _____ can occur when a person holding a position gained by election or appointment steps down, but leaving a position upon the expiration of a term, or choosing not to seek an additional term, is not considered _____ .

Exam Probability: **High**

24. *Answer choices:*

(see index for correct answer)

- a. Resignation
- b. personal values
- c. information systems assessment
- d. open system

Guidance: level 1

:: Behaviorism ::

In behavioral psychology, _____ is a consequence applied that will strengthen an organism's future behavior whenever that behavior is preceded by a specific antecedent stimulus. This strengthening effect may be measured as a higher frequency of behavior , longer duration , greater magnitude , or shorter latency . There are two types of _____ , known as positive _____ and negative _____ ; positive is where by a reward is offered on expression of the wanted behaviour and negative is taking away an undesirable element in the persons environment whenever the desired behaviour is achieved.

Exam Probability: **Medium**

25. *Answer choices:*

(see index for correct answer)

- a. chaining
- b. Matching Law
- c. contingency management
- d. social facilitation

Guidance: level 1

:: Business law ::

An _____ is a natural person, business, or corporation that provides goods or services to another entity under terms specified in a contract or within a verbal agreement. Unlike an employee, an _____ does not work regularly for an employer but works as and when required, during which time they may be subject to law of agency. _____ s are usually paid on a freelance basis. Contractors often work through a limited company or franchise, which they themselves own, or may work through an umbrella company.

Exam Probability: **Low**

26. *Answer choices:*

(see index for correct answer)

- a. Business method patent

- b. License
- c. Bulk transfer
- d. Independent contractor

Guidance: level 1

:: Validity (statistics) ::

_____ is "the degree to which a test measures what it claims, or purports, to be measuring." In the classical model of test validity, _____ is one of three main types of validity evidence, alongside content validity and criterion validity. Modern validity theory defines _____ as the overarching concern of validity research, subsuming all other types of validity evidence.

Exam Probability: **Low**

27. *Answer choices:*
(see index for correct answer)

- a. Construct validity
- b. Criterion validity
- c. Validation
- d. Predictive validity

Guidance: level 1

:: ::

_____ is the administration of an organization, whether it is a business, a not-for-profit organization, or government body. _____ includes the activities of setting the strategy of an organization and coordinating the efforts of its employees to accomplish its objectives through the application of available resources, such as financial, natural, technological, and human resources. The term "_____" may also refer to those people who manage an organization.

Exam Probability: **High**

28. *Answer choices:*

(see index for correct answer)

- a. Sarbanes-Oxley act of 2002
- b. Management
- c. information systems assessment
- d. surface-level diversity

Guidance: level 1

:: ::

_____ is the combination of structured planning and the active management choice of one's own professional career. _____ was first defined in a social work doctoral thesis by Mary Valentich as the implementation of a career strategy through application of career tactics in relation to chosen career orientation . Career orientation referred to the overall design or pattern of one's career, shaped by particular goals and interests and identifiable by particular positions that embody these goals and interests. Career strategy pertains to the individual's general approach to the realization of career goals, and to the specificity of the goals themselves. Two general strategy approaches are adaptive and planned. Career tactics are actions to maintain oneself in a satisfactory employment situation. Tactics may be more or less assertive, with assertiveness in the work situation referring to actions taken to advance one's career interests or to exercise one's legitimate rights while respecting the rights of others.

Exam Probability: **High**

29. *Answer choices:*

(see index for correct answer)

- a. cultural
- b. interpersonal communication
- c. Sarbanes-Oxley act of 2002
- d. Career management

Guidance: level 1

:: ::

_____ is an experience a person may have when one moves to a cultural environment which is different from one's own; it is also the personal disorientation a person may feel when experiencing an unfamiliar way of life due to immigration or a visit to a new country, a move between social environments, or simply transition to another type of life. One of the most common causes of _____ involves individuals in a foreign environment. _____ can be described as consisting of at least one of four distinct phases: honeymoon, negotiation, adjustment, and adaptation.

Exam Probability: **Low**

30. *Answer choices:*

(see index for correct answer)

- a. cultural
- b. corporate values
- c. process perspective
- d. Culture shock

Guidance: level 1

:: Trade unions ::

A _____ is an association of workers forming a legal unit or legal personhood, usually called a "bargaining unit", which acts as bargaining agent and legal representative for a unit of employees in all matters of law or right arising from or in the administration of a collective agreement. Labour unions typically fund the formal organisation, head office, and legal team functions of the labour union through regular fees or union dues. The delegate staff of the labour union representation in the workforce are made up of workplace volunteers who are appointed by members in democratic elections.

Exam Probability: **Low**

31. *Answer choices:*

(see index for correct answer)

- a. Bump
- b. Unionized cooperative
- c. Trade union
- d. International Centre for Trade Union Rights

Guidance: level 1

:: Human resource management ::

_____ refers to the ability of an organization to retain its employees. _____ can be represented by a simple statistic . However, many consider _____ as relating to the efforts by which employers attempt to retain the employees in their workforce. In this sense, retention becomes the strategies rather than the outcome.

32. *Answer choices:*

(see index for correct answer)

- a. Job analysis
- b. Employee retention
- c. E-HRM
- d. Pay in lieu of notice

Guidance: level 1

:: Evaluation methods ::

In social psychology, _____ is the process of looking at oneself in order to assess aspects that are important to one's identity. It is one of the motives that drive self-evaluation, along with self-verification and self-enhancement. Sedikides suggests that the _____ motive will prompt people to seek information to confirm their uncertain self-concept rather than their certain self-concept and at the same time people use _____ to enhance their certainty of their own self-knowledge. However, the _____ motive could be seen as quite different from the other two self-evaluation motives. Unlike the other two motives through _____ people are interested in the accuracy of their current self view, rather than improving their self-view. This makes _____ the only self-evaluative motive that may cause a person's self-esteem to be damaged.

33. *Answer choices:*

(see index for correct answer)

- a. Conformity assessment
- b. Self-assessment
- c. SAT Subject Tests
- d. Transformative assessment

Guidance: level 1

:: Business law ::

_____ or employment relations is the multidisciplinary academic field that studies the employment relationship; that is, the complex interrelations between employers and employees, labor/trade unions, employer organizations and the state.

Exam Probability: **Medium**

34. *Answer choices:*

(see index for correct answer)

- a. Rules of origin
- b. Industrial relations
- c. United Kingdom commercial law
- d. Bulk sale

:: ::

_____ is an enduring pattern of romantic or sexual attraction to persons of the opposite sex or gender, the same sex or gender, or to both sexes or more than one gender. These attractions are generally subsumed under heterosexuality, homosexuality, and bisexuality, while asexuality is sometimes identified as the fourth category.

Exam Probability: **Low**

35. *Answer choices:*

(see index for correct answer)

- a. Sexual orientation
- b. co-culture
- c. hierarchical perspective
- d. personal values

:: Television terminology ::

Distance education or long- _____ is the education of students who may not always be physically present at a school. Traditionally, this usually involved correspondence courses wherein the student corresponded with the school via post. Today it involves online education. Courses that are conducted are either hybrid, blended or 100% _____ . Massive open online courses , offering large-scale interactive participation and open access through the World Wide Web or other network technologies, are recent developments in distance education. A number of other terms are used roughly synonymously with distance education.

Exam Probability: **Medium**

36. *Answer choices:*

(see index for correct answer)

- a. multiplexing
- b. Distance learning
- c. Satellite television
- d. nonprofit

Guidance: level 1

:: Unemployment ::

In economics, a _____ is a business cycle contraction when there is a general decline in economic activity. Macroeconomic indicators such as GDP , investment spending, capacity utilization, household income, business profits, and inflation fall, while bankruptcies and the unemployment rate rise. In the United Kingdom, it is defined as a negative economic growth for two consecutive quarters.

Exam Probability: **Medium**

37. *Answer choices:*

(see index for correct answer)

- a. NAIRU
- b. Frictional unemployment
- c. Unemployment Convention, 1919
- d. Mount Street Club

Guidance: level 1

:: ::

_____ is the amount of time someone works beyond normal working hours. The term is also used for the pay received for this time. Normal hours may be determined in several ways.

Exam Probability: **Medium**

38. *Answer choices:*

(see index for correct answer)

- a. open system
- b. Sarbanes-Oxley act of 2002
- c. Overtime
- d. levels of analysis

Guidance: level 1

:: ::

In business strategy, _____ is establishing a competitive advantage by having the lowest cost of operation in the industry. _____ is often driven by company efficiency, size, scale, scope and cumulative experience .A _____ strategy aims to exploit scale of production, well-defined scope and other economies , producing highly standardized products, using advanced technology.In recent years, more and more companies have chosen a strategic mix to achieve market leadership. These patterns consist of simultaneous _____ , superior customer service and product leadership. Walmart has succeeded across the world due to its _____ strategy. The company has cut down on exesses at every point of production and thus are able to provide the consumers with quality products at low prices.

Exam Probability: **High**

39. *Answer choices:*

(see index for correct answer)

- a. functional perspective
- b. Sarbanes-Oxley act of 2002
- c. Cost leadership
- d. levels of analysis

Guidance: level 1

:: ::

A _____ is a technical analysis of a biological specimen, for example urine, hair, blood, breath, sweat, and/or oral fluid/saliva—to determine the presence or absence of specified parent drugs or their metabolites. Major applications of _____ ing include detection of the presence of performance enhancing steroids in sport, employers and parole/probation officers screening for drugs prohibited by law and police officers testing for the presence and concentration of alcohol in the blood commonly referred to as BAC. BAC tests are typically administered via a breathalyzer while urinalysis is used for the vast majority of _____ ing in sports and the workplace. Numerous other methods with varying degrees of accuracy, sensitivity, and detection periods exist.

Exam Probability: **High**

40. *Answer choices:*

(see index for correct answer)

- a. hierarchical
- b. process perspective
- c. Drug test

- d. interpersonal communication

Guidance: level 1

:: Labour law ::

A _____ is a legal contract that is meant to limit the liability of an employer whose employees are romantically involved. An employer may choose to require a _____ when a romantic relationship within the company becomes known, in order to indemnify the company in case the employees' romantic relationship fails, primarily so that one party can't bring a sexual harassment lawsuit against the company. To that end, the _____ states that the relationship is consensual, and both parties of the relationship must sign it. The _____ may also stipulate rules for acceptable romantic behavior in the workplace.

Exam Probability: **Low**

41. *Answer choices:*
(see index for correct answer)

- a. Core Labor Standards
- b. Love contract
- c. Negligent hiring
- d. Bharat Forge Co Ltd v Uttam Manohar Nakate

Guidance: level 1

:: Business ethics ::

In United States labor law, a _____ exists when one's behavior within a workplace creates an environment that is difficult or uncomfortable for another person to work in, due to discrimination. Common complaints in sexual harassment lawsuits include fondling, suggestive remarks, sexually-suggestive photos displayed in the workplace, use of sexual language, or off-color jokes. Small matters, annoyances, and isolated incidents are usually not considered to be statutory violations of the discrimination laws. For a violation to impose liability, the conduct must create a work environment that would be intimidating, hostile, or offensive to a reasonable person. An employer can be held liable for failing to prevent these workplace conditions, unless it can prove that it attempted to prevent the harassment and that the employee failed to take advantage of existing harassment counter-measures or tools provided by the employer.

Exam Probability: **Low**

42. *Answer choices:*

(see index for correct answer)

- a. Integrity management
- b. Evolution of corporate social responsibility in India
- c. Surface Transportation Assistance Act
- d. Philosophy of business

Guidance: level 1

:: Human resource management ::

_____ is a process for identifying and developing new leaders who can replace old leaders when they leave, retire or die. _____ increases the availability of experienced and capable employees that are prepared to assume these roles as they become available. Taken narrowly, "replacement planning" for key roles is the heart of _____ .

Exam Probability: **Low**

43. *Answer choices:*

(see index for correct answer)

- a. Recruitment process outsourcing
- b. Succession planning
- c. Human relations movement
- d. Job design

Guidance: level 1

:: Labour relations ::

_____ is the practice of hiring more workers than are needed to perform a given job, or to adopt work procedures which appear pointless, complex and time-consuming merely to employ additional workers. The term "make-work" is sometimes used as a synonym for _____ .

Exam Probability: **High**

44. *Answer choices:*

(see index for correct answer)

- a. Social dialogue
- b. Eurocadres
- c. Featherbedding
- d. Acas

Guidance: level 1

:: Business planning ::

_____ is an organization's process of defining its strategy, or direction, and making decisions on allocating its resources to pursue this strategy. It may also extend to control mechanisms for guiding the implementation of the strategy. _____ became prominent in corporations during the 1960s and remains an important aspect of strategic management. It is executed by strategic planners or strategists, who involve many parties and research sources in their analysis of the organization and its relationship to the environment in which it competes.

Exam Probability: **Medium**

45. *Answer choices:*

(see index for correct answer)

- a. Strategic planning
- b. Gap analysis

- c. Open Options Corporation
- d. Exit planning

:: Labour relations ::

A _____ , also known as a post-entry closed shop, is a form of a union security clause. Under this, the employer agrees to either only hire labor union members or to require that any new employees who are not already union members become members within a certain amount of time. Use of the _____ varies widely from nation to nation, depending on the level of protection given trade unions in general.

Exam Probability: **Medium**

46. *Answer choices:*

(see index for correct answer)

- a. Labor relations
- b. Jesse Simons
- c. United Students Against Sweatshops
- d. Union shop

Guidance: level 1

:: Income ::

A _____ is a unit in systems of monetary compensation for employment. It is commonly used in public service, both civil and military, but also for companies of the private sector. _____ s facilitate the employment process by providing a fixed framework of salary ranges, as opposed to a free negotiation. Typically, _____ s encompass two dimensions: a "vertical" range where each level corresponds to the responsibility of, and requirements needed for a certain position; and a "horizontal" range within this scale to allow for monetary incentives rewarding the employee`s quality of performance or length of service. Thus, an employee progresses within the horizontal and vertical ranges upon achieving positive appraisal on a regular basis. In most cases, evaluation is done annually and encompasses more than one method.

Exam Probability: **Low**

47. *Answer choices:*

(see index for correct answer)

- a. Creative real estate investing
- b. Pay grade
- c. Income earner
- d. Per capita income

Guidance: level 1

:: Business ethics cases ::

_____ , 477 U.S. 57 , is a US labor law case, where the United States Supreme Court, in a 9-0 decision, recognized sexual harassment as a violation of Title VII of the Civil Rights Act of 1964. The case was the first of its kind to reach the Supreme Court and would redefine sexual harassment in the workplace.

Exam Probability: **Medium**

48. *Answer choices:*

(see index for correct answer)

- a. Brent Walker
- b. Meritor Savings Bank v. Vinson
- c. Bank of Credit and Commerce International
- d. Oncale v. Sundowner Offshore Services

Guidance: level 1

:: ::

_____ involves the development of an action plan designed to motivate and guide a person or group toward a goal. _____ can be guided by goal-setting criteria such as SMART criteria. _____ is a major component of personal-development and management literature.

Exam Probability: **Medium**

49. *Answer choices:*

(see index for correct answer)

- a. Goal setting
- b. co-culture
- c. hierarchical perspective
- d. levels of analysis

Guidance: level 1

:: Power (social and political) ::

In a notable study of power conducted by social psychologists John R. P. French and Bertram Raven in 1959, power is divided into five separate and distinct forms. In 1965 Raven revised this model to include a sixth form by separating the informational power base as distinct from the _____ base.

Exam Probability: **Low**

50. *Answer choices:*

(see index for correct answer)

- a. need for power
- b. Hard power
- c. Referent power

Guidance: level 1

:: Recruitment ::

_____ is a specialized recruitment service which organizations pay to seek out and recruit highly qualified candidates for senior-level and executive jobs . Headhunters may also seek out and recruit other highly specialized and/or skilled positions in organizations for which there is strong competition in the job market for the top talent, such as senior data analysts or computer programmers. The method usually involves commissioning a third-party organization, typically an _____ firm, but possibly a standalone consultant or consulting firm, to research the availability of suitable qualified candidates working for competitors or related businesses or organizations. Having identified a shortlist of qualified candidates who match the client's requirements, the _____ firm may act as an intermediary to contact the individual and see if they might be interested in moving to a new employer. The _____ firm may also carry out initial screening of the candidate, negotiations on remuneration and benefits, and preparing the employment contract. In some markets there has been a move towards using _____ for lower positions driven by the fact that there are less candidates for some positions even on lower levels than executive.

Exam Probability: **Medium**

51. *Answer choices:*
(see index for correct answer)

- a. HResume
- b. Silicon Milkroundabout
- c. Executive search
- d. Haigui

Guidance: level 1

:: Economic globalization ::

_____ is an agreement in which one company hires another company to be responsible for a planned or existing activity that is or could be done internally.and sometimes involves transferring employees and assets from one firm to another.

Exam Probability: **Medium**

52. *Answer choices:*

(see index for correct answer)

- a. global financial
- b. reshoring

Guidance: level 1

:: Trade unions ::

A _____ , in North America, or union branch , in the United Kingdom and other countries, is a local branch of a usually national trade union. The terms used for sub-branches of _____ s vary from country to country and include "shop committee", "shop floor committee", "board of control", "chapel", and others.

Exam Probability: **Medium**

53. *Answer choices:*

(see index for correct answer)

- a. Local union
- b. Independent union
- c. Scope clause
- d. International Labour Sports Federation

Guidance: level 1

:: Employment ::

A flat organization has an organizational structure with few or no levels of middle management between staff and executives. An organization's structure refers to the nature of the distribution of the units and positions within it, also to the nature of the relationships among those units and positions. Tall and flat organizations differ based on how many levels of management are present in the organization, and how much control managers are endowed with.

Exam Probability: **High**

54. *Answer choices:*

(see index for correct answer)

- a. Supernumerary
- b. Job shadow
- c. Delayering
- d. Academic job market

:: ::

_____ is a form of development in which a person called a coach supports a learner or client in achieving a specific personal or professional goal by providing training and guidance. The learner is sometimes called a coachee. Occasionally, _____ may mean an informal relationship between two people, of whom one has more experience and expertise than the other and offers advice and guidance as the latter learns; but _____ differs from mentoring in focusing on specific tasks or objectives, as opposed to more general goals or overall development.

Exam Probability: **Medium**

55. *Answer choices:*

(see index for correct answer)

- a. levels of analysis
- b. process perspective
- c. interpersonal communication
- d. similarity-attraction theory

:: Validity (statistics) ::

In psychometrics, _____ refers to the extent to which a measure represents all facets of a given construct. For example, a depression scale may lack _____ if it only assesses the affective dimension of depression but fails to take into account the behavioral dimension. An element of subjectivity exists in relation to determining _____ , which requires a degree of agreement about what a particular personality trait such as extraversion represents. A disagreement about a personality trait will prevent the gain of a high _____ .

Exam Probability: **Low**

56. *Answer choices:*

(see index for correct answer)

- a. Verification and validation
- b. Content validity
- c. Nomological network
- d. External validity

Guidance: level 1

:: Organizational behavior ::

_____ is the state or fact of exclusive rights and control over property, which may be an object, land/real estate or intellectual property. _____ involves multiple rights, collectively referred to as title, which may be separated and held by different parties.

57. *Answer choices:*

(see index for correct answer)

- a. Ownership
- b. Achievement Motivation Inventory
- c. Organizational commitment
- d. Collaborative partnerships

Guidance: level 1

:: Bankruptcy ::

_____ is the concept of a person or group of people taking precedence over another person or group because the former is either older than the latter or has occupied a particular position longer than the latter. _____ is present between parents and children and may be present in other common relationships, such as among siblings of different ages or between workers and their managers.

Exam Probability: **Medium**

58. *Answer choices:*

(see index for correct answer)

- a. Seniority
- b. Bankruptcy tourism

- c. Strategic bankruptcy
- d. Bankruptcy prediction

Guidance: level 1

:: ::

An _____ is a person temporarily or permanently residing in a country other than their native country. In common usage, the term often refers to professionals, skilled workers, or artists taking positions outside their home country, either independently or sent abroad by their employers, who can be companies, universities, governments, or non-governmental organisations. Effectively migrant workers, they usually earn more than they would at home, and less than local employees. However, the term ` _____ ` is also used for retirees and others who have chosen to live outside their native country. Historically, it has also referred to exiles.

Exam Probability: **Medium**

59. *Answer choices:*
(see index for correct answer)

- a. functional perspective
- b. hierarchical
- c. information systems assessment
- d. Expatriate

Guidance: level 1

Information systems

Information systems (IS) are formal, sociotechnical, organizational systems designed to collect, process, store, and distribute information. In a sociotechnical perspective Information Systems are composed by four components: technology, process, people and organizational structure.

:: Information technology audit ::

_____ is the act of using a computer to take or alter electronic data, or to gain unlawful use of a computer or system. In the United States, _____ is specifically proscribed by the _____ and Abuse Act, which criminalizes computer-related acts under federal jurisdiction. Types of _____ include.

1. *Answer choices:*

(see index for correct answer)

- a. SekChek Local
- b. Computer fraud
- c. Information technology audit
- d. ACL

Guidance: level 1

:: Identity management ::

_____ is the ability of an individual or group to seclude themselves, or information about themselves, and thereby express themselves selectively. The boundaries and content of what is considered private differ among cultures and individuals, but share common themes. When something is private to a person, it usually means that something is inherently special or sensitive to them. The domain of _____ partially overlaps with security , which can include the concepts of appropriate use, as well as protection of information. _____ may also take the form of bodily integrity.

Exam Probability: **Low**

2. *Answer choices:*

(see index for correct answer)

- a. Privacy
- b. Directory information tree
- c. Mobile signature
- d. Group

Guidance: level 1

:: Survey methodology ::

A _____ is the procedure of systematically acquiring and recording information about the members of a given population. The term is used mostly in connection with national population and housing _____ es; other common _____ es include agriculture, business, and traffic _____ es. The United Nations defines the essential features of population and housing _____ es as "individual enumeration, universality within a defined territory, simultaneity and defined periodicity", and recommends that population _____ es be taken at least every 10 years. United Nations recommendations also cover _____ topics to be collected, official definitions, classifications and other useful information to co-ordinate international practice.

Exam Probability: **Medium**

3. *Answer choices:*

(see index for correct answer)

- a. Census
- b. Enterprise feedback management
- c. Survey research

- d. Scale analysis

Guidance: level 1

:: Commercial item transport and distribution ::

In commerce, supply-chain management , the management of the flow of goods
and services, involves the movement and storage of raw materials, of
work-in-process inventory, and of finished goods from point of origin to point
of consumption. Interconnected or interlinked networks, channels and node
businesses combine in the provision of products and services required by end
customers in a supply chain. Supply-chain management has been defined as the
"design, planning, execution, control, and monitoring of supply-chain
activities with the objective of creating net value, building a competitive
infrastructure, leveraging worldwide logistics, synchronizing supply with
demand and measuring performance globally."SCM practice draws heavily from the
areas of industrial engineering, systems engineering, operations management,
logistics, procurement, information technology, and marketing and strives for
an integrated approach. Marketing channels play an important role in
supply-chain management. Current research in supply-chain management is
concerned with topics related to sustainability and risk management, among
others. Some suggest that the "people dimension" of SCM, ethical issues,
internal integration, transparency/visibility, and human capital/talent
management are topics that have, so far, been underrepresented on the research
agenda.

Exam Probability: **Low**

4. *Answer choices:*

(see index for correct answer)

- a. Supply chain management

- b. Toll Global Forwarding
- c. Wharf
- d. Courier software

Guidance: level 1

:: Virtual reality ::

_____ is an experience taking place within simulated and immersive environments that can be similar to or completely different from the real world. Applications of _____ can include entertainment and educational purposes . Other, distinct types of VR style technology include augmented reality and mixed reality.

Exam Probability: **Low**

5. *Answer choices:*

(see index for correct answer)

- a. Outernet
- b. Virtway
- c. Virtual reality
- d. International Stereoscopic Union

Guidance: level 1

:: Information systems ::

_____ s are information systems that are developed in response to corporate business initiative. They are intended to give competitive advantage to the organization. They may deliver a product or service that is at a lower cost, that is differentiated, that focuses on a particular market segment, or is innovative.

Exam Probability: **High**

6. *Answer choices:*

(see index for correct answer)

- a. Automated information system
- b. Resistance Database Initiative
- c. Censhare
- d. Strategic information system

Guidance: level 1

:: Strategic management ::

In marketing strategy, first-mover advantage is the advantage gained by the initial significant occupant of a market segment. First-mover advantage may be gained by technological leadership, or early purchase of resources.

Exam Probability: **High**

7. *Answer choices:*

(see index for correct answer)

- a. First mover advantage
- b. Keiretsu
- c. BSC SWOT
- d. Strategic Technology Plan

Guidance: level 1

:: Information technology management ::

_____ is a good-practice framework created by international professional association ISACA for information technology management and IT governance. _____ provides an implementable "set of controls over information technology and organizes them around a logical framework of IT-related processes and enablers."

Exam Probability: **High**

8. *Answer choices:*

(see index for correct answer)

- a. Microsoft Customer Care Framework
- b. Prolifics
- c. Soluto
- d. IT Project Coordinator

:: World Wide Web Consortium standards ::

_____ is a markup language that defines a set of rules for encoding documents in a format that is both human-readable and machine-readable. The W3C's XML 1.0 Specification and several other related specifications—all of them free open standards—define XML.

Exam Probability: **Medium**

9. *Answer choices:*

(see index for correct answer)

- a. Hypertext markup language
- b. Hyper Text Markup Language

:: Networking hardware ::

A network interface controller is a computer hardware component that connects a computer to a computer network.

Exam Probability: **Medium**

10. *Answer choices:*

(see index for correct answer)

- a. Console server
- b. Network interface card
- c. bridging

Guidance: level 1

:: Data management ::

A _____ , or metadata repository, as defined in the IBM Dictionary of Computing, is a "centralized repository of information about data such as meaning, relationships to other data, origin, usage, and format". Oracle defines it as a collection of tables with metadata. The term can have one of several closely related meanings pertaining to databases and database management systems .

Exam Probability: **Medium**

11. *Answer choices:*

(see index for correct answer)

- a. Cognos ReportNet
- b. Data dictionary
- c. Edge data integration
- d. Linear medium

:: ::

_____ is software designed to provide a platform for other software. Examples of _____ include operating systems like macOS, Ubuntu and Microsoft Windows, computational science software, game engines, industrial automation, and software as a service applications.

Exam Probability: **Medium**

12. *Answer choices:*

(see index for correct answer)

- a. similarity-attraction theory
- b. levels of analysis
- c. empathy
- d. System software

:: Data ::

_____ is a branch of mathematics working with data collection, organization, analysis, interpretation and presentation. In applying _____ to, for example, a scientific, industrial, or social problem, it is conventional to begin with a statistical population or a statistical model process to be studied. Populations can be diverse topics such as "all people living in a country" or "every atom composing a crystal". _____ deals with every aspect of data, including the planning of data collection in terms of the design of surveys and experiments. See glossary of probability and _____ .

Exam Probability: **Low**

13. *Answer choices:*

(see index for correct answer)

- a. Data acquisition
- b. Humanities Indicators
- c. Statistics
- d. primary data

Guidance: level 1

:: Computer memory ::

_____ is an electronic non-volatile computer storage medium that can be electrically erased and reprogrammed.

Exam Probability: **Low**

14. *Answer choices:*

(see index for correct answer)

- a. U61000
- b. Flash memory
- c. SDRAM latency
- d. Page address register

Guidance: level 1

:: Data management ::

_____ , or IG, is the management of information at an organization. _____ balances the use and security of information. _____ helps with legal compliance, operational transparency, and reducing expenditures associated with legal discovery. An organization can establish a consistent and logical framework for employees to handle data through their _____ policies and procedures. These policies guide proper behavior regarding how organizations and their employees handle electronically stored information .

Exam Probability: **High**

15. *Answer choices:*

(see index for correct answer)

- a. Rainbow Storage
- b. Concurrency control
- c. Reference table

- d. Information governance

Guidance: level 1

:: Business models ::

_____ , a portmanteau of the words "free" and "premium", is a pricing strategy by which a product or service is provided free of charge, but money is charged for additional features, services, or virtual or physical goods. The business model has been in use by the software industry since the 1980s as a licensing scheme. A subset of this model used by the video game industry is called free-to-play.

Exam Probability: **High**

16. *Answer choices:*
(see index for correct answer)

- a. Sustainable business
- b. Subsidiary
- c. Artel
- d. Co-operative Wholesale Society

Guidance: level 1

:: E-commerce ::

Electronic governance or e-governance is the application of information and communication technology for delivering government services, exchange of information, communication transactions, integration of various stand-alone systems and services between government-to-citizen , government-to-business , _____ , government-to-employees as well as back-office processes and interactions within the entire government framework. Through e-governance, government services are made available to citizens in a convenient, efficient, and transparent manner. The three main target groups that can be distinguished in governance concepts are government, citizens, andbusinesses/interest groups. In e-governance, there are no distinct boundaries.

Exam Probability: **High**

17. *Answer choices:*

(see index for correct answer)

- a. Virtual workplace
- b. Online shopping
- c. Government-to-government
- d. Location-based commerce

Guidance: level 1

:: Survey methodology ::

An _____ is a conversation where questions are asked and answers are given. In common parlance, the word " _____ " refers to a one-on-one conversation between an _____ er and an _____ ee. The _____ er asks questions to which the _____ ee responds, usually so information may be transferred from _____ ee to _____ er . Sometimes, information can be transferred in both directions. It is a communication, unlike a speech, which produces a one-way flow of information.

Exam Probability: **Medium**

18. *Answer choices:*

(see index for correct answer)

- a. Survey sampling
- b. Census
- c. Interview
- d. Public opinion

Guidance: level 1

:: E-commerce ::

_____ is the activity of buying or selling of products on online services or over the Internet. Electronic commerce draws on technologies such as mobile commerce, electronic funds transfer, supply chain management, Internet marketing, online transaction processing, electronic data interchange , inventory management systems, and automated data collection systems.

19. *Answer choices:*

(see index for correct answer)

- a. Online shopping
- b. Cyber Black Friday
- c. KonaKart
- d. E-commerce

Guidance: level 1

:: ::

The _____ is the global system of interconnected computer networks that use the _____ protocol suite to link devices worldwide. It is a network of networks that consists of private, public, academic, business, and government networks of local to global scope, linked by a broad array of electronic, wireless, and optical networking technologies. The _____ carries a vast range of information resources and services, such as the inter-linked hypertext documents and applications of the World Wide Web , electronic mail, telephony, and file sharing.

Exam Probability: **Low**

20. *Answer choices:*

(see index for correct answer)

- a. Internet
- b. co-culture
- c. empathy
- d. personal values

Guidance: level 1

:: Cryptography ::

In cryptography, _____ is the process of encoding a message or information in such a way that only authorized parties can access it and those who are not authorized cannot. _____ does not itself prevent interference, but denies the intelligible content to a would-be interceptor. In an _____ scheme, the intended information or message, referred to as plaintext, is encrypted using an _____ algorithm – a cipher – generating ciphertext that can be read only if decrypted. For technical reasons, an _____ scheme usually uses a pseudo-random _____ key generated by an algorithm. It is in principle possible to decrypt the message without possessing the key, but, for a well-designed _____ scheme, considerable computational resources and skills are required. An authorized recipient can easily decrypt the message with the key provided by the originator to recipients but not to unauthorized users.

Exam Probability: **Low**

21. *Answer choices:*

(see index for correct answer)

- a. Electronic Signature
- b. ciphertext

- c. Encryption
- d. plaintext

Guidance: level 1

:: Information technology management ::

In information technology to _____ means to move from one place to another, information to detailed data by focusing in on something. In a GUI-environment, "drilling-down" may involve clicking on some representation in order to reveal more detail.

Exam Probability: **Low**

22. *Answer choices:*
(see index for correct answer)

- a. Problem management
- b. Drill down
- c. Software asset management
- d. Storage hypervisor

Guidance: level 1

:: Enterprise modelling ::

_____ are large-scale application software packages that support business processes, information flows, reporting, and data analytics in complex organizations. While ES are generally packaged enterprise application software systems they can also be bespoke, custom developed systems created to support a specific organization's needs.

Exam Probability: **Low**

23. *Answer choices:*

(see index for correct answer)

- a. Enterprise systems
- b. Object-oriented business engineering
- c. BiZZdesign Architect
- d. Governance, risk management, and compliance

Guidance: level 1

:: Market structure and pricing ::

_____ is a term denoting that a product includes permission to use its source code, design documents, or content. It most commonly refers to the open-source model, in which open-source software or other products are released under an open-source license as part of the open-source-software movement. Use of the term originated with software, but has expanded beyond the software sector to cover other open content and forms of open collaboration.

Exam Probability: **Low**

24. *Answer choices:*

(see index for correct answer)

- a. Installed base
- b. Liberalization
- c. Open source
- d. Open-source economics

Guidance: level 1

:: Marketing ::

_____ is a business model in which consumers create value and businesses consume that value. For example, when a consumer writes reviews or when a consumer gives a useful idea for new product development then that consumer is creating value for the business if the business adopts the input.
In the C2B model, a reverse auction or demand collection model, enables buyers to name or demand their own price, which is often binding, for a specific good or service. Inside of a consumer to business market the roles involved in the transaction must be established and the consumer must offer something of value to the business.

Exam Probability: **High**

25. *Answer choices:*

(see index for correct answer)

- a. Cumulative prospect theory
- b. Product category volume

- c. Branding national myths and symbols
- d. Consumer-to-business

Guidance: level 1

:: Data privacy ::

_____ is the relationship between the collection and dissemination of data, technology, the public expectation of privacy, legal and political issues surrounding them. It is also known as data privacy or data protection.

Exam Probability: **Medium**

26. *Answer choices:*
(see index for correct answer)

- a. Deutsche Telekom eavesdropping controversy
- b. Unclick
- c. Information privacy
- d. Genetic exceptionalism

Guidance: level 1

:: Supply chain management ::

_____ is the removal of intermediaries in economics from a supply chain, or cutting out the middlemen in connection with a transaction or a series of transactions. Instead of going through traditional distribution channels, which had some type of intermediary , companies may now deal with customers directly, for example via the Internet. Hence, the use of factory direct and direct from the factory to mean the same thing.

Exam Probability: **High**

27. *Answer choices:*

(see index for correct answer)

- a. Murphy Warehouse Company
- b. National Centre for Cold-chain Development
- c. Pacific Access
- d. Logistics Bureau

Guidance: level 1

:: Industrial design ::

Across the many fields concerned with _____ , including information science, computer science, human-computer interaction, communication, and industrial design, there is little agreement over the meaning of the term " _____ ", although all are related to interaction with computers and other machines with a user interface.

Exam Probability: **High**

28. *Answer choices:*

(see index for correct answer)

- a. Fab Lab Barcelona
- b. WikID
- c. Sports engineering
- d. Experience design

Guidance: level 1

:: Global Positioning System ::

A _____ is a mechanism for determining the location of an object in space. Technologies for this task exist ranging from worldwide coverage with meter accuracy to workspace coverage with sub-millimetre accuracy.

Exam Probability: **High**

29. *Answer choices:*

(see index for correct answer)

- a. Navizon
- b. SiRFstarIII
- c. Positioning system
- d. GPSBabel

Guidance: level 1

:: Internet advertising ::

_____ , according to the United States federal law known as the Anti _____ Consumer Protection Act, is registering, trafficking in, or using an Internet domain name with bad faith intent to profit from the goodwill of a trademark belonging to someone else. The cybersquatter then offers to sell the domain to the person or company who owns a trademark contained within the name at an inflated price.

Exam Probability: **Low**

30. *Answer choices:*

(see index for correct answer)

- a. Video ad platform
- b. Pay per play
- c. Value Per Action
- d. Cybersquatting

Guidance: level 1

:: Information science ::

_____ is the resolution of uncertainty; it is that which answers the question of "what an entity is" and thus defines both its essence and nature of its characteristics. _____ relates to both data and knowledge, as data is meaningful _____ representing values attributed to parameters, and knowledge signifies understanding of a concept. _____ is uncoupled from an observer, which is an entity that can access _____ and thus discern what it specifies; _____ exists beyond an event horizon for example. In the case of knowledge, the _____ itself requires a cognitive observer to be obtained.

Exam Probability: **Low**

31. *Answer choices:*

(see index for correct answer)

- a. ISO 15926
- b. BioCreative
- c. Information
- d. Engineering informatics

Guidance: level 1

:: Business process ::

A _____ or business method is a collection of related, structured activities or tasks by people or equipment which in a specific sequence produce a service or product for a particular customer or customers. _____ es occur at all organizational levels and may or may not be visible to the customers. A _____ may often be visualized as a flowchart of a sequence of activities with interleaving decision points or as a process matrix of a sequence of activities with relevance rules based on data in the process. The benefits of using _____ es include improved customer satisfaction and improved agility for reacting to rapid market change. Process-oriented organizations break down the barriers of structural departments and try to avoid functional silos.

Exam Probability: **Medium**

32. *Answer choices:*

(see index for correct answer)

- a. Extended Enterprise Modeling Language
- b. Business process outsourcing
- c. Business operations
- d. Business process

Guidance: level 1

:: Economic globalization ::

_____ is an agreement in which one company hires another company to be responsible for a planned or existing activity that is or could be done internally,and sometimes involves transferring employees and assets from one firm to another.

Exam Probability: **Medium**

33. *Answer choices:*

(see index for correct answer)

- a. Outsourcing
- b. global financial

Guidance: level 1

:: Industrial design ::

In physics and mathematics, the _____ of a mathematical space is informally defined as the minimum number of coordinates needed to specify any point within it. Thus a line has a _____ of one because only one coordinate is needed to specify a point on it for example, the point at 5 on a number line. A surface such as a plane or the surface of a cylinder or sphere has a _____ of two because two coordinates are needed to specify a point on it for example, both a latitude and longitude are required to locate a point on the surface of a sphere. The inside of a cube, a cylinder or a sphere is three- _____ al because three coordinates are needed to locate a point within these spaces.

Exam Probability: **Medium**

34. *Answer choices:*

(see index for correct answer)

- a. Slow design
- b. Form factor
- c. User interface design
- d. Dimension

Guidance: level 1

:: Costs ::

In economics, _____ is the total economic cost of production and is made up of variable cost, which varies according to the quantity of a good produced and includes inputs such as labour and raw materials, plus fixed cost, which is independent of the quantity of a good produced and includes inputs that cannot be varied in the short term: fixed costs such as buildings and machinery, including sunk costs if any. Since cost is measured per unit of time, it is a flow variable.

Exam Probability: **Low**

35. *Answer choices:*

(see index for correct answer)

- a. Cost curve
- b. Average cost
- c. Opportunity cost of capital

- d. Further processing cost

Guidance: level 1

:: Automatic identification and data capture ::

_____ is the trademark for a type of matrix barcode first designed in 1994 for the automotive industry in Japan. A barcode is a machine-readable optical label that contains information about the item to which it is attached. In practice, _____ s often contain data for a locator, identifier, or tracker that points to a website or application. A _____ uses four standardized encoding modes to store data efficiently; extensions may also be used.

Exam Probability: **Low**

36. *Answer choices:*

(see index for correct answer)

- a. Chipless RFID
- b. QR code
- c. Barcode reader
- d. Retriever Communications

Guidance: level 1

:: Information systems ::

A _____ is an information system that supports business or organizational decision-making activities. DSSs serve the management, operations and planning levels of an organization and help people make decisions about problems that may be rapidly changing and not easily specified in advance—i.e. unstructured and semi-structured decision problems. _____ s can be either fully computerized or human-powered, or a combination of both.

Exam Probability: **Medium**

37. *Answer choices:*

(see index for correct answer)

- a. Decision support system
- b. Expert systems for mortgages
- c. Website Meta Language
- d. Ucode system

Guidance: level 1

:: Infographics ::

A _____ is a symbolic representation of information according to visualization technique. _____ s have been used since ancient times, but became more prevalent during the Enlightenment. Sometimes, the technique uses a three-dimensional visualization which is then projected onto a two-dimensional surface. The word graph is sometimes used as a synonym for _____ .

Exam Probability: **High**

38. *Answer choices:*

- a. Teaching method
- b. Diagram
- c. Signage systems
- d. Storyboard

Guidance: level 1

:: Virtual reality ::

A _____ is a computer-based simulated environment which may be populated by many users who can create a personal avatar, and simultaneously and independently explore the _____ , participate in its activities and communicate with others. These avatars can be textual, two or three-dimensional graphical representations, or live video avatars with auditory and touch sensations. In general, _____ s allow for multiple users but single player computer games, such as Skyrim, can also be considered a type of _____ .

Exam Probability: **Low**

39. *Answer choices:*

- a. Transformed social interaction
- b. Virtual world
- c. Motion simulator
- d. Google Street View

Guidance: level 1

:: Security compliance ::

_____ refers to the inability to withstand the effects of a hostile environment. A window of _____ is a time frame within which defensive measures are diminished, compromised or lacking.

Exam Probability: **High**

40. *Answer choices:*

(see index for correct answer)

- a. Federal Information Security Management Act of 2002
- b. Vulnerability
- c. Vulnerability management
- d. Information assurance vulnerability alert

Guidance: level 1

:: Computer security standards ::

The _____ for Information Technology Security Evaluation is an international standard for computer security certification. It is currently in version 3.1 revision 5.

Exam Probability: **Low**

41. *Answer choices:*

(see index for correct answer)

- a. Trusted Computer System Evaluation Criteria
- b. FIPS 199
- c. Blacker
- d. AFSSI-5020

Guidance: level 1

:: Stochastic processes ::

_____ in its modern meaning is a "new idea, creative thoughts, new imaginations in form of device or method". _____ is often also viewed as the application of better solutions that meet new requirements, unarticulated needs, or existing market needs. Such _____ takes place through the provision of more-effective products, processes, services, technologies, or business models that are made available to markets, governments and society. An _____ is something original and more effective and, as a consequence, new, that "breaks into" the market or society. _____ is related to, but not the same as, invention, as _____ is more apt to involve the practical implementation of an invention to make a meaningful impact in the market or society, and not all _____ s require an invention. _____ often manifests itself via the engineering process, when the problem being solved is of a technical or scientific nature. The opposite of _____ is exnovation.

Exam Probability: **Low**

42. *Answer choices:*

(see index for correct answer)

- a. Random measure
- b. Nuisance variable
- c. Product-form solution
- d. Innovation

Guidance: level 1

:: Computer data ::

In computer science, _____ is the ability to access an arbitrary element of a sequence in equal time or any datum from a population of addressable elements roughly as easily and efficiently as any other, no matter how many elements may be in the set. It is typically contrasted to sequential access.

Exam Probability: **Low**

43. *Answer choices:*

(see index for correct answer)

- a. 18-bit
- b. Random access
- c. Termcap
- d. Hex editor

Guidance: level 1

:: E-commerce ::

Electronic governance or e-governance is the application of information and communication technology for delivering government services, exchange of information, communication transactions, integration of various stand-alone systems and services between government-to-citizen , _____ , government-to-government , government-to-employees as well as back-office processes and interactions within the entire government framework. Through e-governance, government services are made available to citizens in a convenient, efficient, and transparent manner. The three main target groups that can be distinguished in governance concepts are government, citizens, andbusinesses/interest groups. In e-governance, there are no distinct boundaries.

Exam Probability: **Low**

44. *Answer choices:*

(see index for correct answer)

- a. Paywall
- b. Maritime E-Commerce Association
- c. BuildDirect
- d. Government-to-business

Guidance: level 1

:: Payment systems ::

An _____ is an electronic telecommunications device that enables customers of financial institutions to perform financial transactions, such as cash withdrawals, deposits, transfer funds, or obtaining account information, at any time and without the need for direct interaction with bank staff.

Exam Probability: **Low**

45. *Answer choices:*

(see index for correct answer)

- a. TIPANET
- b. ACI Worldwide
- c. Automated teller machine
- d. ToDDaSO

Guidance: level 1

:: Virtual economies ::

_____ is an online virtual world, developed and owned by the San Francisco-based firm Linden Lab and launched on June 23, 2003. By 2013, _____ had approximately one million regular users; at the end of 2017 active user count totals "between 800,000 and 900,000". In many ways, _____ is similar to massively multiplayer online role-playing games; however, Linden Lab is emphatic that their creation is not a game: "There is no manufactured conflict, no set objective".

Exam Probability: **Medium**

46. *Answer choices:*

(see index for correct answer)

- a. Cabal Online
- b. Second Life
- c. World of Warcraft
- d. The Sims Online

Guidance: level 1

:: Remote administration software ::

_____ is a protocol used on the Internet or local area network to provide a bidirectional interactive text-oriented communication facility using a virtual terminal connection. User data is interspersed in-band with _____ control information in an 8-bit byte oriented data connection over the Transmission Control Protocol .

Exam Probability: **High**

47. *Answer choices:*

(see index for correct answer)

- a. LanSchool
- b. Virtual Machine Manager
- c. Telnet
- d. GoToMyPC

:: Data quality ::

_____ is the maintenance of, and the assurance of the accuracy and consistency of, data over its entire life-cycle, and is a critical aspect to the design, implementation and usage of any system which stores, processes, or retrieves data. The term is broad in scope and may have widely different meanings depending on the specific context even under the same general umbrella of computing. It is at times used as a proxy term for data quality, while data validation is a pre-requisite for _____ . _____ is the opposite of data corruption. The overall intent of any _____ technique is the same: ensure data is recorded exactly as intended and upon later retrieval, ensure the data is the same as it was when it was originally recorded. In short, _____ aims to prevent unintentional changes to information. _____ is not to be confused with data security, the discipline of protecting data from unauthorized parties.

Exam Probability: **Low**

48. *Answer choices:*

(see index for correct answer)

- a. Data validation
- b. Data corruption
- c. Data degradation
- d. Data integrity

:: E-commerce ::

The phrase _____ was originally coined in 1997 by Kevin Duffey at the launch of the Global _____ Forum, to mean "the delivery of electronic commerce capabilities directly into the consumer's hand, anywhere, via wireless technology." Many choose to think of _____ as meaning "a retail outlet in your customer's pocket."

Exam Probability: **Medium**

49. *Answer choices:*

(see index for correct answer)

- a. Mobile commerce
- b. Location-based commerce
- c. Network Security Services
- d. Free Shipping Day

Guidance: level 1

:: Data quality ::

_____ or data cleaning is the process of detecting and correcting corrupt or inaccurate records from a record set, table, or database and refers to identifying incomplete, incorrect, inaccurate or irrelevant parts of the data and then replacing, modifying, or deleting the dirty or coarse data. _____ may be performed interactively with data wrangling tools, or as batch processing through scripting.

50. *Answer choices:*

(see index for correct answer)

- a. Declarative Referential Integrity
- b. Referential integrity
- c. Data cleansing
- d. Data Quality Campaign

Guidance: level 1

:: Computing input devices ::

In computing, an _____ is a piece of computer hardware equipment used to provide data and control signals to an information processing system such as a computer or information appliance. Examples of _____ s include keyboards, mouse, scanners, digital cameras and joysticks. Audio _____ s may be used for purposes including speech recognition. Many companies are utilizing speech recognition to help assist users to use their device.

Exam Probability: **Low**

51. *Answer choices:*

(see index for correct answer)

- a. SteelSeries
- b. Input device

- c. Ergonomic keyboard
- d. Novint Technologies

Guidance: level 1

:: Computer access control protocols ::

An _____ is a type of computer communications protocol or cryptographic protocol specifically designed for transfer of authentication data between two entities. It allows the receiving entity to authenticate the connecting entity as well as authenticate itself to the connecting entity by declaring the type of information needed for authentication as well as syntax. It is the most important layer of protection needed for secure communication within computer networks.

Exam Probability: **High**

52. *Answer choices:*
(see index for correct answer)

- a. Authentication protocol
- b. TACACS
- c. NTLMSSP
- d. CRAM-MD5

Guidance: level 1

:: Management ::

_____ is the identification of an organization's assets , followed by the development, documentation, and implementation of policies and procedures for protecting these assets.

Exam Probability: **High**

53. *Answer choices:*

(see index for correct answer)

- a. Community-based management
- b. Security management
- c. Success trap
- d. Business value

Guidance: level 1

:: Management ::

A _____ describes the rationale of how an organization creates, delivers, and captures value, in economic, social, cultural or other contexts. The process of _____ construction and modification is also called _____ innovation and forms a part of business strategy.

Exam Probability: **Medium**

54. *Answer choices:*

(see index for correct answer)

- a. Business model
- b. Reverse innovation
- c. Relational view
- d. Marketing management

Guidance: level 1

:: Contract law ::

_____ refers to a situation where a statement's author cannot successfully dispute its authorship or the validity of an associated contract. The term is often seen in a legal setting when the authenticity of a signature is being challenged. In such an instance, the authenticity is being "repudiated".

Exam Probability: **Medium**

55. *Answer choices:*

(see index for correct answer)

- a. Frustration of purpose
- b. Cover
- c. Convention on the Law Applicable to Contractual Obligations 1980
- d. Non-repudiation

:: SQL ::

SQL is a domain-specific language used in programming and designed for managing data held in a relational database management system , or for stream processing in a relational data stream management system . It is particularly useful in handling structured data where there are relations between different entities/variables of the data. SQL offers two main advantages over older read/write APIs like ISAM or VSAM. First, it introduced the concept of accessing many records with one single command; and second, it eliminates the need to specify how to reach a record, e.g. with or without an index.

Exam Probability: **Low**

56. *Answer choices:*

(see index for correct answer)

- a. Correlated subquery
- b. Structured query language
- c. Call Level Interface
- d. Structured type

:: Data ::

_____ is viewed by many disciplines as a modern equivalent of visual communication. It involves the creation and study of the visual representation of data.

Exam Probability: **Medium**

57. *Answer choices:*

(see index for correct answer)

- a. Dummy data
- b. Statistics
- c. Data Transmission
- d. Data visualization

Guidance: level 1

:: User interfaces ::

_____ , keystroke biometrics, typing dynamics and lately typing biometrics, is the detailed timing information which describes exactly when each key was pressed and when it was released as a person is typing at a computer keyboard.

Exam Probability: **Medium**

58. *Answer choices:*

(see index for correct answer)

- a. Social interface
- b. Command
- c. Multi-monitor
- d. Physical computing

Guidance: level 1

:: Human–computer interaction ::

_____ is a database query language for relational databases. It was devised by Moshé M. Zloof at IBM Research during the mid-1970s, in parallel to the development of SQL. It is the first graphical query language, using visual tables where the user would enter commands, example elements and conditions. Many graphical front-ends for databases use the ideas from QBE today. Originally limited only for the purpose of retrieving data, QBE was later extended to allow other operations, such as inserts, deletes and updates, as well as creation of temporary tables.

Exam Probability: **Low**

59. *Answer choices:*
(see index for correct answer)

- a. Bad Day
- b. Implicit data collection
- c. First-time user experience
- d. Query by Example

Marketing

Marketing is the study and management of exchange relationships. Marketing is the business process of creating relationships with and satisfying customers. With its focus on the customer, marketing is one of the premier components of business management.

Marketing is defined by the American Marketing Association as "the activity, set of institutions, and processes for creating, communicating, delivering, and exchanging offerings that have value for customers, clients, partners, and society at large."

:: ::

_____ consists of using generic or ad hoc methods in an orderly manner to find solutions to problems. Some of the problem-solving techniques developed and used in philosophy, artificial intelligence, computer science, engineering, mathematics, or medicine are related to mental problem-solving techniques studied in psychology.

Exam Probability: **Low**

1. *Answer choices:*

(see index for correct answer)

- a. cultural
- b. co-culture
- c. empathy
- d. Problem Solving

Guidance: level 1

:: Marketing ::

_____ s are structured marketing strategies designed by merchants to encourage customers to continue to shop at or use the services of businesses associated with each program. These programs exist covering most types of commerce, each one having varying features and rewards-schemes.

Exam Probability: **Low**

2. *Answer choices:*

(see index for correct answer)

- a. Digital native
- b. Place branding
- c. Ayelet Gneezy
- d. Loyalty program

Guidance: level 1

:: Behaviorism ::

In behavioral psychology, _____ is a consequence applied that will strengthen an organism's future behavior whenever that behavior is preceded by a specific antecedent stimulus. This strengthening effect may be measured as a higher frequency of behavior , longer duration , greater magnitude , or shorter latency . There are two types of _____ , known as positive _____ and negative _____ ; positive is where by a reward is offered on expression of the wanted behaviour and negative is taking away an undesirable element in the persons environment whenever the desired behaviour is achieved.

Exam Probability: **Medium**

3. *Answer choices:*

(see index for correct answer)

- a. Programmed instruction
- b. Matching Law

- c. social facilitation
- d. Reinforcement

Guidance: level 1

:: ::

A _____ service is an online platform which people use to build social networks or social relationship with other people who share similar personal or career interests, activities, backgrounds or real-life connections.

Exam Probability: **Medium**

4. *Answer choices:*
(see index for correct answer)

- a. Social networking
- b. process perspective
- c. levels of analysis
- d. hierarchical

Guidance: level 1

:: ::

_____ s are formal, sociotechnical, organizational systems designed to collect, process, store, and distribute information. In a sociotechnical perspective, _____ s are composed by four components: task, people, structure , and technology.

Exam Probability: **Low**

5. *Answer choices:*

(see index for correct answer)

- a. functional perspective
- b. personal values
- c. deep-level diversity
- d. open system

Guidance: level 1

:: Business terms ::

_____ occurs when a sales representative meets with a potential client for the purpose of transacting a sale. Many sales representatives rely on a sequential sales process that typically includes nine steps. Some sales representatives develop scripts for all or part of the sales process. The sales process can be used in face-to-face encounters and in telemarketing.

Exam Probability: **Low**

6. *Answer choices:*

(see index for correct answer)

- a. Personal selling
- b. organic growth
- c. granular
- d. centralization

Guidance: level 1

:: Business models ::

_____ es are privately owned corporations, partnerships, or sole proprietorships that have fewer employees and/or less annual revenue than a regular-sized business or corporation. Businesses are defined as "small" in terms of being able to apply for government support and qualify for preferential tax policy varies depending on the country and industry. _____ es range from fifteen employees under the Australian Fair Work Act 2009, fifty employees according to the definition used by the European Union, and fewer than five hundred employees to qualify for many U.S. _____ Administration programs. While _____ es can also be classified according to other methods, such as annual revenues, shipments, sales, assets, or by annual gross or net revenue or net profits, the number of employees is one of the most widely used measures.

Exam Probability: **Low**

7. *Answer choices:*

(see index for correct answer)

- a. Cooperative
- b. The India Way
- c. Very small business
- d. Free-to-play

Guidance: level 1

:: Evaluation methods ::

_____ is a scientific method of observation to gather non-numerical data. This type of research "refers to the meanings, concepts definitions, characteristics, metaphors, symbols, and description of things" and not to their "counts or measures." This research answers why and how a certain phenomenon may occur rather than how often. _____ approaches are employed across many academic disciplines, focusing particularly on the human elements of the social and natural sciences; in less academic contexts, areas of application include qualitative market research, business, service demonstrations by non-profits, and journalism.

Exam Probability: **Medium**

8. *Answer choices:*
(see index for correct answer)

- a. Business excellence
- b. Event correlation
- c. Alternative assessment
- d. Qualitative research

:: ::

_____ is both a research area and a practical skill encompassing the ability of an individual or organization to "lead" or guide other individuals, teams, or entire organizations. Specialist literature debates various viewpoints, contrasting Eastern and Western approaches to _____ , and also United States versus European approaches. U.S. academic environments define _____ as "a process of social influence in which a person can enlist the aid and support of others in the accomplishment of a common task".

Exam Probability: **Low**

9. *Answer choices:*

(see index for correct answer)

- a. information systems assessment
- b. levels of analysis
- c. similarity-attraction theory
- d. Leadership

:: Information technology management ::

B2B is often contrasted with business-to-consumer . In B2B commerce, it is often the case that the parties to the relationship have comparable negotiating power, and even when they do not, each party typically involves professional staff and legal counsel in the negotiation of terms, whereas B2C is shaped to a far greater degree by economic implications of information asymmetry. However, within a B2B context, large companies may have many commercial, resource and information advantages over smaller businesses. The United Kingdom government, for example, created the post of Small Business Commissioner under the Enterprise Act 2016 to "enable small businesses to resolve disputes" and "consider complaints by small business suppliers about payment issues with larger businesses that they supply."

Exam Probability: **Medium**

10. *Answer choices:*
(see index for correct answer)

- a. Business-to-business
- b. Accelops
- c. Shadow system
- d. Open Cobalt

Guidance: level 1

:: Health promotion ::

_____ , as defined by the World _____ Organization , is "a state of complete physical, mental and social well-being and not merely the absence of disease or infirmity." This definition has been subject to controversy, as it may have limited value for implementation. _____ may be defined as the ability to adapt and manage physical, mental and social challenges throughout life.

Exam Probability: **Low**

11. *Answer choices:*

(see index for correct answer)

- a. Maria Gomori
- b. Social marketing
- c. Alliance for Healthy Cities
- d. Health

Guidance: level 1

:: Management ::

The term _____ refers to measures designed to increase the degree of autonomy and self-determination in people and in communities in order to enable them to represent their interests in a responsible and self-determined way, acting on their own authority. It is the process of becoming stronger and more confident, especially in controlling one's life and claiming one's rights. _____ as action refers both to the process of self-_____ and to professional support of people, which enables them to overcome their sense of powerlessness and lack of influence, and to recognize and use their resources. To do work with power.

Exam Probability: **Medium**

12. *Answer choices:*

(see index for correct answer)

- a. Empowerment
- b. Energy monitoring and targeting
- c. Industrial market segmentation
- d. Event chain methodology

Guidance: level 1

:: Business models ::

A _____ is "an autonomous association of persons united voluntarily to meet their common economic, social, and cultural needs and aspirations through a jointly-owned and democratically-controlled enterprise". _____ s may include.

13. *Answer choices:*

(see index for correct answer)

- a. Cooperative
- b. Revenue model
- c. Component business model
- d. Paid To Click

Guidance: level 1

:: ::

_____ is the process whereby a business sets the price at which it will sell its products and services, and may be part of the business's marketing plan. In setting prices, the business will take into account the price at which it could acquire the goods, the manufacturing cost, the market place, competition, market condition, brand, and quality of product.

Exam Probability: **Low**

14. *Answer choices:*

(see index for correct answer)

- a. co-culture
- b. levels of analysis

- c. Pricing
- d. functional perspective

Guidance: level 1

:: Product management ::

` _____ ` is a phrase used in the marketing industry which describes the value of having a well-known brand name, based on the idea that the owner of a well-known brand name can generate more revenue simply from brand recognition; that is from products with that brand name than from products with a less well known name, as consumers believe that a product with a well-known name is better than products with less well-known names.

Exam Probability: **High**

15. *Answer choices:*

(see index for correct answer)

- a. Tipping point
- b. Brand equity
- c. Trademark
- d. Requirement prioritization

Guidance: level 1

:: Advertising ::

A _____ is a large outdoor advertising structure , typically found in high-traffic areas such as alongside busy roads. _____ s present large advertisements to passing pedestrians and drivers. Typically showing witty slogans and distinctive visuals, _____ s are highly visible in the top designated market areas.

Exam Probability: **Low**

16. *Answer choices:*

(see index for correct answer)

- a. Billboard
- b. Issue advocacy ads
- c. Restaurant media
- d. Pennysaver

Guidance: level 1

:: ::

In legal terminology, a _____ is any formal legal document that sets out the facts and legal reasons that the filing party or parties believes are sufficient to support a claim against the party or parties against whom the claim is brought that entitles the plaintiff to a remedy . For example, the Federal Rules of Civil Procedure that govern civil litigation in United States courts provide that a civil action is commenced with the filing or service of a pleading called a _____ . Civil court rules in states that have incorporated the Federal Rules of Civil Procedure use the same term for the same pleading.

17. *Answer choices:*

(see index for correct answer)

- a. functional perspective
- b. personal values
- c. Complaint
- d. co-culture

Guidance: level 1

:: Market research ::

_____ is "the process or set of processes that links the producers, customers, and end users to the marketer through information used to identify and define marketing opportunities and problems; generate, refine, and evaluate marketing actions; monitor marketing performance; and improve understanding of marketing as a process. _____ specifies the information required to address these issues, designs the method for collecting information, manages and implements the data collection process, analyzes the results, and communicates the findings and their implications."

Exam Probability: **Low**

18. *Answer choices:*

(see index for correct answer)

- a. Marketing research
- b. Qualtrics
- c. TNS NIPO
- d. IModerate

Guidance: level 1

:: Brokered programming ::

An _____ is a form of television commercial, which generally includes a toll-free telephone number or website. Most often used as a form of direct response television , long-form _____ s are typically 28:30 or 58:30 minutes in length. _____ s are also known as paid programming . This phenomenon started in the United States, where _____ s were typically shown overnight , outside peak prime time hours for commercial broadcasters. Some television stations chose to air _____ s as an alternative to the former practice of signing off. Some channels air _____ s 24 hours. Some stations also choose to air _____ s during the daytime hours mostly on weekends to fill in for unscheduled network or syndicated programming. By 2009, most _____ spending in the U.S. occurred during the early morning, daytime and evening hours, or in the afternoon. Stations in most countries around the world have instituted similar media structures. The _____ industry is worth over $200 billion.

Exam Probability: **Low**

19. *Answer choices:*

(see index for correct answer)

- a. Brokered programming

- b. Leased access
- c. Infomercial
- d. Toonzai

Guidance: level 1

:: Types of marketing ::

_____ was first defined as a form of marketing developed from direct response marketing campaigns which emphasizes customer retention and satisfaction, rather than a focus on sales transactions.

Exam Probability: **Medium**

20. *Answer choices:*

(see index for correct answer)

- a. Relationship marketing
- b. Social pull marketing
- c. Ambush marketing
- d. Account planning

Guidance: level 1

:: bad_topic ::

Sponsoring something is the act of supporting an event, activity, person, or organization financially or through the provision of products or services. The individual or group that provides the support, similar to a benefactor, is known as sponsor.

Exam Probability: **High**

21. *Answer choices:*

(see index for correct answer)

- a. Vision statement
- b. Sponsorship
- c. MBNA Corporation
- d. equity interest

Guidance: level 1

:: ::

According to the philosopher Piyush Mathur , "Tangibility is the property that a phenomenon exhibits if it has and/or transports mass and/or energy and/or momentum".

Exam Probability: **High**

22. *Answer choices:*

(see index for correct answer)

- a. functional perspective
- b. empathy
- c. Tangible
- d. Sarbanes-Oxley act of 2002

Guidance: level 1

:: ::

_____ , known in Europe as research and technological development , refers to innovative activities undertaken by corporations or governments in developing new services or products, or improving existing services or products. _____ constitutes the first stage of development of a potential new service or the production process.

Exam Probability: **Low**

23. *Answer choices:*

(see index for correct answer)

- a. deep-level diversity
- b. empathy
- c. open system
- d. hierarchical

Guidance: level 1

:: Marketing ::

_____ is a market strategy in which a firm decides to ignore market segment differences and appeal the whole market with one offer or one strategy, which supports the idea of broadcasting a message that will reach the largest number of people possible. Traditionally _____ has focused on radio, television and newspapers as the media used to reach this broad audience. By reaching the largest audience possible, exposure to the product is maximized, and in theory this would directly correlate with a larger number of sales or buys into the product.

Exam Probability: **Medium**

24. *Answer choices:*

(see index for correct answer)

- a. Mass marketing
- b. Hakan Okay
- c. In-game advertising
- d. LIDA

Guidance: level 1

:: Competition regulators ::

The _____ is an independent agency of the United States government, established in 1914 by the _____ Act. Its principal mission is the promotion of consumer protection and the elimination and prevention of anticompetitive business practices, such as coercive monopoly. It is headquartered in the _____ Building in Washington, D.C.

Exam Probability: **High**

25. *Answer choices:*

(see index for correct answer)

- a. Fair Trade Commission
- b. Queensland Competition Authority
- c. Federal Trade Commission
- d. Commerce Commission

Guidance: level 1

:: ::

_____ is a marketing communication that employs an openly sponsored, non-personal message to promote or sell a product, service or idea. Sponsors of _____ are typically businesses wishing to promote their products or services. _____ is differentiated from public relations in that an advertiser pays for and has control over the message. It differs from personal selling in that the message is non-personal, i.e., not directed to a particular individual. _____ is communicated through various mass media, including traditional media such as newspapers, magazines, television, radio, outdoor _____ or direct mail; and new media such as search results, blogs, social media, websites or text messages. The actual presentation of the message in a medium is referred to as an advertisement, or "ad" or advert for short.

Exam Probability: **Low**

26. *Answer choices:*

(see index for correct answer)

- a. imperative
- b. corporate values
- c. process perspective
- d. functional perspective

Guidance: level 1

:: ::

An _____ is the production of goods or related services within an economy. The major source of revenue of a group or company is the indicator of its relevant _____ . When a large group has multiple sources of revenue generation, it is considered to be working in different industries. Manufacturing _____ became a key sector of production and labour in European and North American countries during the Industrial Revolution, upsetting previous mercantile and feudal economies. This came through many successive rapid advances in technology, such as the production of steel and coal.

Exam Probability: **Low**

27. *Answer choices:*

(see index for correct answer)

- a. hierarchical perspective
- b. Industry
- c. Sarbanes-Oxley act of 2002
- d. surface-level diversity

Guidance: level 1

:: ::

In financial markets, a share is a unit used as mutual funds, limited partnerships, and real estate investment trusts. The owner of _____ in the corporation/company is a shareholder of the corporation. A share is an indivisible unit of capital, expressing the ownership relationship between the company and the shareholder. The denominated value of a share is its face value, and the total of the face value of issued _____ represent the capital of a company, which may not reflect the market value of those _____ .

28. *Answer choices:*

(see index for correct answer)

- a. co-culture
- b. Character
- c. information systems assessment
- d. Shares

Guidance: level 1

:: Materials ::

A _____ , also known as a feedstock, unprocessed material, or primary commodity, is a basic material that is used to produce goods, finished products, energy, or intermediate materials which are feedstock for future finished products. As feedstock, the term connotes these materials are bottleneck assets and are highly important with regard to producing other products. An example of this is crude oil, which is a _____ and a feedstock used in the production of industrial chemicals, fuels, plastics, and pharmaceutical goods; lumber is a _____ used to produce a variety of products including all types of furniture. The term " _____ " denotes materials in minimally processed or unprocessed in states; e.g., raw latex, crude oil, cotton, coal, raw biomass, iron ore, air, logs, or water i.e. "...any product of agriculture, forestry, fishing and any other mineral that is in its natural form or which has undergone the transformation required to prepare it for internationally marketing in substantial volumes."

Exam Probability: **High**

29. *Answer choices:*

(see index for correct answer)

- a. Food contact materials
- b. Raw material
- c. Superhard material
- d. Propolis

Guidance: level 1

:: Trade associations ::

A _____ , also known as an industry trade group, business association, sector association or industry body, is an organization founded and funded by businesses that operate in a specific industry. An industry _____ participates in public relations activities such as advertising, education, political donations, lobbying and publishing, but its focus is collaboration between companies. Associations may offer other services, such as producing conferences, networking or charitable events or offering classes or educational materials. Many associations are non-profit organizations governed by bylaws and directed by officers who are also members.

Exam Probability: **Medium**

30. *Answer choices:*

(see index for correct answer)

- a. Rubber Trade Association of Penang
- b. Trade association
- c. SD Association
- d. Lighting Association

Guidance: level 1

:: Progressive Era in the United States ::

The Clayton Antitrust Act of 1914 , was a part of United States antitrust law with the goal of adding further substance to the U.S. antitrust law regime; the _____ sought to prevent anticompetitive practices in their incipiency. That regime started with the Sherman Antitrust Act of 1890, the first Federal law outlawing practices considered harmful to consumers . The _____ specified particular prohibited conduct, the three-level enforcement scheme, the exemptions, and the remedial measures.

Exam Probability: **High**

31. *Answer choices:*

(see index for correct answer)

- a. Clayton Antitrust Act
- b. Clayton Act
- c. Mann Act

Guidance: level 1

:: Consumer behaviour ::

Convenient procedures, products and services are those intended to increase ease in accessibility, save resources and decrease frustration. A modern _____ is a labor-saving device, service or substance which make a task easier or more efficient than a traditional method. _____ is a relative concept, and depends on context. For example, automobiles were once considered a _____ , yet today are regarded as a normal part of life.

Exam Probability: **Medium**

32. *Answer choices:*

(see index for correct answer)

- a. Convenience
- b. Mociology
- c. Self-brand
- d. Intertemporal choice

Guidance: level 1

:: ::

In law, a _____ is a coming together of parties to a dispute, to present information in a tribunal, a formal setting with the authority to adjudicate claims or disputes. One form of tribunal is a court. The tribunal, which may occur before a judge, jury, or other designated trier of fact, aims to achieve a resolution to their dispute.

Exam Probability: **Medium**

33. *Answer choices:*

(see index for correct answer)

- a. process perspective
- b. deep-level diversity

- c. Trial
- d. corporate values

Guidance: level 1

:: Television commercials ::

_____ is a characteristic that distinguishes physical entities that have biological processes, such as signaling and self-sustaining processes, from those that do not, either because such functions have ceased , or because they never had such functions and are classified as inanimate. Various forms of _____ exist, such as plants, animals, fungi, protists, archaea, and bacteria. The criteria can at times be ambiguous and may or may not define viruses, viroids, or potential synthetic _____ as "living". Biology is the science concerned with the study of _____ .

Exam Probability: **Low**

34. *Answer choices:*

(see index for correct answer)

- a. Life
- b. Batman OnStar commercials
- c. Blipvert
- d. NoitulovE

Guidance: level 1

:: Marketing ::

A _____ is something that is necessary for an organism to live a healthy life. _____ s are distinguished from wants in that, in the case of a _____ , a deficiency causes a clear adverse outcome: a dysfunction or death. In other words, a _____ is something required for a safe, stable and healthy life while a want is a desire, wish or aspiration. When _____ s or wants are backed by purchasing power, they have the potential to become economic demands.

Exam Probability: **Medium**

35. *Answer choices:*

(see index for correct answer)

- a. Need
- b. City marketing
- c. Albuquerque Craft Beer Market
- d. Health marketing

Guidance: level 1

:: ::

A _____ or sample _____ is a single measure of some attribute of a sample . It is calculated by applying a function to the values of the items of the sample, which are known together as a set of data.

36. *Answer choices:*

(see index for correct answer)

- a. hierarchical perspective
- b. surface-level diversity
- c. process perspective
- d. Statistic

Guidance: level 1

:: Marketing ::

A _____ is a group of customers within a business's serviceable available market at which a business aims its marketing efforts and resources. A _____ is a subset of the total market for a product or service. The _____ typically consists of consumers who exhibit similar characteristics and are considered most likely to buy a business's market offerings or are likely to be the most profitable segments for the business to service.

Exam Probability: **Low**

37. *Answer choices:*

(see index for correct answer)

- a. Cola Wars
- b. Call to action

- c. Existing visitor optimisation
- d. Target market

Guidance: level 1

:: Business ::

In commerce, _____ is the product of an interaction between an organization and a customer over the duration of their relationship. This interaction is made up of three parts: the customer journey, the brand touchpoints the customer interacts with, and the environments the _____ s during their experience. A good _____ means that the individual's experience during all points of contact matches the individual's expectations. Gartner asserts the importance of managing the customer's experience.

Exam Probability: **Low**

38. *Answer choices:*
(see index for correct answer)

- a. Customer experience
- b. EPG Model
- c. Kingdomality
- d. Family business

Guidance: level 1

:: Advertising by type ::

_____ or advertising war is an advertisement in which a particular product, or service, specifically mentions a competitor by name for the express purpose of showing why the competitor is inferior to the product naming it. Also referred to as "knocking copy", it is loosely defined as advertising where "the advertised brand is explicitly compared with one or more competing brands and the comparison is obvious to the audience."

Exam Probability: **Low**

39. *Answer choices:*
(see index for correct answer)

- a. Shock advertising
- b. Out-of-home advertising
- c. Space advertising
- d. Comparative advertising

Guidance: level 1

:: ::

_____ is the means to see, hear, or become aware of something or someone through our fundamental senses. The term _____ derives from the Latin word perceptio, and is the organization, identification, and interpretation of sensory information in order to represent and understand the presented information, or the environment.

40. *Answer choices:*

(see index for correct answer)

- a. hierarchical perspective
- b. deep-level diversity
- c. cultural
- d. Perception

Guidance: level 1

:: Meetings ::

A _____ is a body of one or more persons that is subordinate to a deliberative assembly. Usually, the assembly sends matters into a _____ as a way to explore them more fully than would be possible if the assembly itself were considering them. _____ s may have different functions and their type of work differ depending on the type of the organization and its needs.

41. *Answer choices:*

(see index for correct answer)

- a. Committee
- b. Future workshop

- c. Carlton Club meeting
- d. Annual Georgia European Union Summit

Guidance: level 1

:: National accounts ::

_____ is a monetary measure of the market value of all the final goods and services produced in a period of time, often annually. GDP per capita does not, however, reflect differences in the cost of living and the inflation rates of the countries; therefore using a basis of GDP per capita at purchasing power parity is arguably more useful when comparing differences in living standards between nations.

Exam Probability: **Medium**

42. *Answer choices:*

(see index for correct answer)

- a. Gross domestic product
- b. capital formation
- c. National Income

Guidance: level 1

:: Stock market ::

_____ is freedom from, or resilience against, potential harm caused by others. Beneficiaries of _____ may be of persons and social groups, objects and institutions, ecosystems or any other entity or phenomenon vulnerable to unwanted change by its environment.

Exam Probability: **High**

43. *Answer choices:*

(see index for correct answer)

- a. Squeeze out
- b. Security
- c. Stop price
- d. London Stock Exchange Group

Guidance: level 1

:: Mereology ::

_____ , in the abstract, is what belongs to or with something, whether as an attribute or as a component of said thing. In the context of this article, it is one or more components , whether physical or incorporeal, of a person's estate; or so belonging to, as in being owned by, a person or jointly a group of people or a legal entity like a corporation or even a society. Depending on the nature of the _____ , an owner of _____ has the right to consume, alter, share, redefine, rent, mortgage, pawn, sell, exchange, transfer, give away or destroy it, or to exclude others from doing these things, as well as to perhaps abandon it; whereas regardless of the nature of the _____ , the owner thereof has the right to properly use it , or at the very least exclusively keep it.

Exam Probability: **High**

44. *Answer choices:*

(see index for correct answer)

- a. Mereology
- b. Gunk
- c. Mereological nihilism
- d. Meronomy

Guidance: level 1

:: Graphic design ::

An _____ is an artifact that depicts visual perception, such as a photograph or other two-dimensional picture, that resembles a subject—usually a physical object—and thus provides a depiction of it. In the context of signal processing, an _____ is a distributed amplitude of color.

Exam Probability: **High**

45. *Answer choices:*

(see index for correct answer)

- a. Gestalt psychology
- b. Image
- c. Iris printer
- d. Illustria Designs

Guidance: level 1

:: Income ::

In business and accounting, net income is an entity's income minus cost of goods sold, expenses and taxes for an accounting period. It is computed as the residual of all revenues and gains over all expenses and losses for the period, and has also been defined as the net increase in shareholders' equity that results from a company's operations. In the context of the presentation of financial statements, the IFRS Foundation defines net income as synonymous with profit and loss. The difference between revenue and the cost of making a product or providing a service, before deducting overheads, payroll, taxation, and interest payments. This is different from operating income .

46. *Answer choices:*

(see index for correct answer)

- a. Creative real estate investing
- b. Trinity study
- c. Bottom line
- d. Real income

Guidance: level 1

:: ::

The _____ is an agreement signed by Canada, Mexico, and the United States, creating a trilateral trade bloc in North America. The agreement came into force on January 1, 1994, and superseded the 1988 Canada–United States Free Trade Agreement between the United States and Canada. The NAFTA trade bloc is one of the largest trade blocs in the world by gross domestic product.

47. *Answer choices:*

(see index for correct answer)

- a. interpersonal communication
- b. corporate values

- c. information systems assessment
- d. North American Free Trade Agreement

:: Marketing ::

_____ is research conducted for a problem that has not been studied more clearly, intended to establish priorities, develop operational definitions and improve the final research design. _____ helps determine the best research design, data-collection method and selection of subjects. It should draw definitive conclusions only with extreme caution. Given its fundamental nature, _____ often relies on techniques such as.

Exam Probability: **High**

48. *Answer choices:*

(see index for correct answer)

- a. Multichannel marketing
- b. European Information Technology Observatory
- c. Exploratory research
- d. Cause-related loyalty marketing

:: Evaluation methods ::

In natural and social sciences, and sometimes in other fields, _____ is the systematic empirical investigation of observable phenomena via statistical, mathematical, or computational techniques. The objective of _____ is to develop and employ mathematical models, theories, and hypotheses pertaining to phenomena. The process of measurement is central to _____ because it provides the fundamental connection between empirical observation and mathematical expression of quantitative relationships.

Exam Probability: **Medium**

49. *Answer choices:*

(see index for correct answer)

- a. Question-focused dataset
- b. Pick chart
- c. Moral statistics
- d. Quantitative research

Guidance: level 1

:: Business law ::

A _____ is an arrangement where parties, known as partners, agree to cooperate to advance their mutual interests. The partners in a _____ may be individuals, businesses, interest-based organizations, schools, governments or combinations. Organizations may partner to increase the likelihood of each achieving their mission and to amplify their reach. A _____ may result in issuing and holding equity or may be only governed by a contract.

50. *Answer choices:*

(see index for correct answer)

- a. Installment sale
- b. Court auction
- c. Partnership
- d. Board of directors

Guidance: level 1

:: Marketing ::

_____ is a marketing practice of individuals or organizations . It
allows them to sell products or services to other companies or organizations
that resell them, use them in their products or services or use them to support
their works.

Exam Probability: **High**

51. *Answer choices:*

(see index for correct answer)

- a. Commodity chain
- b. Consumer-to-business
- c. Business marketing

- d. Jobbing house

Guidance: level 1

:: Marketing ::

_____ is a pricing strategy where the price of a product is initially set low to rapidly reach a wide fraction of the market and initiate word of mouth. The strategy works on the expectation that customers will switch to the new brand because of the lower price. _____ is most commonly associated with marketing objectives of enlarging market share and exploiting economies of scale or experience.

Exam Probability: **High**

52. *Answer choices:*
(see index for correct answer)

- a. Customer interaction tracker
- b. Brand content management
- c. Penetration pricing
- d. Purchase funnel

Guidance: level 1

:: ::

A _____ consists of one people who live in the same dwelling and share meals. It may also consist of a single family or another group of people. A dwelling is considered to contain multiple _____ s if meals or living spaces are not shared. The _____ is the basic unit of analysis in many social, microeconomic and government models, and is important to economics and inheritance.

Exam Probability: **Medium**

53. *Answer choices:*

(see index for correct answer)

- a. imperative
- b. Household
- c. levels of analysis
- d. deep-level diversity

Guidance: level 1

:: Library science ::

_____ refers to data which is collected by someone who is someone other than the user. Common sources of _____ for social science include censuses, information collected by government departments, organizational records and data that was originally collected for other research purposes. Primary data, by contrast, are collected by the investigator conducting the research.

54. *Answer choices:*

(see index for correct answer)

- a. John Sessions Memorial Award
- b. Library science
- c. OpenURL
- d. Western Waters Digital Library

Guidance: level 1

:: Social psychology ::

_____ s is a qualitative methodology used to describe consumers on psychological attributes. _____ s have been applied to the study of personality, values, opinions, attitudes, interests, and lifestyles. While _____ s are often equated with lifestyle research, it has been argued that _____ s should apply to the study of cognitive attributes such as attitudes, interests, opinions, and beliefs while lifestyle should apply to the study of overt behavior . Because this area of research focuses on activities, interests, and opinions, _____ factors are sometimes abbreviated to `AIO variables`.

Exam Probability: **Medium**

55. *Answer choices:*

(see index for correct answer)

- a. Production blocking
- b. Psychographic
- c. Social penetration
- d. Social character

Guidance: level 1

:: ::

_____ refers to a diverse array of media technologies that reach a large audience via mass communication. The technologies through which this communication takes place include a variety of outlets.

Exam Probability: **Medium**

56. *Answer choices:*

(see index for correct answer)

- a. similarity-attraction theory
- b. process perspective
- c. Mass media
- d. interpersonal communication

Guidance: level 1

:: Management accounting ::

In economics, _____ s, indirect costs or overheads are business expenses that are not dependent on the level of goods or services produced by the business. They tend to be time-related, such as interest or rents being paid per month, and are often referred to as overhead costs. This is in contrast to variable costs, which are volume-related and unknown at the beginning of the accounting year. For a simple example, such as a bakery, the monthly rent for the baking facilities, and the monthly payments for the security system and basic phone line are _____ s, as they do not change according to how much bread the bakery produces and sells. On the other hand, the wage costs of the bakery are variable, as the bakery will have to hire more workers if the production of bread increases. Economists reckon _____ as a entry barrier for new entrepreneurs.

Exam Probability: **Low**

57. *Answer choices:*

(see index for correct answer)

- a. Contribution margin
- b. Fixed cost
- c. Environmental full-cost accounting
- d. Invested capital

Guidance: level 1

:: Product management ::

A _____ is a professional role which is responsible for the development of products for an organization, known as the practice of product management. _____ s own the business strategy behind a product , specify its functional requirements and generally manage the launch of features. They coordinate work done by many other functions and are ultimately responsible for the business success of the product.

Exam Probability: **Low**

58. *Answer choices:*

- a. Obsolescence
- b. Product manager
- c. Scarcity Development Cycle
- d. Control chart

Guidance: level 1

:: ::

In marketing jargon, product lining is offering several related products for sale individually. Unlike product bundling, where several products are combined into one group, which is then offered for sale as a units, product lining involves offering the products for sale separately. A line can comprise related products of various sizes, types, colors, qualities, or prices. Line depth refers to the number of subcategories a category has. Line consistency refers to how closely related the products that make up the line are. Line vulnerability refers to the percentage of sales or profits that are derived from only a few products in the line.

Exam Probability: **Medium**

59. *Answer choices:*

(see index for correct answer)

- a. cultural
- b. open system
- c. Product line
- d. Character

Guidance: level 1

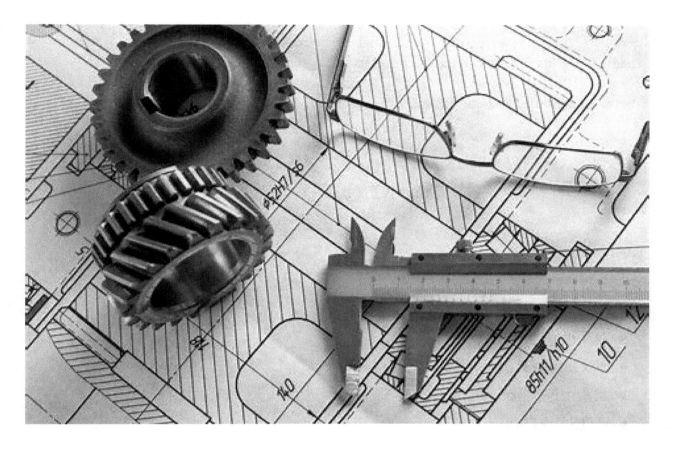

Manufacturing

Manufacturing is the production of merchandise for use or sale using labor and machines, tools, chemical and biological processing, or formulation. The term may refer to a range of human activity, from handicraft to high tech, but is most commonly applied to industrial design , in which raw materials are transformed into finished goods on a large scale. Such finished goods may be sold to other manufacturers for the production of other, more complex products, such as aircraft, household appliances, furniture, sports equipment or automobiles, or sold to wholesalers, who in turn sell them to retailers, who then sell them to end users and consumers.

:: Project management ::

A _____ is a type of bar chart that illustrates a project schedule, named after its inventor, Henry Gantt , who designed such a chart around the years 1910–1915. Modern _____ s also show the dependency relationships between activities and current schedule status.

Exam Probability: **High**

1. *Answer choices:*

(see index for correct answer)

- a. Financial plan
- b. Gantt chart
- c. Project governance
- d. ISO 21500

Guidance: level 1

:: Management ::

_____ is the identification, evaluation, and prioritization of risks followed by coordinated and economical application of resources to minimize, monitor, and control the probability or impact of unfortunate events or to maximize the realization of opportunities.

Exam Probability: **High**

2. *Answer choices:*

(see index for correct answer)

- a. Stovepipe
- b. Project cost management
- c. Flat organization
- d. Place management

Guidance: level 1

:: Metalworking ::

A _____ is a round object with various uses. It is used in _____ games, where the play of the game follows the state of the _____ as it is hit, kicked or thrown by players. _____ s can also be used for simpler activities, such as catch or juggling. _____ s made from hard-wearing materials are used in engineering applications to provide very low friction bearings, known as _____ bearings. Black-powder weapons use stone and metal _____ s as projectiles.

Exam Probability: **High**

3. *Answer choices:*

(see index for correct answer)

- a. Semi-solid metal casting
- b. Ball
- c. Mokume-gane
- d. Ironwork

:: ::

_____ refers to the confirmation of certain characteristics of an object, person, or organization. This confirmation is often, but not always, provided by some form of external review, education, assessment, or audit. Accreditation is a specific organization's process of _____ . According to the National Council on Measurement in Education, a _____ test is a credentialing test used to determine whether individuals are knowledgeable enough in a given occupational area to be labeled "competent to practice" in that area.

Exam Probability: **Medium**

4. *Answer choices:*
(see index for correct answer)

- a. similarity-attraction theory
- b. empathy
- c. surface-level diversity
- d. Certification

:: Costs ::

In process improvement efforts, _____ or cost of quality is a means to quantify the total cost of quality-related efforts and deficiencies. It was first described by Armand V. Feigenbaum in a 1956 Harvard Business Review article.

Exam Probability: **High**

5. *Answer choices:*

(see index for correct answer)

- a. labor cost
- b. Quality costs
- c. Average variable cost
- d. Cost of products sold

Guidance: level 1

:: Production and manufacturing ::

_____ is a systematic method to improve the "value" of goods or products and services by using an examination of function. Value, as defined, is the ratio of function to cost. Value can therefore be manipulated by either improving the function or reducing the cost. It is a primary tenet of _____ that basic functions be preserved and not be reduced as a consequence of pursuing value improvements.

Exam Probability: **Low**

6. *Answer choices:*

(see index for correct answer)

- a. PA512
- b. Product data record
- c. Detailed division of labor
- d. Value engineering

Guidance: level 1

:: Lean manufacturing ::

_____ is the Sino-Japanese word for "improvement". In business, _____ refers to activities that continuously improve all functions and involve all employees from the CEO to the assembly line workers. It also applies to processes, such as purchasing and logistics, that cross organizational boundaries into the supply chain. It has been applied in healthcare, psychotherapy, life-coaching, government, and banking.

Exam Probability: **Low**

7. *Answer choices:*

(see index for correct answer)

- a. Supply chain responsiveness matrix
- b. Continuous improvement
- c. Fixed Repeating Schedule
- d. Agent-assisted automation

:: ::

A _____ is a covering that is applied to the surface of an object, usually referred to as the substrate. The purpose of applying the _____ may be decorative, functional, or both. The _____ itself may be an all-over _____ , completely covering the substrate, or it may only cover parts of the substrate. An example of all of these types of _____ is a product label on many drinks bottles- one side has an all-over functional _____ and the other side has one or more decorative _____ s in an appropriate pattern to form the words and images.

Exam Probability: **Low**

8. *Answer choices:*

(see index for correct answer)

- a. hierarchical
- b. Coating
- c. hierarchical perspective
- d. imperative

:: Information technology management ::

_____ within quality management systems and information technology systems is a process—either formal or informal—used to ensure that changes to a product or system are introduced in a controlled and coordinated manner. It reduces the possibility that unnecessary changes will be introduced to a system without forethought, introducing faults into the system or undoing changes made by other users of software. The goals of a _____ procedure usually include minimal disruption to services, reduction in back-out activities, and cost-effective utilization of resources involved in implementing change.

Exam Probability: **Medium**

9. *Answer choices:*

(see index for correct answer)

- a. Change control
- b. Electronic document and records management system
- c. IT cost transparency
- d. IT risk

Guidance: level 1

:: E-commerce ::

_____ is the activity of buying or selling of products on online services or over the Internet. Electronic commerce draws on technologies such as mobile commerce, electronic funds transfer, supply chain management, Internet marketing, online transaction processing, electronic data interchange , inventory management systems, and automated data collection systems.

10. *Answer choices:*

(see index for correct answer)

- a. AsiaPay
- b. Shopping directory
- c. Very
- d. Video commerce

Guidance: level 1

:: Project management ::

_____ is a marketing activity that does an aggregate plan for the production process, in advance of 6 to 18 months, to give an idea to management as to what quantity of materials and other resources are to be procured and when, so that the total cost of operations of the organization is kept to the minimum over that period.

Exam Probability: **Medium**

11. *Answer choices:*

(see index for correct answer)

- a. Aggregate planning
- b. Axelos

- c. Project cancellation
- d. Time to completion

Guidance: level 1

:: Management ::

_____ is the practice of initiating, planning, executing, controlling, and closing the work of a team to achieve specific goals and meet specific success criteria at the specified time.

Exam Probability: **Medium**

12. *Answer choices:*
(see index for correct answer)

- a. Enterprise planning system
- b. Vorstand
- c. Managerial economics
- d. Business model

Guidance: level 1

:: Project management ::

Rolling-wave planning is the process of project planning in waves as the project proceeds and later details become clearer; similar to the techniques used in agile software development approaches like Scrum..

Exam Probability: **Low**

13. *Answer choices:*

(see index for correct answer)

- a. Effective Development Group
- b. Gold plating
- c. Rolling Wave planning
- d. Cone of Uncertainty

Guidance: level 1

:: Fault-tolerant computer systems ::

_____ decision-making is a group decision-making process in which group members develop, and agree to support a decision in the best interest of the whole group or common goal. _____ may be defined professionally as an acceptable resolution, one that can be supported, even if not the "favourite" of each individual. It has its origin in the Latin word consensus , which is from consentio meaning literally feel together. It is used to describe both the decision and the process of reaching a decision. _____ decision-making is thus concerned with the process of deliberating and finalizing a decision, and the social, economic, legal, environmental and political effects of applying this process.

14. *Answer choices:*

(see index for correct answer)

- a. Consensus
- b. Single point of failure
- c. Superstabilization
- d. Paxos

Guidance: level 1

:: Project management ::

A _____ is the approximation of the cost of a program, project, or operation. The _____ is the product of the cost estimating process. The _____ has a single total value and may have identifiable component values. A problem with a cost overrun can be avoided with a credible, reliable, and accurate _____ . A cost estimator is the professional who prepares _____ s. There are different types of cost estimators, whose title may be preceded by a modifier, such as building estimator, or electrical estimator, or chief estimator. Other professionals such as quantity surveyors and cost engineers may also prepare _____ s or contribute to _____ s. In the US, according to the Bureau of Labor Statistics, there were 185,400 cost estimators in 2010. There are around 75,000 professional quantity surveyors working in the UK.

15. *Answer choices:*

(see index for correct answer)

- a. Sustainable event management
- b. Cost estimate
- c. Libyan Project Management Association
- d. Integrated product team

Guidance: level 1

:: ::

_____ is the production of products for use or sale using labour and machines, tools, chemical and biological processing, or formulation. The term may refer to a range of human activity, from handicraft to high tech, but is most commonly applied to industrial design, in which raw materials are transformed into finished goods on a large scale. Such finished goods may be sold to other manufacturers for the production of other, more complex products, such as aircraft, household appliances, furniture, sports equipment or automobiles, or sold to wholesalers, who in turn sell them to retailers, who then sell them to end users and consumers.

Exam Probability: **Medium**

16. *Answer choices:*

(see index for correct answer)

- a. Manufacturing
- b. process perspective

- c. interpersonal communication
- d. hierarchical perspective

Guidance: level 1

:: Gas technologies ::

A _____ is a device used to transfer heat between two or more fluids. _____ s are used in both cooling and heating processes. The fluids may be separated by a solid wall to prevent mixing or they may be in direct contact. They are widely used in space heating, refrigeration, air conditioning, power stations, chemical plants, petrochemical plants, petroleum refineries, natural-gas processing, and sewage treatment. The classic example of a _____ is found in an internal combustion engine in which a circulating fluid known as engine coolant flows through radiator coils and air flows past the coils, which cools the coolant and heats the incoming air. Another example is the heat sink, which is a passive _____ that transfers the heat generated by an electronic or a mechanical device to a fluid medium, often air or a liquid coolant.

Exam Probability: **Medium**

17. *Answer choices:*
(see index for correct answer)

- a. Air pump
- b. Heat exchanger
- c. Gas mantle
- d. Gas stove

:: Quality ::

_____ is a concept first outlined by quality expert Joseph M. Juran in publications, most notably Juran on _____ . Designing for quality and innovation is one of the three universal processes of the Juran Trilogy, in which Juran describes what is required to achieve breakthroughs in new products, services, and processes. Juran believed that quality could be planned, and that most quality crises and problems relate to the way in which quality was planned.

Exam Probability: **Medium**

18. *Answer choices:*

(see index for correct answer)

- a. American Society for Quality
- b. Ringtest
- c. Cleaning validation
- d. Quality by Design

Guidance: level 1

:: Waste ::

_____ are unwanted or unusable materials. _____ is any substance which is discarded after primary use, or is worthless, defective and of no use. A by-product by contrast is a joint product of relatively minor economic value. A _____ product may become a by-product, joint product or resource through an invention that raises a _____ product`s value above zero.

Exam Probability: **Low**

19. *Answer choices:*

(see index for correct answer)

- a. Zero waste agriculture
- b. Used good
- c. Tailings
- d. Sanitary garden

Guidance: level 1

:: Non-parametric statistics ::

A _____ is an accurate representation of the distribution of numerical data. It is an estimate of the probability distribution of a continuous variable and was first introduced by Karl Pearson. It differs from a bar graph, in the sense that a bar graph relates two variables, but a _____ relates only one. To construct a _____ , the first step is to "bin" the range of values—that is, divide the entire range of values into a series of intervals—and then count how many values fall into each interval. The bins are usually specified as consecutive, non-overlapping intervals of a variable. The bins must be adjacent, and are often of equal size.

Exam Probability: **Low**

20. *Answer choices:*

(see index for correct answer)

- • a. Order statistic
- • b. Van der Waerden test
- • c. Histogram
- • d. Median test

Guidance: level 1

:: Production economics ::

_____ is the joint use of a resource or space. It is also the process of dividing and distributing. In its narrow sense, it refers to joint or alternating use of inherently finite goods, such as a common pasture or a shared residence. Still more loosely, " _____ " can actually mean giving something as an outright gift: for example, to "share" one's food really means to give some of it as a gift. _____ is a basic component of human interaction, and is responsible for strengthening social ties and ensuring a person's well-being.

Exam Probability: **Low**

21. *Answer choices:*

(see index for correct answer)

- a. Multifactor productivity
- b. Industrial production index
- c. Total factor productivity
- d. Diminishing returns

Guidance: level 1

:: Sensitivity analysis ::

_____ is the study of how the uncertainty in the output of a mathematical model or system can be divided and allocated to different sources of uncertainty in its inputs. A related practice is uncertainty analysis, which has a greater focus on uncertainty quantification and propagation of uncertainty; ideally, uncertainty and _____ should be run in tandem.

Exam Probability: **Low**

22. *Answer choices:*
(see index for correct answer)

- a. Tornado diagram
- b. Variance-based sensitivity analysis
- c. Sensitivity analysis
- d. Fourier amplitude sensitivity testing

Guidance: level 1

:: Commercial item transport and distribution ::

In commerce, supply-chain management , the management of the flow of goods and services, involves the movement and storage of raw materials, of work-in-process inventory, and of finished goods from point of origin to point of consumption. Interconnected or interlinked networks, channels and node businesses combine in the provision of products and services required by end customers in a supply chain. Supply-chain management has been defined as the "design, planning, execution, control, and monitoring of supply-chain activities with the objective of creating net value, building a competitive infrastructure, leveraging worldwide logistics, synchronizing supply with demand and measuring performance globally."SCM practice draws heavily from the areas of industrial engineering, systems engineering, operations management, logistics, procurement, information technology, and marketing and strives for an integrated approach. Marketing channels play an important role in supply-chain management. Current research in supply-chain management is concerned with topics related to sustainability and risk management, among others. Some suggest that the "people dimension" of SCM, ethical issues, internal integration, transparency/visibility, and human capital/talent management are topics that have, so far, been underrepresented on the research agenda.

Exam Probability: **Low**

23. *Answer choices:*
(see index for correct answer)

- a. E2open
- b. Semi-trailer truck
- c. Fulfillment house
- d. Retail concentration

Guidance: level 1

:: Management ::

In inventory management, _____ is the order quantity that minimizes the total holding costs and ordering costs. It is one of the oldest classical production scheduling models. The model was developed by Ford W. Harris in 1913, but R. H. Wilson, a consultant who applied it extensively, and K. Andler are given credit for their in-depth analysis.

Exam Probability: **Low**

24. *Answer choices:*

(see index for correct answer)

- a. Systems analysis
- b. Managing stage boundaries
- c. Economic order quantity
- d. Scrum

Guidance: level 1

:: Monopoly (economics) ::

_____ are "efficiencies formed by variety, not volume" . For example, a gas station that sells gasoline can sell soda, milk, baked goods, etc through their customer service representatives and thus achieve gasoline companies _____ .

25. *Answer choices:*

(see index for correct answer)

- a. Municipalization
- b. Contestable market
- c. Economies of scope
- d. Network effect

Guidance: level 1

:: Data management ::

_____ refers to a data-driven improvement cycle used for improving, optimizing and stabilizing business processes and designs. The _____ improvement cycle is the core tool used to drive Six Sigma projects. However, _____ is not exclusive to Six Sigma and can be used as the framework for other improvement applications.

Exam Probability: **High**

26. *Answer choices:*

(see index for correct answer)

- a. Data dictionary
- b. Distributed concurrency control

- c. DMAIC
- d. Semantic integration

:: Metrics ::

_____ is a computer model developed by the University of Idaho, that uses Landsat satellite data to compute and map evapotranspiration . _____ calculates ET as a residual of the surface energy balance, where ET is estimated by keeping account of total net short wave and long wave radiation at the vegetation or soil surface, the amount of heat conducted into soil, and the amount of heat convected into the air above the surface. The difference in these three terms represents the amount of energy absorbed during the conversion of liquid water to vapor, which is ET. _____ expresses near-surface temperature gradients used in heat convection as indexed functions of radio _____ surface temperature, thereby eliminating the need for absolutely accurate surface temperature and the need for air-temperature measurements.

Exam Probability: **Medium**

27. *Answer choices:*

(see index for correct answer)

- a. Key Risk Indicator
- b. Parts-per notation
- c. METRIC
- d. Software metric

:: Industrial processes ::

A _____ is a device used for high-temperature heating. The name derives from Latin word fornax, which means oven. The heat energy to fuel a _____ may be supplied directly by fuel combustion, by electricity such as the electric arc _____ , or through induction heating in induction _____ s.

Exam Probability: **Low**

28. *Answer choices:*

(see index for correct answer)

- a. Furnace
- b. Glass-to-metal seal
- c. Transfer hydrogenation
- d. Turbine Inlet Air Cooling

:: Data interchange standards ::

_____ is the concept of businesses electronically communicating information that was traditionally communicated on paper, such as purchase orders and invoices. Technical standards for EDI exist to facilitate parties transacting such instruments without having to make special arrangements.

Exam Probability: **High**

29. *Answer choices:*

(see index for correct answer)

- a. Interaction protocol
- b. Uniform Communication Standard
- c. Domain Application Protocol
- d. Electronic data interchange

Guidance: level 1

:: Casting (manufacturing) ::

A _____ is a regularity in the world, man-made design, or abstract ideas. As such, the elements of a _____ repeat in a predictable manner. A geometric _____ is a kind of _____ formed of geometric shapes and typically repeated like a wallpaper design.

Exam Probability: **High**

30. *Answer choices:*

(see index for correct answer)

- a. Dross
- b. Pattern
- c. Directional solidification
- d. Porosity sealing

Guidance: level 1

:: Quality control tools ::

A _____ is a type of diagram that represents an algorithm, workflow or process. _____ can also be defined as a diagramatic representation of an algorithm .

Exam Probability: **Low**

31. *Answer choices:*
(see index for correct answer)

- a. Western Electric rules
- b. U-chart
- c. Robustness validation
- d. Flowchart

Guidance: level 1

_____ is the quantity of three-dimensional space enclosed by a closed surface, for example, the space that a substance or shape occupies or contains. _____ is often quantified numerically using the SI derived unit, the cubic metre. The _____ of a container is generally understood to be the capacity of the container; i. e., the amount of fluid that the container could hold, rather than the amount of space the container itself displaces. Three dimensional mathematical shapes are also assigned _____ s. _____ s of some simple shapes, such as regular, straight-edged, and circular shapes can be easily calculated using arithmetic formulas. _____ s of complicated shapes can be calculated with integral calculus if a formula exists for the shape`s boundary. One-dimensional figures and two-dimensional shapes are assigned zero _____ in the three-dimensional space.

Exam Probability: **Low**

32. *Answer choices:*

(see index for correct answer)

- a. Character
- b. hierarchical perspective
- c. imperative
- d. functional perspective

Guidance: level 1

:: Commerce ::

A _____ is an employee within a company, business or other organization who is responsible at some level for buying or approving the acquisition of goods and services needed by the company. Responsible for buying the best quality products, goods and services for their company at the most competitive prices, _____ s work in a wide range of sectors for many different organizations. The position responsibilities may be the same as that of a buyer or purchasing agent, or may include wider supervisory or managerial responsibilities. A _____ may oversee the acquisition of materials needed for production, general supplies for offices and facilities, equipment, or construction contracts. A _____ often supervises purchasing agents and buyers, but in small companies the _____ may also be the purchasing agent or buyer. The _____ position may also carry the title "Procurement Manager" or in the public sector, "Procurement Officer". He or she can come from both an Engineering or Economics background.

Exam Probability: **High**

33. *Answer choices:*

(see index for correct answer)

- a. Shipping list
- b. Trading post
- c. White Elephant Sale
- d. Purchasing manager

Guidance: level 1

:: Risk analysis ::

Supply-chain risk management is "the implementation of strategies to manage both everyday and exceptional risks along the supply chain based on continuous risk assessment with the objective of reducing vulnerability and ensuring continuity".

Exam Probability: **High**

34. *Answer choices:*

(see index for correct answer)

- a. Supply chain risk management
- b. Unintended consequences
- c. Probabilistic risk assessment
- d. Risk analysis

Guidance: level 1

:: Quality management ::

_____ ensures that an organization, product or service is consistent. It has four main components: quality planning, quality assurance, quality control and quality improvement. _____ is focused not only on product and service quality, but also on the means to achieve it. _____ , therefore, uses quality assurance and control of processes as well as products to achieve more consistent quality. What a customer wants and is willing to pay for it determines quality. It is written or unwritten commitment to a known or unknown consumer in the market . Thus, quality can be defined as fitness for intended use or, in other words, how well the product performs its intended function

35. *Answer choices:*

(see index for correct answer)

- a. Indian Register Quality Systems
- b. Quality management system
- c. European Quality in Social Services
- d. Quality management

Guidance: level 1

:: Evaluation ::

_____ is a way of preventing mistakes and defects in manufactured products and avoiding problems when delivering products or services to customers; which ISO 9000 defines as "part of quality management focused on providing confidence that quality requirements will be fulfilled". This defect prevention in _____ differs subtly from defect detection and rejection in quality control and has been referred to as a shift left since it focuses on quality earlier in the process .

Exam Probability: **High**

36. *Answer choices:*

(see index for correct answer)

- a. Transferable skills analysis

- b. Academic equivalency evaluation
- c. Program evaluation
- d. Ecological indicator

Guidance: level 1

:: Semiconductor companies ::

_____ Corporation is a Japanese multinational conglomerate corporation headquartered in Konan, Minato, Tokyo. Its diversified business includes consumer and professional electronics, gaming, entertainment and financial services. The company owns the largest music entertainment business in the world, the largest video game console business and one of the largest video game publishing businesses, and is one of the leading manufacturers of electronic products for the consumer and professional markets, and a leading player in the film and television entertainment industry. _____ was ranked 97th on the 2018 Fortune Global 500 list.

Exam Probability: **Medium**

37. *Answer choices:*
(see index for correct answer)

- a. Nuvoton
- b. Sony
- c. VeriSilicon
- d. GreenPeak Technologies

Guidance: level 1

:: Commercial item transport and distribution ::

_____ in logistics and supply chain management is an organization's use of third-party businesses to outsource elements of its distribution, warehousing, and fulfillment services.

Exam Probability: **Medium**

38. *Answer choices:*

(see index for correct answer)

- a. Dock
- b. Dimensional weight
- c. Tanker
- d. Third-party logistics

Guidance: level 1

:: Lean manufacturing ::

_____ is a scheduling system for lean manufacturing and just-in-time manufacturing . Taiichi Ohno, an industrial engineer at Toyota, developed _____ to improve manufacturing efficiency. _____ is one method to achieve JIT. The system takes its name from the cards that track production within a factory. For many in the automotive sector, _____ is known as the "Toyota nameplate system" and as such the term is not used by some other automakers.

Exam Probability: **Low**

39. *Answer choices:*

(see index for correct answer)

- a. Andon
- b. Kanban
- c. Heijunka box
- d. Overall equipment effectiveness

Guidance: level 1

:: Water ::

_____ is a transparent, tasteless, odorless, and nearly colorless chemical substance, which is the main constituent of Earth's streams, lakes, and oceans, and the fluids of most living organisms. It is vital for all known forms of life, even though it provides no calories or organic nutrients. Its chemical formula is H2O, meaning that each of its molecules contains one oxygen and two hydrogen atoms, connected by covalent bonds. _____ is the name of the liquid state of H2O at standard ambient temperature and pressure. It forms precipitation in the form of rain and aerosols in the form of fog. Clouds are formed from suspended droplets of _____ and ice, its solid state. When finely divided, crystalline ice may precipitate in the form of snow. The gaseous state of _____ is steam or _____ vapor. _____ moves continually through the _____ cycle of evaporation, transpiration, condensation, precipitation, and runoff, usually reaching the sea.

Exam Probability: **High**

40. *Answer choices:*

(see index for correct answer)

- a. Kangaroo Lake
- b. Water quality
- c. Electrolysed water
- d. Water

Guidance: level 1

:: Occupational safety and health ::

_____ is a chemical element with symbol Pb and atomic number 82. It is a heavy metal that is denser than most common materials. _____ is soft and malleable, and also has a relatively low melting point. When freshly cut, _____ is silvery with a hint of blue; it tarnishes to a dull gray color when exposed to air. _____ has the highest atomic number of any stable element and three of its isotopes are endpoints of major nuclear decay chains of heavier elements.

Exam Probability: **High**

41. *Answer choices:*

(see index for correct answer)

- a. Lead
- b. Threshold limit value
- c. Lead safe work practices
- d. Global road safety for workers

Guidance: level 1

:: Quality ::

A _____ is an initiating cause of either a condition or a causal chain that leads to an outcome or effect of interest. The term denotes the earliest, most basic, `deepest`, cause for a given behavior; most often a fault. The idea is that you can only see an error by its manifest signs. Those signs can be widespread, multitudinous, and convoluted, whereas the _____ leading to them often is a lot simpler.

42. *Answer choices:*

(see index for correct answer)

- a. Dualistic Petri nets
- b. Root cause
- c. Shigeo Shingo
- d. Robustification

Guidance: level 1

:: Management ::

_____ is a process by which entities review the quality of all factors involved in production. ISO 9000 defines _____ as "A part of quality management focused on fulfilling quality requirements".

Exam Probability: **Low**

43. *Answer choices:*

(see index for correct answer)

- a. Modes of leadership
- b. Extended enterprise
- c. Information excellence
- d. Risk appetite

:: Debt ::

_____ is the trust which allows one party to provide money or resources to another party wherein the second party does not reimburse the first party immediately , but promises either to repay or return those resources at a later date. In other words, _____ is a method of making reciprocity formal, legally enforceable, and extensible to a large group of unrelated people.

Exam Probability: **High**

44. *Answer choices:*

(see index for correct answer)

- a. Credit
- b. Rule of 72
- c. Sum certain
- d. Odious debt

:: Retailing ::

_____ is the process of selling consumer goods or services to customers through multiple channels of distribution to earn a profit. _____ers satisfy demand identified through a supply chain. The term "_____er" is typically applied where a service provider fills the small orders of a large number of individuals, who are end-users, rather than large orders of a small number of wholesale, corporate or government clientele. Shopping generally refers to the act of buying products. Sometimes this is done to obtain final goods, including necessities such as food and clothing; sometimes it takes place as a recreational activity. Recreational shopping often involves window shopping and browsing: it does not always result in a purchase.

Exam Probability: **Medium**

45. *Answer choices:*

(see index for correct answer)

- a. Sbiten
- b. Window dresser
- c. Strip mall
- d. Diffusion line

Guidance: level 1

:: Management ::

Business _____ is a discipline in operations management in which people use various methods to discover, model, analyze, measure, improve, optimize, and automate business processes. BPM focuses on improving corporate performance by managing business processes. Any combination of methods used to manage a company's business processes is BPM. Processes can be structured and repeatable or unstructured and variable. Though not required, enabling technologies are often used with BPM.

Exam Probability: **Medium**

46. *Answer choices:*

(see index for correct answer)

- a. Enterprise decision management
- b. Business model
- c. Meeting
- d. Management fad

Guidance: level 1

:: Product management ::

_____ s, also known as Shewhart charts or process-behavior charts, are a statistical process control tool used to determine if a manufacturing or business process is in a state of control.

Exam Probability: **Medium**

47. *Answer choices:*

(see index for correct answer)

- a. Requirement prioritization
- b. Crossing the Chasm
- c. Tipping point
- d. Service life

Guidance: level 1

:: Product development ::

In business and engineering, _____ covers the complete process of bringing a new product to market. A central aspect of NPD is product design, along with various business considerations. _____ is described broadly as the transformation of a market opportunity into a product available for sale. The product can be tangible or intangible , though sometimes services and other processes are distinguished from "products." NPD requires an understanding of customer needs and wants, the competitive environment, and the nature of the market.Cost, time and quality are the main variables that drive customer needs. Aiming at these three variables, innovative companies develop continuous practices and strategies to better satisfy customer requirements and to increase their own market share by a regular development of new products. There are many uncertainties and challenges which companies must face throughout the process. The use of best practices and the elimination of barriers to communication are the main concerns for the management of the NPD .

Exam Probability: **High**

48. *Answer choices:*

(see index for correct answer)

- a. DFMA
- b. Material selection
- c. Design brief
- d. New product development

Guidance: level 1

:: Help desk ::

A high-explosive anti-tank warhead is a type of shaped charge explosive that uses the Munroe effect to penetrate thick tank armor. The warhead functions by having the explosive charge collapse a metal liner inside the warhead into a high-velocity superplastic jet. This superplastic jet is capable of penetrating armor steel to a depth of seven or more times the diameter of the charge but is usually used to immobilize or destroy tanks. Due to the way they work, they do not have to be fired as fast as an armor piercing shell, allowing less recoil. Contrary to a widespread misconception , the jet does not melt its way through armor, as its effect is purely kinetic in nature. The _____ warhead has become less effective against tanks and other armored vehicles due to the use of composite armor, explosive-reactive armor, and active protection systems which destroy the _____ warhead before it hits the tank. Even though _____ rounds are less effective against the heavy armor found on 2010s main battle tanks, _____ warheads remain a threat against less-armored parts of a main battle tank and against lighter armored vehicles or unarmored vehicles and helicopters.

Exam Probability: **Low**

49. *Answer choices:*

- a. Web Help Desk
- b. Vitalyst
- c. SysAid Technologies
- d. HEAT

Guidance: level 1

:: Supply chain management ::

_____ is a core supply chain function and includes supply chain planning and supply chain execution capabilities. Specifically, _____ is the capability firms use to plan total material requirements. The material requirements are communicated to procurement and other functions for sourcing. _____ is also responsible for determining the amount of material to be deployed at each stocking location across the supply chain, establishing material replenishment plans, determining inventory levels to hold for each type of inventory , and communicating information regarding material needs throughout the extended supply chain.

Exam Probability: **Low**

50. *Answer choices:*

- a. LLamasoft
- b. Suppliers and Parts database
- c. Global supply-chain finance

- d. Delivery Reliability

Guidance: level 1

:: Consortia ::

A _____ is an association of two or more individuals, companies, organizations or governments with the objective of participating in a common activity or pooling their resources for achieving a common goal.

Exam Probability: **High**

51. *Answer choices:*
(see index for correct answer)

- a. Institute of Geomatics
- b. Blu-ray Disc Association
- c. Asian American and Pacific Islander Policy Research Consortium
- d. Consortium

Guidance: level 1

:: Quality awards ::

The _____ recognizes U.S. organizations in the business, health care, education, and nonprofit sectors for performance excellence. The Baldrige Award is the only formal recognition of the performance excellence of both public and private U.S. organizations given by the President of the United States. It is administered by the Baldrige Performance Excellence Program, which is based at and managed by the National Institute of Standards and Technology , an agency of the U.S. Department of Commerce.

Exam Probability: **Low**

52. *Answer choices:*

(see index for correct answer)

- a. Malcolm Baldrige National Quality Award
- b. Philippine Quality Award
- c. Canada Awards for Excellence
- d. EFQM Excellence Award

Guidance: level 1

:: Business planning ::

_____ is a critical component to the successful delivery of any project, programme or activity. A stakeholder is any individual, group or organization that can affect, be affected by, or perceive itself to be affected by a programme.

Exam Probability: **Medium**

53. *Answer choices:*

(see index for correct answer)

- a. Joint decision trap
- b. Community Futures
- c. Customer Demand Planning
- d. Business war games

Guidance: level 1

:: Supply chain management terms ::

In business and finance, _____ is a system of organizations, people, activities, information, and resources involved in moving a product or service from supplier to customer. _____ activities involve the transformation of natural resources, raw materials, and components into a finished product that is delivered to the end customer. In sophisticated _____ systems, used products may re-enter the _____ at any point where residual value is recyclable. _____ s link value chains.

Exam Probability: **High**

54. *Answer choices:*

(see index for correct answer)

- a. Stockout
- b. Most valuable customers
- c. Overstock

- d. Supply chain

Guidance: level 1

:: Production and manufacturing ::

An _____ is a manufacturing process in which parts are added as the semi-finished assembly moves from workstation to workstation where the parts are added in sequence until the final assembly is produced. By mechanically moving the parts to the assembly work and moving the semi-finished assembly from work station to work station, a finished product can be assembled faster and with less labor than by having workers carry parts to a stationary piece for assembly.

Exam Probability: **Low**

55. *Answer choices:*

(see index for correct answer)

- a. Economic dispatch
- b. Advanced product quality planning
- c. Assembly line
- d. BOMtracker

Guidance: level 1

:: Project management ::

In economics, _____ is the assignment of available resources to various uses. In the context of an entire economy, resources can be allocated by various means, such as markets or central planning.

Exam Probability: **Low**

56. *Answer choices:*

- a. Kickoff meeting
- b. Resource allocation
- c. Australian Institute of Project Management
- d. Design structure matrix

Guidance: level 1

:: Production and manufacturing ::

A BOM can define products as they are designed , as they are ordered , as they are built , or as they are maintained . The different types of BOMs depend on the business need and use for which they are intended. In process industries, the BOM is also known as the formula, recipe, or ingredients list. The phrase "bill of material" is frequently used by engineers as an adjective to refer not to the literal bill, but to the current production configuration of a product, to distinguish it from modified or improved versions under study or in test.

Exam Probability: **Low**

57. *Answer choices:*

(see index for correct answer)

- a. Woodworking machine
- b. Remanufacturing
- c. Queueing theory
- d. Bill of materials

Guidance: level 1

:: Quality management ::

In quality management system, a _____ is a document developed by management to express the directive of the top management with respect to quality. _____ management is a strategic item.

Exam Probability: **High**

58. *Answer choices:*

(see index for correct answer)

- a. Flemish Quality Management Center
- b. Management by wandering around
- c. Quality policy
- d. European Quality in Social Services

Guidance: level 1

:: Costs ::

_____ is the process used by companies to reduce their costs and increase their profits. Depending on a company's services or product, the strategies can vary. Every decision in the product development process affects cost.

Exam Probability: **Low**

59. *Answer choices:*

(see index for correct answer)

- a. Prospective costs
- b. Implicit cost
- c. Quality costs
- d. Cost reduction

Guidance: level 1

Commerce

Commerce relates to "the exchange of goods and services, especially on a large scale." It includes legal, economic, political, social, cultural and technological systems that operate in any country or internationally.

:: Market research ::

_____ is an organized effort to gather information about target markets or customers. It is a very important component of business strategy. The term is commonly interchanged with marketing research; however, expert practitioners may wish to draw a distinction, in that marketing research is concerned specifically about marketing processes, while _____ is concerned specifically with markets.

1. *Answer choices:*

(see index for correct answer)

- a. IRI
- b. AMAI
- c. Landing page optimization
- d. Market research

Guidance: level 1

:: Mereology ::

_____ , in the abstract, is what belongs to or with something, whether as an attribute or as a component of said thing. In the context of this article, it is one or more components , whether physical or incorporeal, of a person's estate; or so belonging to, as in being owned by, a person or jointly a group of people or a legal entity like a corporation or even a society. Depending on the nature of the _____ , an owner of _____ has the right to consume, alter, share, redefine, rent, mortgage, pawn, sell, exchange, transfer, give away or destroy it, or to exclude others from doing these things, as well as to perhaps abandon it; whereas regardless of the nature of the _____ , the owner thereof has the right to properly use it , or at the very least exclusively keep it.

Exam Probability: **Medium**

2. *Answer choices:*

(see index for correct answer)

- a. Mereological essentialism
- b. Non-wellfounded mereology
- c. Property
- d. Simple

Guidance: level 1

:: Game theory ::

To _____ is to make a deal between different parties where each party gives up part of their demand. In arguments, _____ is a concept of finding agreement through communication, through a mutual acceptance of terms—often involving variations from an original goal or desires.

Exam Probability: **High**

3. *Answer choices:*
(see index for correct answer)

- a. Chicken
- b. Metagaming
- c. Compromise
- d. Rational agent

Guidance: level 1

:: Industry ::

_____ describes various measures of the efficiency of production. Often , a _____ measure is expressed as the ratio of an aggregate output to a single input or an aggregate input used in a production process, i.e. output per unit of input. Most common example is the labour _____ measure, e.g., such as GDP per worker. There are many different definitions of _____ and the choice among them depends on the purpose of the _____ measurement and/or data availability. The key source of difference between various _____ measures is also usually related to how the outputs and the inputs are aggregated into scalars to obtain such a ratio-type measure of _____ .

Exam Probability: **High**

4. *Answer choices:*

(see index for correct answer)

- a. Industrial safety system
- b. Reindustrialization
- c. Productivity
- d. United Nations Industrial Development Organization

Guidance: level 1

:: Accounting source documents ::

A _____ is a commercial document and first official offer issued by a buyer to a seller indicating types, quantities, and agreed prices for products or services. It is used to control the purchasing of products and services from external suppliers. _____ s can be an essential part of enterprise resource planning system orders.

Exam Probability: **Medium**

5. *Answer choices:*

(see index for correct answer)

- a. Credit memorandum
- b. Air waybill
- c. Bank statement
- d. Purchase order

Guidance: level 1

:: ::

_____ Corporation is an American multinational technology company with headquarters in Redmond, Washington. It develops, manufactures, licenses, supports and sells computer software, consumer electronics, personal computers, and related services. Its best known software products are the _____ Windows line of operating systems, the _____ Office suite, and the Internet Explorer and Edge Web browsers. Its flagship hardware products are the Xbox video game consoles and the _____ Surface lineup of touchscreen personal computers. As of 2016, it is the world's largest software maker by revenue, and one of the world's most valuable companies. The word "_____" is a portmanteau of "microcomputer" and "software". _____ is ranked No. 30 in the 2018 Fortune 500 rankings of the largest United States corporations by total revenue.

Exam Probability: **Medium**

6. *Answer choices:*

(see index for correct answer)

- a. similarity-attraction theory
- b. empathy
- c. Microsoft
- d. functional perspective

Guidance: level 1

:: Stock market ::

The _____ of a corporation is all of the shares into which ownership of the corporation is divided. In American English, the shares are commonly known as " _____ s". A single share of the _____ represents fractional ownership of the corporation in proportion to the total number of shares. This typically entitles the _____ holder to that fraction of the company's earnings, proceeds from liquidation of assets , or voting power, often dividing these up in proportion to the amount of money each _____ holder has invested. Not all _____ is necessarily equal, as certain classes of _____ may be issued for example without voting rights, with enhanced voting rights, or with a certain priority to receive profits or liquidation proceeds before or after other classes of shareholders.

Exam Probability: **Medium**

7. *Answer choices:*

(see index for correct answer)

- a. Clientele effect
- b. Witching hour
- c. Earnings call
- d. Volume-weighted average price

Guidance: level 1

:: Project management ::

_____ is the right to exercise power, which can be formalized by a state and exercised by way of judges, appointed executives of government, or the ecclesiastical or priestly appointed representatives of a God or other deities.

Exam Probability: **Low**

8. *Answer choices:*

(see index for correct answer)

- a. Trend analysis
- b. Authority
- c. Advanced Integrated Practice
- d. Expected commercial value

Guidance: level 1

:: ::

Competition arises whenever at least two parties strive for a goal which cannot be shared: where one`s gain is the other`s loss .

Exam Probability: **High**

9. *Answer choices:*

(see index for correct answer)

- a. open system
- b. Competitor
- c. cultural
- d. levels of analysis

Guidance: level 1

:: Information technology ::

_____ is the use of computers to store, retrieve, transmit, and manipulate data, or information, often in the context of a business or other enterprise. IT is considered to be a subset of information and communications technology . An _____ system is generally an information system, a communications system or, more specifically speaking, a computer system – including all hardware, software and peripheral equipment – operated by a limited group of users.

Exam Probability: **Low**

10. *Answer choices:*

(see index for correct answer)

- a. PC Supporters
- b. Omniview technology
- c. Micropipelining
- d. Information technology

Guidance: level 1

:: Management ::

_____ is a process by which entities review the quality of all factors involved in production. ISO 9000 defines _____ as "A part of quality management focused on fulfilling quality requirements".

Exam Probability: **Low**

11. *Answer choices:*

(see index for correct answer)

- a. Marketing management
- b. Logistics management
- c. Quality control
- d. Business process mapping

Guidance: level 1

:: Statutory law ::

_____ or statute law is written law set down by a body of legislature or by a singular legislator . This is as opposed to oral or customary law; or regulatory law promulgated by the executive or common law of the judiciary. Statutes may originate with national, state legislatures or local municipalities.

12. *Answer choices:*

(see index for correct answer)

- a. incorporation by reference
- b. ratification
- c. Statutory law
- d. statute law

Guidance: level 1

:: Auctioneering ::

An _____ is a process of buying and selling goods or services by offering them up for bid, taking bids, and then selling the item to the highest bidder. The open ascending price _____ is arguably the most common form of _____ in use today. Participants bid openly against one another, with each subsequent bid required to be higher than the previous bid. An _____ eer may announce prices, bidders may call out their bids themselves , or bids may be submitted electronically with the highest current bid publicly displayed. In a Dutch _____ , the _____ eer begins with a high asking price for some quantity of like items; the price is lowered until a participant is willing to accept the _____ eer`s price for some quantity of the goods in the lot or until the seller`s reserve price is met. While _____ s are most associated in the public imagination with the sale of antiques, paintings, rare collectibles and expensive wines, _____ s are also used for commodities, livestock, radio spectrum and used cars. In economic theory, an _____ may refer to any mechanism or set of trading rules for exchange.

13. *Answer choices:*

(see index for correct answer)

- a. Demsetz auction
- b. Auctionata
- c. Auction
- d. Forward auction

Guidance: level 1

:: Cryptography ::

In cryptography, _____ is the process of encoding a message or information in such a way that only authorized parties can access it and those who are not authorized cannot. _____ does not itself prevent interference, but denies the intelligible content to a would-be interceptor. In an _____ scheme, the intended information or message, referred to as plaintext, is encrypted using an _____ algorithm – a cipher – generating ciphertext that can be read only if decrypted. For technical reasons, an _____ scheme usually uses a pseudo-random _____ key generated by an algorithm. It is in principle possible to decrypt the message without possessing the key, but, for a well-designed _____ scheme, considerable computational resources and skills are required. An authorized recipient can easily decrypt the message with the key provided by the originator to recipients but not to unauthorized users.

Exam Probability: **High**

14. *Answer choices:*

(see index for correct answer)

- a. cryptosystem
- b. Encryption
- c. backdoor
- d. ciphertext

Guidance: level 1

:: Commodities ::

In economics, a _____ is an economic good or service that has full or substantial fungibility: that is, the market treats instances of the good as equivalent or nearly so with no regard to who produced them. Most commodities are raw materials, basic resources, agricultural, or mining products, such as iron ore, sugar, or grains like rice and wheat. Commodities can also be mass-produced unspecialized products such as chemicals and computer memory.

Exam Probability: **Medium**

15. *Answer choices:*

(see index for correct answer)

- a. Sample grade
- b. IRely
- c. Commodity
- d. Commodity pathway diversion

:: Goods ::

In most contexts, the concept of _____ denotes the conduct that should be preferred when posed with a choice between possible actions. _____ is generally considered to be the opposite of evil, and is of interest in the study of morality, ethics, religion and philosophy. The specific meaning and etymology of the term and its associated translations among ancient and contemporary languages show substantial variation in its inflection and meaning depending on circumstances of place, history, religious, or philosophical context.

Exam Probability: **High**

16. *Answer choices:*

(see index for correct answer)

- a. Good
- b. Demerit good
- c. Bad
- d. Search good

:: ::

A _____ consists of one people who live in the same dwelling and share meals. It may also consist of a single family or another group of people. A dwelling is considered to contain multiple _____ s if meals or living spaces are not shared. The _____ is the basic unit of analysis in many social, microeconomic and government models, and is important to economics and inheritance.

Exam Probability: **High**

17. *Answer choices:*

(see index for correct answer)

- a. deep-level diversity
- b. Household
- c. process perspective
- d. empathy

Guidance: level 1

:: Project management ::

In political science, an _____ is a means by which a petition signed by a certain minimum number of registered voters can force a government to choose to either enact a law or hold a public vote in parliament in what is called indirect _____ , or under direct _____ , the proposition is immediately put to a plebiscite or referendum, in what is called a Popular initiated Referendum or citizen-initiated referendum).

18. *Answer choices:*

(see index for correct answer)

- a. Team performance management
- b. Responsibility assignment matrix
- c. Collaborative project management
- d. Initiative

Guidance: level 1

:: ::

The _____ is a U.S. business-focused, English-language international daily newspaper based in New York City. The Journal, along with its Asian and European editions, is published six days a week by Dow Jones & Company, a division of News Corp. The newspaper is published in the broadsheet format and online. The Journal has been printed continuously since its inception on July 8, 1889, by Charles Dow, Edward Jones, and Charles Bergstresser.

Exam Probability: **High**

19. *Answer choices:*

(see index for correct answer)

- a. corporate values
- b. levels of analysis

- c. functional perspective
- d. process perspective

Guidance: level 1

:: Income ::

_____ is a ratio between the net profit and cost of investment resulting from an investment of some resources. A high ROI means the investment's gains favorably to its cost. As a performance measure, ROI is used to evaluate the efficiency of an investment or to compare the efficiencies of several different investments. In purely economic terms, it is one way of relating profits to capital invested. _____ is a performance measure used by businesses to identify the efficiency of an investment or number of different investments.

Exam Probability: **High**

20. *Answer choices:*
(see index for correct answer)

- a. Real income
- b. Return on investment
- c. Stipend
- d. Income earner

Guidance: level 1

:: Business ethics ::

_____ is a type of harassment technique that relates to a sexual nature and the unwelcome or inappropriate promise of rewards in exchange for sexual favors. _____ includes a range of actions from mild transgressions to sexual abuse or assault. Harassment can occur in many different social settings such as the workplace, the home, school, churches, etc. Harassers or victims may be of any gender.

Exam Probability: **Medium**

21. *Answer choices:*

(see index for correct answer)

- a. Perfect Relations
- b. Destructionism
- c. Sweatshop
- d. Smart casual

Guidance: level 1

:: E-commerce ::

A _____ is a hosted service offering that acts as an intermediary between business partners sharing standards based or proprietary data via shared business processes. The offered service is referred to as " _____ services".

Exam Probability: **Low**

22. *Answer choices:*

(see index for correct answer)

- a. Shipping portal
- b. Camgirl
- c. Shopping directory
- d. SAScon

Guidance: level 1

:: ::

In law, an _____ is the process in which cases are reviewed, where parties request a formal change to an official decision. _____ s function both as a process for error correction as well as a process of clarifying and interpreting law. Although appellate courts have existed for thousands of years, common law countries did not incorporate an affirmative right to _____ into their jurisprudence until the 19th century.

Exam Probability: **Low**

23. *Answer choices:*

(see index for correct answer)

- a. interpersonal communication
- b. empathy

- c. Appeal
- d. hierarchical perspective

Guidance: level 1

:: Dot-com bubble ::

Yahoo! _____ was a web hosting service. It was founded in November 1994 by David Bohnett and John Rezner, and was called Beverly Hills Internet for a very short time before being named _____ .

Exam Probability: **High**

24. *Answer choices:*
(see index for correct answer)

- a. E-Dreams
- b. Dot com party
- c. GeoCities
- d. Fucked Company

Guidance: level 1

:: Direct marketing ::

_____ is a form of advertising where organizations communicate directly to customers through a variety of media including cell phone text messaging, email, websites, online adverts, database marketing, fliers, catalog distribution, promotional letters, targeted television, newspapers, magazine advertisements, and outdoor advertising. Among practitioners, it is also known as direct response marketing.

Exam Probability: **Medium**

25. *Answer choices:*

(see index for correct answer)

- a. Boardroom, Inc.
- b. DVD club
- c. Forced Free Trial
- d. American Family Publishers

Guidance: level 1

:: ::

_____ is a type of government support for the citizens of that society. _____ may be provided to people of any income level, as with social security , but it is usually intended to ensure that the poor can meet their basic human needs such as food and shelter. _____ attempts to provide poor people with a minimal level of well-being, usually either a free- or a subsidized-supply of certain goods and social services, such as healthcare, education, and vocational training.

26. *Answer choices:*

(see index for correct answer)

- a. information systems assessment
- b. hierarchical
- c. similarity-attraction theory
- d. functional perspective

Guidance: level 1

:: International trade ::

_____ involves the transfer of goods or services from one person or entity to another, often in exchange for money. A system or network that allows _____ is called a market.

Exam Probability: **High**

27. *Answer choices:*

(see index for correct answer)

- a. Competitiveness Policy Council
- b. International Organisation of Employers
- c. Endaka
- d. UNeDocs

:: ::

A _____ manages, commands, directs, or regulates the behavior of other devices or systems using control loops. It can range from a single home heating controller using a thermostat controlling a domestic boiler to large Industrial _____ s which are used for controlling processes or machines.

Exam Probability: **Low**

28. *Answer choices:*

(see index for correct answer)

- a. Control system
- b. cultural
- c. Sarbanes-Oxley act of 2002
- d. empathy

:: E-commerce ::

_____ Inc. was an electronic money corporation founded by David Chaum in 1989. _____ transactions were unique in that they were anonymous due to a number of cryptographic protocols developed by its founder. _____ declared bankruptcy in 1998, and subsequently sold its assets to eCash Technologies, another digital currency company, which was acquired by InfoSpace on Feb. 19, 2002.

Exam Probability: **Medium**

29. *Answer choices:*

(see index for correct answer)

- a. DigiCash
- b. UN/CEFACT
- c. Public key certificate
- d. UsedSoft

Guidance: level 1

:: Insolvency ::

_____ is the process in accounting by which a company is brought to an end in the United Kingdom, Republic of Ireland and United States. The assets and property of the company are redistributed. _____ is also sometimes referred to as winding-up or dissolution, although dissolution technically refers to the last stage of _____ . The process of _____ also arises when customs, an authority or agency in a country responsible for collecting and safeguarding customs duties, determines the final computation or ascertainment of the duties or drawback accruing on an entry.

30. *Answer choices:*

(see index for correct answer)

- a. Personal Insolvency Arrangement
- b. Financial distress
- c. Liquidation
- d. Insolvency law of Russia

Guidance: level 1

:: Workplace ::

_____ is asystematic determination of a subject`s merit, worth and significance, using criteria governed by a set of standards. It can assist an organization, program, design, project or any other intervention or initiative to assess any aim, realisable concept/proposal, or any alternative, to help in decision-making; or to ascertain the degree of achievement or value in regard to the aim and objectives and results of any such action that has been completed. The primary purpose of _____ , in addition to gaining insight into prior or existing initiatives, is to enable reflection and assist in the identification of future change.

Exam Probability: **Low**

31. *Answer choices:*

(see index for correct answer)

- a. 360-degree feedback
- b. Workplace incivility
- c. Occupational stress
- d. Evaluation

Guidance: level 1

:: Costs ::

In economics, _____ is the total economic cost of production and is made up of variable cost, which varies according to the quantity of a good produced and includes inputs such as labour and raw materials, plus fixed cost, which is independent of the quantity of a good produced and includes inputs that cannot be varied in the short term: fixed costs such as buildings and machinery, including sunk costs if any. Since cost is measured per unit of time, it is a flow variable.

Exam Probability: **High**

32. *Answer choices:*
(see index for correct answer)

- a. Implicit cost
- b. Travel and subsistence
- c. Total cost
- d. Average variable cost

Guidance: level 1

A _____ is an individual or institution that legally owns one or more shares of stock in a public or private corporation. _____ s may be referred to as members of a corporation. Legally, a person is not a _____ in a corporation until their name and other details are entered in the corporation's register of _____ s or members.

Exam Probability: **High**

33. *Answer choices:*

(see index for correct answer)

- a. corporate values
- b. Shareholder
- c. deep-level diversity
- d. Character

Guidance: level 1

:: Management ::

In business, a _____ is the attribute that allows an organization to outperform its competitors. A _____ may include access to natural resources, such as high-grade ores or a low-cost power source, highly skilled labor, geographic location, high entry barriers, and access to new technology.

34. *Answer choices:*

(see index for correct answer)

- a. Power to the edge
- b. Total security management
- c. Meeting
- d. Middle management

Guidance: level 1

:: ::

_____ is the social science that studies the production, distribution, and consumption of goods and services.

Exam Probability: **High**

35. *Answer choices:*

(see index for correct answer)

- a. information systems assessment
- b. imperative
- c. surface-level diversity
- d. co-culture

:: Confidence tricks ::

_____ is the fraudulent attempt to obtain sensitive information such as usernames, passwords and credit card details by disguising oneself as a trustworthy entity in an electronic communication. Typically carried out by email spoofing or instant messaging, it often directs users to enter personal information at a fake website which matches the look and feel of the legitimate site.

Exam Probability: **High**

36. *Answer choices:*

(see index for correct answer)

- a. Reloading scam
- b. Phishing
- c. Gem scam
- d. Enzyte

:: ::

A _____ is monetary compensation paid by an employer to an employee in exchange for work done. Payment may be calculated as a fixed amount for each task completed , or at an hourly or daily rate , or based on an easily measured quantity of work done.

Exam Probability: **Low**

37. *Answer choices:*

(see index for correct answer)

- a. Sarbanes-Oxley act of 2002
- b. interpersonal communication
- c. Wage
- d. cultural

Guidance: level 1

:: Minimum wage ::

A _____ is the lowest remuneration that employers can legally pay their workers—the price floor below which workers may not sell their labor. Most countries had introduced _____ legislation by the end of the 20th century.

Exam Probability: **High**

38. *Answer choices:*

(see index for correct answer)

- a. Working poor
- b. Minimum wage in the United States
- c. Minimum wage
- d. Minimum wage in Taiwan

Guidance: level 1

:: Marketing ::

The _____ is a foundation model for businesses. The _____ has been defined as the "set of marketing tools that the firm uses to pursue its marketing objectives in the target market". Thus the _____ refers to four broad levels of marketing decision, namely: product, price, place, and promotion. Marketing practice has been occurring for millennia, but marketing theory emerged in the early twentieth century. The contemporary _____ , or the 4 Ps, which has become the dominant framework for marketing management decisions, was first published in 1960. In services marketing, an extended _____ is used, typically comprising 7 Ps, made up of the original 4 Ps extended by process, people, and physical evidence. Occasionally service marketers will refer to 8 Ps, comprising these 7 Ps plus performance.

Exam Probability: **Medium**

39. *Answer choices:*

(see index for correct answer)

- a. Market overhang

- b. Marketing mix
- c. John Neeson
- d. elaboration likelihood model

Guidance: level 1

:: Customs duties ::

A _____ is a tax on imports or exports between sovereign states. It is a form of regulation of foreign trade and a policy that taxes foreign products to encourage or safeguard domestic industry. _____ s are the simplest and oldest instrument of trade policy. Traditionally, states have used them as a source of income. Now, they are among the most widely used instruments of protection, along with import and export quotas.

Exam Probability: **Low**

40. *Answer choices:*

(see index for correct answer)

- a. Tariff
- b. Tariff-rate quota
- c. Specific rate duty
- d. Wines in bond

Guidance: level 1

:: Service industries ::

_____ is travel for pleasure or business; also the theory and practice of touring, the business of attracting, accommodating, and entertaining tourists, and the business of operating tours. _____ may be international, or within the traveller's country. The World _____ Organization defines _____ more generally, in terms which go "beyond the common perception of _____ as being limited to holiday activity only", as people "traveling to and staying in places outside their usual environment for not more than one consecutive year for leisure and not less than 24 hours, business and other purposes".

Exam Probability: **Medium**

41. *Answer choices:*

(see index for correct answer)

- a. Inn sign
- b. Tourism
- c. Financial services in South Korea
- d. Graham Company

Guidance: level 1

:: Production economics ::

In economics long run is a theoretical concept where all markets are in equilibrium, and all prices and quantities have fully adjusted and are in equilibrium. The long run contrasts with the _____ where there are some constraints and markets are not fully in equilibrium.

Exam Probability: **Low**

42. *Answer choices:*
(see index for correct answer)

- a. Short run
- b. Producer's risk
- c. Division of work
- d. Marginal product

Guidance: level 1

:: Quality management ::

_____ ensures that an organization, product or service is consistent. It has four main components: quality planning, quality assurance, quality control and quality improvement. _____ is focused not only on product and service quality, but also on the means to achieve it. _____ , therefore, uses quality assurance and control of processes as well as products to achieve more consistent quality. What a customer wants and is willing to pay for it determines quality. It is written or unwritten commitment to a known or unknown consumer in the market . Thus, quality can be defined as fitness for intended use or, in other words, how well the product performs its intended function

43. *Answer choices:*

(see index for correct answer)

- a. Dana Ulery
- b. Informal Methods
- c. European Quality in Social Services
- d. Common Assessment Framework

Guidance: level 1

:: E-commerce ::

_____ is a United States-based payment gateway service provider allowing merchants to accept credit card and electronic check payments through their website and over an Internet Protocol connection. Founded in 1996, _____ is now a subsidiary of Visa Inc. Its service permits customers to enter credit card and shipping information directly onto a web page, in contrast to some alternatives that require the customer to sign up for a payment service before performing a transaction.

Exam Probability: **Medium**

44. *Answer choices:*

(see index for correct answer)

- a. GamersGate

- b. Seja online
- c. Friend-to-friend
- d. IBill

Guidance: level 1

:: ::

In international relations, _____ is – from the perspective of governments – a voluntary transfer of resources from one country to another.

Exam Probability: **Medium**

45. *Answer choices:*

(see index for correct answer)

- a. information systems assessment
- b. interpersonal communication
- c. Sarbanes-Oxley act of 2002
- d. Aid

Guidance: level 1

:: E-commerce ::

An _____ , or automated clearinghouse, is an electronic network for financial transactions, generally domestic low value payments. An ACH is a computer-based clearing house and settlement facility established to process the exchange of electronic transactions between participating financial institutions. It is a form of clearing house that is specifically for payments and may support both credit transfers and direct debits.

Exam Probability: **Low**

46. *Answer choices:*

(see index for correct answer)

- a. Zingiri
- b. The Cluetrain Manifesto
- c. UN/CEFACT
- d. Customer Access and Retrieval System

Guidance: level 1

:: ::

A _____ is an organization, usually a group of people or a company, authorized to act as a single entity and recognized as such in law. Early incorporated entities were established by charter . Most jurisdictions now allow the creation of new _____ s through registration.

Exam Probability: **Medium**

47. *Answer choices:*

(see index for correct answer)

- a. Corporation
- b. levels of analysis
- c. personal values
- d. process perspective

Guidance: level 1

:: Marketing ::

_____ is the percentage of a market accounted for by a specific entity. In a survey of nearly 200 senior marketing managers, 67% responded that they found the revenue- "dollar _____ " metric very useful, while 61% found "unit _____ " very useful.

Exam Probability: **Medium**

48. *Answer choices:*

(see index for correct answer)

- a. Democratized transactional giving
- b. Market share
- c. Adobe Media Optimizer
- d. Buyer decision process

Guidance: level 1

:: ::

Advertising is a marketing communication that employs an openly sponsored, non-personal message to promote or sell a product, service or idea. Sponsors of advertising are typically businesses wishing to promote their products or services. Advertising is differentiated from public relations in that an advertiser pays for and has control over the message. It differs from personal selling in that the message is non-personal, i.e., not directed to a particular individual.Advertising is communicated through various mass media, including traditional media such as newspapers, magazines, television, radio, outdoor advertising or direct mail; and new media such as search results, blogs, social media, websites or text messages. The actual presentation of the message in a medium is referred to as an _____ , or "ad" or advert for short.

Exam Probability: **Medium**

49. *Answer choices:*

(see index for correct answer)

- a. surface-level diversity
- b. hierarchical
- c. co-culture
- d. Advertisement

Guidance: level 1

:: Scientific method ::

In the social sciences and life sciences, a _____ is a research method involving an up-close, in-depth, and detailed examination of a subject of study , as well as its related contextual conditions.

Exam Probability: **Low**

50. *Answer choices:*

(see index for correct answer)

- a. explanatory research
- b. pilot project
- c. Case study
- d. Causal research

Guidance: level 1

:: Basic financial concepts ::

_____ is a sustained increase in the general price level of goods and services in an economy over a period of time. When the general price level rises, each unit of currency buys fewer goods and services; consequently, _____ reflects a reduction in the purchasing power per unit of money a loss of real value in the medium of exchange and unit of account within the economy. The measure of _____ is the _____ rate, the annualized percentage change in a general price index, usually the consumer price index, over time. The opposite of _____ is deflation.

51. *Answer choices:*

(see index for correct answer)

- a. Present value of costs
- b. Base effect
- c. Inflation
- d. Tax shield

Guidance: level 1

:: Supply chain management ::

A _____ is a type of auction in which the traditional roles of buyer and seller are reversed. Thus, there is one buyer and many potential sellers. In an ordinary auction , buyers compete to obtain goods or services by offering increasingly higher prices. In contrast, in a _____ , the sellers compete to obtain business from the buyer and prices will typically decrease as the sellers underbid each other.

Exam Probability: **Medium**

52. *Answer choices:*

(see index for correct answer)

- a. Service parts pricing
- b. Enterprise carbon accounting

- c. ICON-SCM
- d. Reverse auction

Guidance: level 1

:: ::

In marketing jargon, product lining is offering several related products for sale individually. Unlike product bundling, where several products are combined into one group, which is then offered for sale as a units, product lining involves offering the products for sale separately. A line can comprise related products of various sizes, types, colors, qualities, or prices. Line depth refers to the number of subcategories a category has. Line consistency refers to how closely related the products that make up the line are. Line vulnerability refers to the percentage of sales or profits that are derived from only a few products in the line.

Exam Probability: **Low**

53. *Answer choices:*

(see index for correct answer)

- a. hierarchical perspective
- b. cultural
- c. surface-level diversity
- d. Product mix

Guidance: level 1

:: Market structure and pricing ::

_____ has historically emerged in two separate types of discussions in economics, that of Adam Smith on the one hand, and that of Karl Marx on the other hand. Adam Smith in his writing on economics stressed the importance of laissez-faire principles outlining the operation of the market in the absence of dominant political mechanisms of control, while Karl Marx discussed the working of the market in the presence of a controlled economy sometimes referred to as a command economy in the literature. Both types of _____ have been in historical evidence throughout the twentieth century and twenty-first century.

Exam Probability: **High**

54. *Answer choices:*

(see index for correct answer)

- a. Liberalization
- b. Installed base
- c. Open-source economics
- d. Open source

Guidance: level 1

:: International trade ::

A _____ is a document issued by a carrier to acknowledge receipt of cargo for shipment. Although the term historically related only to carriage by sea, a _____ may today be used for any type of carriage of goods.

Exam Probability: **Low**

55. *Answer choices:*

(see index for correct answer)

- a. Bill of lading
- b. Transfer problem
- c. Debt moratorium
- d. Kennedy Round

Guidance: level 1

:: Project management ::

Contemporary business and science treat as a _____ any undertaking, carried out individually or collaboratively and possibly involving research or design, that is carefully planned to achieve a particular aim.

Exam Probability: **High**

56. *Answer choices:*

(see index for correct answer)

- a. LibrePlan
- b. Big Hairy Audacious Goal
- c. Agile management
- d. Doctor of Project Management

Guidance: level 1

:: Service industries ::

_____ are the economic services provided by the finance industry, which encompasses a broad range of businesses that manage money, including credit unions, banks, credit-card companies, insurance companies, accountancy companies, consumer-finance companies, stock brokerages, investment funds, individual managers and some government-sponsored enterprises. _____ companies are present in all economically developed geographic locations and tend to cluster in local, national, regional and international financial centers such as London, New York City, and Tokyo.

Exam Probability: **Low**

57. *Answer choices:*

(see index for correct answer)

- a. Financial services
- b. Graham Company
- c. Financial services in Singapore
- d. Independent Financial Adviser

:: Marketing ::

_____ comes from the Latin neg and otsia referring to businessmen who, unlike the patricians, had no leisure time in their industriousness; it held the meaning of business until the 17th century when it took on the diplomatic connotation as a dialogue between two or more people or parties intended to reach a beneficial outcome over one or more issues where a conflict exists with respect to at least one of these issues. Thus, _____ is a process of combining divergent positions into a joint agreement under a decision rule of unanimity.

Exam Probability: **Low**

58. *Answer choices:*

(see index for correct answer)

- a. Discounting
- b. Negotiation
- c. Predatory pricing
- d. Marketspace

:: ::

_____ is an American restaurant chain and international franchise which was founded in 1958 by Dan and Frank Carney. The company is known for its Italian-American cuisine menu, including pizza and pasta, as well as side dishes and desserts. _____ has 18,431 restaurants worldwide as of December 31, 2018, making it the world's largest pizza chain in terms of locations. It is a subsidiary of Yum! Brands, Inc., one of the world's largest restaurant companies.

Exam Probability: **Medium**

59. *Answer choices:*

(see index for correct answer)

- a. hierarchical perspective
- b. Pizza Hut
- c. process perspective
- d. corporate values

Guidance: level 1

Business ethics

Business ethics (also known as corporate ethics) is a form of applied ethics or professional ethics, that examines ethical principles and moral or ethical problems that can arise in a business environment. It applies to all aspects of business conduct and is relevant to the conduct of individuals and entire organizations. These ethics originate from individuals, organizational statements or from the legal system. These norms, values, ethical, and unethical practices are what is used to guide business. They help those businesses maintain a better connection with their stakeholders.

:: Progressive Era in the United States ::

The Clayton Antitrust Act of 1914 , was a part of United States antitrust law with the goal of adding further substance to the U.S. antitrust law regime; the _____ sought to prevent anticompetitive practices in their incipiency. That regime started with the Sherman Antitrust Act of 1890, the first Federal law outlawing practices considered harmful to consumers . The _____ specified particular prohibited conduct, the three-level enforcement scheme, the exemptions, and the remedial measures.

Exam Probability: **Low**

1. *Answer choices:*

(see index for correct answer)

- a. Clayton Act
- b. Mann Act
- c. pragmatism

Guidance: level 1

:: ::

The _____ to Fight AIDS, Tuberculosis and Malaria is an international financing organization that aims to "attract, leverage and invest additional resources to end the epidemics of HIV/AIDS, tuberculosis and malaria to support attainment of the Sustainable Development Goals established by the United Nations." A public-private partnership, the organization maintains its secretariat in Geneva, Switzerland. The organization began operations in January 2002. Microsoft founder Bill Gates was one of the first private foundations among many bilateral donors to provide seed money for the partnership.

Exam Probability: **Medium**

2. *Answer choices:*
(see index for correct answer)

- a. Sarbanes-Oxley act of 2002
- b. process perspective
- c. Global Fund
- d. interpersonal communication

Guidance: level 1

:: Corporate governance ::

_____ refers to the practice of members of a corporate board of directors serving on the boards of multiple corporations. A person that sits on multiple boards is known as a multiple director. Two firms have a direct interlock if a director or executive of one firm is also a director of the other, and an indirect interlock if a director of each sits on the board of a third firm. This practice, although widespread and lawful, raises questions about the quality and independence of board decisions.

Exam Probability: **Medium**

3. *Answer choices:*

(see index for correct answer)

- a. Institute of Directors
- b. Integrated reporting
- c. Chief privacy officer
- d. Australian Institute of Company Directors

Guidance: level 1

:: Data management ::

_____ is a form of intellectual property that grants the creator of an original creative work an exclusive legal right to determine whether and under what conditions this original work may be copied and used by others, usually for a limited term of years. The exclusive rights are not absolute but limited by limitations and exceptions to _____ law, including fair use. A major limitation on _____ on ideas is that _____ protects only the original expression of ideas, and not the underlying ideas themselves.

4. *Answer choices:*

(see index for correct answer)

- a. Copyright
- b. Savepoint
- c. Data auditing
- d. Lean integration

Guidance: level 1

:: Leadership ::

_____ is leadership that is directed by respect for ethical beliefs and values and for the dignity and rights of others. It is thus related to concepts such as trust, honesty, consideration, charisma, and fairness.

Exam Probability: **Medium**

5. *Answer choices:*

(see index for correct answer)

- a. BTS Group
- b. Transformational leadership
- c. Authentic leadership
- d. Ethical leadership

:: Labour relations ::

_____ is a field of study that can have different meanings depending on the context in which it is used. In an international context, it is a subfield of labor history that studies the human relations with regard to work – in its broadest sense – and how this connects to questions of social inequality. It explicitly encompasses unregulated, historical, and non-Western forms of labor. Here, _____ define "for or with whom one works and under what rules. These rules determine the type of work, type and amount of remuneration, working hours, degrees of physical and psychological strain, as well as the degree of freedom and autonomy associated with the work."

Exam Probability: **High**

6. *Answer choices:*

(see index for correct answer)

- a. Acas
- b. Labor relations
- c. Work Order Act
- d. Worker center

:: ::

The _____ of 1906 was the first of a series of significant consumer protection laws which was enacted by Congress in the 20th century and led to the creation of the Food and Drug Administration. Its main purpose was to ban foreign and interstate traffic in adulterated or mislabeled food and drug products, and it directed the U.S. Bureau of Chemistry to inspect products and refer offenders to prosecutors. It required that active ingredients be placed on the label of a drug's packaging and that drugs could not fall below purity levels established by the United States Pharmacopeia or the National Formulary. The Jungle by Upton Sinclair with its graphic and revolting descriptions of unsanitary conditions and unscrupulous practices rampant in the meatpacking industry, was an inspirational piece that kept the public's attention on the important issue of unhygienic meat processing plants that later led to food inspection legislation. Sinclair quipped, "I aimed at the public's heart and by accident I hit it in the stomach," as outraged readers demanded and got the pure food law.

Exam Probability: **High**

7. *Answer choices:*

(see index for correct answer)

- a. Character
- b. information systems assessment
- c. co-culture
- d. functional perspective

Guidance: level 1

:: ::

_____ in the United States is a federal and state program that helps with medical costs for some people with limited income and resources. _____ also offers benefits not normally covered by Medicare, including nursing home care and personal care services. The Health Insurance Association of America describes _____ as "a government insurance program for persons of all ages whose income and resources are insufficient to pay for health care." _____ is the largest source of funding for medical and health-related services for people with low income in the United States, providing free health insurance to 74 million low-income and disabled people as of 2017. It is a means-tested program that is jointly funded by the state and federal governments and managed by the states, with each state currently having broad leeway to determine who is eligible for its implementation of the program. States are not required to participate in the program, although all have since 1982. _____ recipients must be U.S. citizens or qualified non-citizens, and may include low-income adults, their children, and people with certain disabilities. Poverty alone does not necessarily qualify someone for _____.

Exam Probability: **High**

8. *Answer choices:*

(see index for correct answer)

- a. open system
- b. empathy
- c. surface-level diversity
- d. corporate values

Guidance: level 1

:: Electronic feedback ::

_____ occurs when outputs of a system are routed back as inputs as part of a chain of cause-and-effect that forms a circuit or loop. The system can then be said to feed back into itself. The notion of cause-and-effect has to be handled carefully when applied to _____ systems.

Exam Probability: **Low**

9. *Answer choices:*

(see index for correct answer)

- a. Feedback
- b. feedback loop

Guidance: level 1

:: Ethically disputed business practices ::

_____ is the trading of a public company's stock or other securities by individuals with access to nonpublic information about the company. In various countries, some kinds of trading based on insider information is illegal. This is because it is seen as unfair to other investors who do not have access to the information, as the investor with insider information could potentially make larger profits than a typical investor could make. The rules governing _____ are complex and vary significantly from country to country. The extent of enforcement also varies from one country to another. The definition of insider in one jurisdiction can be broad, and may cover not only insiders themselves but also any persons related to them, such as brokers, associates and even family members. A person who becomes aware of non-public information and trades on that basis may be guilty of a crime.

10. *Answer choices:*

(see index for correct answer)

- a. Copyright troll
- b. Insider trading
- c. American Market
- d. anti-competitive

Guidance: level 1

:: Business ethics ::

A _____ is a person who exposes any kind of information or activity that is deemed illegal, unethical, or not correct within an organization that is either private or public. The information of alleged wrongdoing can be classified in many ways: violation of company policy/rules, law, regulation, or threat to public interest/national security, as well as fraud, and corruption. Those who become _____ s can choose to bring information or allegations to surface either internally or externally. Internally, a _____ can bring his/her accusations to the attention of other people within the accused organization such as an immediate supervisor. Externally, a _____ can bring allegations to light by contacting a third party outside of an accused organization such as the media, government, law enforcement, or those who are concerned. _____ s, however, take the risk of facing stiff reprisal and retaliation from those who are accused or alleged of wrongdoing.

11. *Answer choices:*

(see index for correct answer)

- a. Perfect Relations
- b. Equator Principles
- c. Surface Transportation Assistance Act
- d. Whistleblower

Guidance: level 1

:: ::

An _____ is the release of a liquid petroleum hydrocarbon into the environment, especially the marine ecosystem, due to human activity, and is a form of pollution. The term is usually given to marine _____ s, where oil is released into the ocean or coastal waters, but spills may also occur on land. _____ s may be due to releases of crude oil from tankers, offshore platforms, drilling rigs and wells, as well as spills of refined petroleum products and their by-products, heavier fuels used by large ships such as bunker fuel, or the spill of any oily refuse or waste oil.

Exam Probability: **Low**

12. *Answer choices:*

(see index for correct answer)

- a. co-culture
- b. Oil spill

- c. functional perspective
- d. surface-level diversity

Guidance: level 1

:: Fraud ::

In law, _____ is intentional deception to secure unfair or unlawful gain, or to deprive a victim of a legal right. _____ can violate civil law , a criminal law , or it may cause no loss of money, property or legal right but still be an element of another civil or criminal wrong. The purpose of _____ may be monetary gain or other benefits, for example by obtaining a passport, travel document, or driver's license, or mortgage _____ , where the perpetrator may attempt to qualify for a mortgage by way of false statements.

Exam Probability: **Medium**

13. *Answer choices:*
(see index for correct answer)

- a. SHERIFF
- b. Plastic shaman
- c. Fraud
- d. Medicare fraud

Guidance: level 1

:: ::

A _____ service is an online platform which people use to build social networks or social relationship with other people who share similar personal or career interests, activities, backgrounds or real-life connections.

Exam Probability: **Medium**

14. *Answer choices:*

(see index for correct answer)

- a. personal values
- b. similarity-attraction theory
- c. Sarbanes-Oxley act of 2002
- d. Social networking

Guidance: level 1

:: Auditing ::

_____ is a general term that can reflect various types of evaluations intended to identify environmental compliance and management system implementation gaps, along with related corrective actions. In this way they perform an analogous function to financial audits. There are generally two different types of _____ s: compliance audits and management systems audits. Compliance audits tend to be the primary type in the US or within US-based multinationals.

15. *Answer choices:*

(see index for correct answer)

- a. Chartered Institute of Internal Auditors
- b. Environmental audit
- c. Mazars
- d. Legal auditing

Guidance: level 1

:: ::

_____ is "property consisting of land and the buildings on it, along with its natural resources such as crops, minerals or water; immovable property of this nature; an interest vested in this an item of real property, buildings or housing in general. Also: the business of _____ ; the profession of buying, selling, or renting land, buildings, or housing." It is a legal term used in jurisdictions whose legal system is derived from English common law, such as India, England, Wales, Northern Ireland, United States, Canada, Pakistan, Australia, and New Zealand.

Exam Probability: **Medium**

16. *Answer choices:*

(see index for correct answer)

- a. Real estate
- b. similarity-attraction theory
- c. process perspective
- d. hierarchical perspective

Guidance: level 1

:: Anti-capitalism ::

_____ is a range of economic and social systems characterised by social ownership of the means of production and workers' self-management, as well as the political theories and movements associated with them. Social ownership can be public, collective or cooperative ownership, or citizen ownership of equity. There are many varieties of _____ and there is no single definition encapsulating all of them, with social ownership being the common element shared by its various forms.

Exam Probability: **Low**

17. *Answer choices:*

(see index for correct answer)

- a. Social anarchism
- b. Soviet democracy
- c. Socialism
- d. Communism

Guidance: level 1

:: Criminal law ::

_____ is the body of law that relates to crime. It proscribes conduct perceived as threatening, harmful, or otherwise endangering to the property, health, safety, and moral welfare of people inclusive of one's self. Most _____ is established by statute, which is to say that the laws are enacted by a legislature. _____ includes the punishment and rehabilitation of people who violate such laws. _____ varies according to jurisdiction, and differs from civil law, where emphasis is more on dispute resolution and victim compensation, rather than on punishment or rehabilitation. Criminal procedure is a formalized official activity that authenticates the fact of commission of a crime and authorizes punitive or rehabilitative treatment of the offender.

Exam Probability: **High**

18. *Answer choices:*

(see index for correct answer)

- a. complicit
- b. Mala prohibita
- c. Self-incrimination
- d. Criminal law

Guidance: level 1

:: Hazard analysis ::

Broadly speaking, a _____ is the combined effort of 1. identifying and analyzing potential events that may negatively impact individuals, assets, and/or the environment ; and 2. making judgments "on the tolerability of the risk on the basis of a risk analysis" while considering influencing factors . Put in simpler terms, a _____ analyzes what can go wrong, how likely it is to happen, what the potential consequences are, and how tolerable the identified risk is. As part of this process, the resulting determination of risk may be expressed in a quantitative or qualitative fashion. The _____ is an inherent part of an overall risk management strategy, which attempts to, after a _____ , "introduce control measures to eliminate or reduce" any potential risk-related consequences.

Exam Probability: **High**

19. *Answer choices:*

(see index for correct answer)

- a. Hazard
- b. Risk assessment
- c. Swiss cheese model
- d. Hazardous Materials Identification System

Guidance: level 1

:: Separation of investment and commercial banking ::

The _____ refers to § 619 of the Dodd–Frank Wall Street Reform and Consumer Protection Act . The rule was originally proposed by American economist and former United States Federal Reserve Chairman Paul Volcker to restrict United States banks from making certain kinds of speculative investments that do not benefit their customers. Volcker argued that such speculative activity played a key role in the financial crisis of 2007–2008. The rule is often referred to as a ban on proprietary trading by commercial banks, whereby deposits are used to trade on the bank's own accounts, although a number of exceptions to this ban were included in the Dodd-Frank law.

Exam Probability: **High**

20. *Answer choices:*

(see index for correct answer)

- a. Bank holding company
- b. Volcker Rule
- c. investment bank
- d. Speculation

Guidance: level 1

:: Public relations terminology ::

_____ , also called "green sheen", is a form of spin in which green PR or green marketing is deceptively used to promote the perception that an organization's products, aims or policies are environmentally friendly. Evidence that an organization is _____ often comes from pointing out the spending differences: when significantly more money or time has been spent advertising being "green" , than is actually spent on environmentally sound practices. _____ efforts can range from changing the name or label of a product to evoke the natural environment on a product that contains harmful chemicals to multimillion-dollar marketing campaigns portraying highly polluting energy companies as eco-friendly.Publicized accusations of _____ have contributed to the term's increasing use.

Exam Probability: **High**

21. *Answer choices:*

(see index for correct answer)

- a. Photo op
- b. No comment
- c. Junk science
- d. Greenwashing

Guidance: level 1

:: ::

A _____ is a form of business network, for example, a local organization of businesses whose goal is to further the interests of businesses. Business owners in towns and cities form these local societies to advocate on behalf of the business community. Local businesses are members, and they elect a board of directors or executive council to set policy for the chamber. The board or council then hires a President, CEO or Executive Director, plus staffing appropriate to size, to run the organization.

Exam Probability: **High**

22. *Answer choices:*

(see index for correct answer)

- a. interpersonal communication
- b. Chamber of Commerce
- c. co-culture
- d. empathy

Guidance: level 1

:: ::

Oriental Nicety, formerly _____ , Exxon Mediterranean, SeaRiver Mediterranean, S/R Mediterranean, Mediterranean, and Dong Fang Ocean, was an oil tanker that gained notoriety after running aground in Prince William Sound spilling hundreds of thousands of barrels of crude oil in Alaska. On March 24, 1989, while owned by the former Exxon Shipping Company, and captained by Joseph Hazelwood and First Mate James Kunkel bound for Long Beach, California, the vessel ran aground on the Bligh Reef resulting in the second largest oil spill in United States history. The size of the spill is estimated to have been 40,900 to 120,000 m3 , or 257,000 to 750,000 barrels. In 1989, the _____ oil spill was listed as the 54th largest spill in history.

Exam Probability: **High**

23. *Answer choices:*

(see index for correct answer)

- a. hierarchical
- b. interpersonal communication
- c. personal values
- d. Exxon Valdez

Guidance: level 1

:: Majority–minority relations ::

It was established as axiomatic in anthropological research by Franz Boas in the first few decades of the 20th century and later popularized by his students. Boas first articulated the idea in 1887: "civilization is not something absolute, but ... is relative, and ... our ideas and conceptions are true only so far as our civilization goes". However, Boas did not coin the term.

Exam Probability: **High**

24. *Answer choices:*

(see index for correct answer)

- a. cultural dissonance
- b. Affirmative action
- c. positive discrimination

Guidance: level 1

:: United Kingdom labour law ::

The _____ was a series of programs, public work projects, financial reforms, and regulations enacted by President Franklin D. Roosevelt in the United States between 1933 and 1936. It responded to needs for relief, reform, and recovery from the Great Depression. Major federal programs included the Civilian Conservation Corps , the Civil Works Administration , the Farm Security Administration , the National Industrial Recovery Act of 1933 and the Social Security Administration . They provided support for farmers, the unemployed, youth and the elderly. The _____ included new constraints and safeguards on the banking industry and efforts to re-inflate the economy after prices had fallen sharply. _____ programs included both laws passed by Congress as well as presidential executive orders during the first term of the presidency of Franklin D. Roosevelt.

Exam Probability: **High**

25. *Answer choices:*
(see index for correct answer)

- a. Truck Acts
- b. Special register body
- c. New Deal
- d. Collective Redundancies Directive

Guidance: level 1

:: Supply chain management terms ::

In business and finance, _____ is a system of organizations, people, activities, information, and resources involved in moving a product or service from supplier to customer. _____ activities involve the transformation of natural resources, raw materials, and components into a finished product that is delivered to the end customer. In sophisticated _____ systems, used products may re-enter the _____ at any point where residual value is recyclable. _____ s link value chains.

Exam Probability: **High**

26. *Answer choices:*

(see index for correct answer)

- a. inventory management
- b. Most valuable customers
- c. Widget
- d. Consumables

Guidance: level 1

:: Corporate crime ::

_____ LLP, based in Chicago, was an American holding company. Formerly one of the "Big Five" accounting firms , the firm had provided auditing, tax, and consulting services to large corporations. By 2001, it had become one of the world's largest multinational companies.

Exam Probability: **Medium**

27. *Answer choices:*

(see index for correct answer)

- a. Compass Group
- b. Anti-corporate
- c. Arthur Andersen
- d. NatWest Three

Guidance: level 1

:: ::

The Federal National Mortgage Association , commonly known as _____ , is a United States government-sponsored enterprise and, since 1968, a publicly traded company. Founded in 1938 during the Great Depression as part of the New Deal, the corporation's purpose is to expand the secondary mortgage market by securitizing mortgage loans in the form of mortgage-backed securities , allowing lenders to reinvest their assets into more lending and in effect increasing the number of lenders in the mortgage market by reducing the reliance on locally based savings and loan associations . Its brother organization is the Federal Home Loan Mortgage Corporation , better known as Freddie Mac. As of 2018, _____ is ranked #21 on the Fortune 500 rankings of the largest United States corporations by total revenue.

Exam Probability: **Medium**

28. *Answer choices:*

(see index for correct answer)

- a. corporate values
- b. hierarchical perspective
- c. surface-level diversity
- d. information systems assessment

Guidance: level 1

:: Labor rights ::

The _____ is the concept that people have a human _____ , or engage in productive employment, and may not be prevented from doing so. The _____ is enshrined in the Universal Declaration of Human Rights and recognized in international human rights law through its inclusion in the International Covenant on Economic, Social and Cultural Rights, where the _____ emphasizes economic, social and cultural development.

Exam Probability: **Medium**

29. *Answer choices:*

(see index for correct answer)

- a. Swift raids
- b. Right to work
- c. Labor rights
- d. China Labor Watch

Guidance: level 1

:: Socialism ::

_____ is a label used to define the first currents of modern socialist thought as exemplified by the work of Henri de Saint-Simon, Charles Fourier, Étienne Cabet and Robert Owen.

Exam Probability: **High**

30. *Answer choices:*

(see index for correct answer)

- a. Liberal socialism
- b. Utopian socialism
- c. Scientific socialism
- d. African socialism

Guidance: level 1

:: Professional ethics ::

In the mental health field, a _____ is a situation where multiple roles exist between a therapist, or other mental health practitioner, and a client. _____ s are also referred to as multiple relationships, and these two terms are used interchangeably in the research literature. The American Psychological Association Ethical Principles of Psychologists and Code of Conduct is a resource that outlines ethical standards and principles to which practitioners are expected to adhere. Standard 3.05 of the APA ethics code outlines the definition of multiple relationships. Dual or multiple relationships occur when.

Exam Probability: **Low**

31. *Answer choices:*

(see index for correct answer)

- a. professional conduct
- b. Dual relationship
- c. Continuous professional development

Guidance: level 1

:: Management ::

_____ or executive pay is composed of the financial compensation and other non-financial awards received by an executive from their firm for their service to the organization. It is typically a mixture of salary, bonuses, shares of or call options on the company stock, benefits, and perquisites, ideally configured to take into account government regulations, tax law, the desires of the organization and the executive, and rewards for performance.

Exam Probability: **Medium**

32. *Answer choices:*

(see index for correct answer)

- a. Performance indicator
- b. Failure demand
- c. Executive compensation
- d. Authoritarian leadership style

Guidance: level 1

:: Corporate scandals ::

Exxon Mobil Corporation, doing business as _____ , is an American multinational oil and gas corporation headquartered in Irving, Texas. It is the largest direct descendant of John D. Rockefeller's Standard Oil Company, and was formed on November 30, 1999 by the merger of Exxon and Mobil . _____ 's primary brands are Exxon, Mobil, Esso, and _____ Chemical.

Exam Probability: **High**

33. *Answer choices:*

(see index for correct answer)

- a. Great Phenol Plot
- b. Patent encumbrance of large automotive NiMH batteries

- c. Overseas Trust Bank
- d. Yield Burning

Guidance: level 1

:: Fraud ::

In the United States, _____ is the claiming of Medicare health care reimbursement to which the claimant is not entitled. There are many different types of _____ , all of which have the same goal: to collect money from the Medicare program illegitimately.

Exam Probability: **High**

34. *Answer choices:*

(see index for correct answer)

- a. Claims Conference
- b. Certified Fraud Examiner
- c. Medicare fraud
- d. SHERIFF

Guidance: level 1

:: Coal ::

_____ is a combustible black or brownish-black sedimentary rock, formed as rock strata called _____ seams. _____ is mostly carbon with variable amounts of other elements; chiefly hydrogen, sulfur, oxygen, and nitrogen. _____ is formed if dead plant matter decays into peat and over millions of years the heat and pressure of deep burial converts the peat into _____ . Vast deposits of _____ originates in former wetlands—called _____ forests—that covered much of the Earth's tropical land areas during the late Carboniferous and Permian times.

Exam Probability: **High**

35. *Answer choices:*

(see index for correct answer)

- a. Char
- b. World Coal Association
- c. Coalbed methane
- d. Densified coal

Guidance: level 1

:: Ethical banking ::

A _____ or community development finance institution - abbreviated in
both cases to CDFI - is a financial institution that provides credit and
financial services to underserved markets and populations, primarily in the USA
but also in the UK. A CDFI may be a community development bank, a community
development credit union , a community development loan fund , a community
development venture capital fund , a microenterprise development loan fund, or
a community development corporation.

Exam Probability: High

36. *Answer choices:*

(see index for correct answer)

- a. Alfred Rexroth
- b. Community development financial institution
- c. Cultura Sparebank
- d. Triodos Bank

Guidance: level 1

:: Market-based policy instruments ::

Cause marketing is defined as a type of corporate social responsibility, in
which a company's promotional campaign has the dual purpose of increasing
profitability while bettering society.

Exam Probability: Low

37. *Answer choices:*

(see index for correct answer)

- a. Energy Tax Act
- b. Cause-related marketing
- c. Feebate
- d. Tax choice

Guidance: level 1

:: Competition regulators ::

The _____ is an independent agency of the United States government, established in 1914 by the _____ Act. Its principal mission is the promotion of consumer protection and the elimination and prevention of anticompetitive business practices, such as coercive monopoly. It is headquartered in the _____ Building in Washington, D.C.

Exam Probability: **High**

38. *Answer choices:*

(see index for correct answer)

- a. Federal Trade Commission
- b. Netherlands Competition Authority
- c. Commerce Commission
- d. Federal Cartel Office

:: Corporate scandals ::

_____ was a bank based in the Caribbean, which operated from 1986 to 2009 when it went into receivership. It was an affiliate of the Stanford Financial Group and failed when the its parent was seized by United States authorities in early 2009 as part of the investigation into Allen Stanford.

Exam Probability: **Low**

39. *Answer choices:*

(see index for correct answer)

- a. S-Chips Scandals
- b. Eurest Support Services
- c. Baptist Foundation of Arizona
- d. Petters Group Worldwide

:: Renewable energy ::

_____ is the conversion of energy from sunlight into electricity, either directly using photovoltaics , indirectly using concentrated _____ , or a combination. Concentrated _____ systems use lenses or mirrors and tracking systems to focus a large area of sunlight into a small beam. Photovoltaic cells convert light into an electric current using the photovoltaic effect.

Exam Probability: **Low**

40. *Answer choices:*

(see index for correct answer)

- a. Variable renewable energy
- b. Carbon neutrality
- c. Human power
- d. Solar power

Guidance: level 1

:: ::

_____ refers to a business initiative to increase the access between a company and their current and potential customers through the use of the Internet. The Internet allows the company to market themselves and attract new customers to their website where they can provide product information and better customer service. Customers can place orders electronically, therefore reducing expensive long distant phone calls and postage costs of placing orders, while saving time on behalf of the customer and company.

41. *Answer choices:*

(see index for correct answer)

- a. empathy
- b. levels of analysis
- c. similarity-attraction theory
- d. Global reach

Guidance: level 1

:: Business ethics ::

_____ is a type of international private business self-regulation. While once it was possible to describe CSR as an internal organisational policy or a corporate ethic strategy, that time has passed as various international laws have been developed and various organisations have used their authority to push it beyond individual or even industry-wide initiatives. While it has been considered a form of corporate self-regulation for some time, over the last decade or so it has moved considerably from voluntary decisions at the level of individual organisations, to mandatory schemes at regional, national and even transnational levels.

Exam Probability: **High**

42. *Answer choices:*

(see index for correct answer)

- a. Altruistic corporate social responsibility
- b. Corruption of Foreign Public Officials Act
- c. Corporate social responsibility
- d. Hostile work environment

Guidance: level 1

:: Offshoring ::

A _____ is the temporary suspension or permanent termination of employment of an employee or, more commonly, a group of employees for business reasons, such as personnel management or downsizing an organization. Originally, _____ referred exclusively to a temporary interruption in work, or employment but this has evolved to a permanent elimination of a position in both British and US English, requiring the addition of "temporary" to specify the original meaning of the word. A _____ is not to be confused with wrongful termination. Laid off workers or displaced workers are workers who have lost or left their jobs because their employer has closed or moved, there was insufficient work for them to do, or their position or shift was abolished . Downsizing in a company is defined to involve the reduction of employees in a workforce. Downsizing in companies became a popular practice in the 1980s and early 1990s as it was seen as a way to deliver better shareholder value as it helps to reduce the costs of employers . Indeed, recent research on downsizing in the U.S., UK, and Japan suggests that downsizing is being regarded by management as one of the preferred routes to help declining organizations, cutting unnecessary costs, and improve organizational performance. Usually a _____ occurs as a cost cutting measure.

Exam Probability: **High**

43. *Answer choices:*

(see index for correct answer)

- a. Sourcing advisory
- b. Offshoring Research Network
- c. Programmers Guild
- d. Nearshoring

Guidance: level 1

:: Law ::

_____ is a body of law which defines the role, powers, and structure of different entities within a state, namely, the executive, the parliament or legislature, and the judiciary; as well as the basic rights of citizens and, in federal countries such as the United States and Canada, the relationship between the central government and state, provincial, or territorial governments.

Exam Probability: **Low**

44. *Answer choices:*
(see index for correct answer)

- a. Constitutional law
- b. Comparative law

Guidance: level 1

:: Leadership ::

_____ is a theory of leadership where a leader works with teams to identify needed change, creating a vision to guide the change through inspiration, and executing the change in tandem with committed members of a group; it is an integral part of the Full Range Leadership Model. _____ serves to enhance the motivation, morale, and job performance of followers through a variety of mechanisms; these include connecting the follower's sense of identity and self to a project and to the collective identity of the organization; being a role model for followers in order to inspire them and to raise their interest in the project; challenging followers to take greater ownership for their work, and understanding the strengths and weaknesses of followers, allowing the leader to align followers with tasks that enhance their performance.

Exam Probability: **Medium**

45. *Answer choices:*
(see index for correct answer)

- a. Transformational leadership
- b. Three levels of leadership model
- c. Integral leadership
- d. Ethical leadership

Guidance: level 1

:: ::

In regulatory jurisdictions that provide for it , _____ is a group of laws and organizations designed to ensure the rights of consumers as well as fair trade, competition and accurate information in the marketplace. The laws are designed to prevent the businesses that engage in fraud or specified unfair practices from gaining an advantage over competitors. They may also provides additional protection for those most vulnerable in society. _____ laws are a form of government regulation that aim to protect the rights of consumers. For example, a government may require businesses to disclose detailed information about products—particularly in areas where safety or public health is an issue, such as food.

Exam Probability: **Low**

46. *Answer choices:*

(see index for correct answer)

- a. personal values
- b. process perspective
- c. Character
- d. Consumer Protection

Guidance: level 1

:: Business ethics ::

_____ is a persistent pattern of mistreatment from others in the workplace that causes either physical or emotional harm. It can include such tactics as verbal, nonverbal, psychological, physical abuse and humiliation. This type of workplace aggression is particularly difficult because, unlike the typical school bully, workplace bullies often operate within the established rules and policies of their organization and their society. In the majority of cases, bullying in the workplace is reported as having been by someone who has authority over their victim. However, bullies can also be peers, and occasionally subordinates. Research has also investigated the impact of the larger organizational context on bullying as well as the group-level processes that impact on the incidence and maintenance of bullying behaviour. Bullying can be covert or overt. It may be missed by superiors; it may be known by many throughout the organization. Negative effects are not limited to the targeted individuals, and may lead to a decline in employee morale and a change in organizational culture. It can also take place as overbearing supervision, constant criticism, and blocking promotions.

Exam Probability: **Low**

47. *Answer choices:*

(see index for correct answer)

- a. Third-party technique
- b. Workplace bullying
- c. Being Globally Responsible Conference
- d. Unfree labour

Guidance: level 1

:: United States federal labor legislation ::

The _____ of 1988 is a United States federal law that generally prevents employers from using polygraph tests, either for pre-employment screening or during the course of employment, with certain exemptions.

Exam Probability: **Low**

48. *Answer choices:*

(see index for correct answer)

- a. Erdman Act
- b. Financial core
- c. Alien Contract Labor Law
- d. Title 29 of the United States Code

Guidance: level 1

:: Timber industry ::

The _____ is an international non-profit, multi-stakeholder organization established in 1993 to promote responsible management of the world's forests. The FSC does this by setting standards on forest products, along with certifying and labeling them as eco-friendly.

Exam Probability: **Medium**

49. *Answer choices:*

(see index for correct answer)

- a. Susquehanna Boom
- b. Wood warping
- c. Forest Stewardship Council
- d. Brettstapel

Guidance: level 1

:: Occupational safety and health ::

_____ is a chemical element with symbol Pb and atomic number 82. It is a heavy metal that is denser than most common materials. _____ is soft and malleable, and also has a relatively low melting point. When freshly cut, _____ is silvery with a hint of blue; it tarnishes to a dull gray color when exposed to air. _____ has the highest atomic number of any stable element and three of its isotopes are endpoints of major nuclear decay chains of heavier elements.

Exam Probability: **Medium**

50. *Answer choices:*

(see index for correct answer)

- a. Lead
- b. Canadian Registered Safety Professional
- c. Contact dermatitis
- d. Global road safety for workers

:: Human resource management ::

_____ is the ethics of an organization, and it is how an organization responds to an internal or external stimulus. _____ is interdependent with the organizational culture. Although it is akin to both organizational behavior and industrial and organizational psychology as well as business ethics on the micro and macro levels, _____ is neither OB or I/O psychology, nor is it solely business ethics . _____ express the values of an organization to its employees and/or other entities irrespective of governmental and/or regulatory laws.

Exam Probability: **Low**

51. *Answer choices:*

(see index for correct answer)

- a. Diversity Icebreaker
- b. Organizational ethics
- c. Cultural capital
- d. Selection ratio

:: Management ::

_____ is the identification, evaluation, and prioritization of risks followed by coordinated and economical application of resources to minimize, monitor, and control the probability or impact of unfortunate events or to maximize the realization of opportunities.

Exam Probability: **High**

52. *Answer choices:*

(see index for correct answer)

- a. I-VMS
- b. Risk management
- c. Bed management
- d. Total security management

Guidance: level 1

:: ::

The _____ was a severe worldwide economic depression that took place mostly during the 1930s, beginning in the United States. The timing of the _____ varied across nations; in most countries it started in 1929 and lasted until the late-1930s. It was the longest, deepest, and most widespread depression of the 20th century. In the 21st century, the _____ is commonly used as an example of how intensely the world's economy can decline.

Exam Probability: **Medium**

53. *Answer choices:*

(see index for correct answer)

- a. co-culture
- b. deep-level diversity
- c. Sarbanes-Oxley act of 2002
- d. Great Depression

Guidance: level 1

:: ::

The _____ is an institution of the European Union, responsible for proposing legislation, implementing decisions, upholding the EU treaties and managing the day-to-day business of the EU. Commissioners swear an oath at the European Court of Justice in Luxembourg City, pledging to respect the treaties and to be completely independent in carrying out their duties during their mandate. Unlike in the Council of the European Union, where members are directly and indirectly elected, and the European Parliament, where members are directly elected, the Commissioners are proposed by the Council of the European Union, on the basis of suggestions made by the national governments, and then appointed by the European Council after the approval of the European Parliament.

Exam Probability: **High**

54. *Answer choices:*

(see index for correct answer)

- a. similarity-attraction theory
- b. European Commission
- c. surface-level diversity
- d. deep-level diversity

Guidance: level 1

:: ::

A _____ is a set of rules, often written, with regards to clothing.
_____ s are created out of social perceptions and norms, and vary based on purpose, circumstances and occasions. Different societies and cultures are likely to have different _____ s.

Exam Probability: **High**

55. *Answer choices:*
(see index for correct answer)

- a. corporate values
- b. functional perspective
- c. Dress code
- d. interpersonal communication

Guidance: level 1

:: ::

The Catholic Church, also known as the Roman Catholic Church, is the largest
Christian church, with approximately 1.3 billion baptised Catholics worldwide
as of 2017. As the world's oldest continuously functioning international
institution, it has played a prominent role in the history and development of
Western civilisation. The church is headed by the Bishop of Rome, known as the
pope. Its central administration, the Holy See, is in the Vatican City, an
enclave within the city of Rome in Italy.

Exam Probability: **Low**

56. *Answer choices:*

(see index for correct answer)

- a. hierarchical
- b. deep-level diversity
- c. Sarbanes-Oxley act of 2002
- d. Catholicism

Guidance: level 1

:: ::

A _____ is an astronomical body orbiting a star or stellar remnant that
is massive enough to be rounded by its own gravity, is not massive enough to
cause thermonuclear fusion, and has cleared its neighbouring region of
_____ esimals.

Exam Probability: **High**

57. *Answer choices:*

(see index for correct answer)

- a. information systems assessment
- b. similarity-attraction theory
- c. Planet
- d. hierarchical

Guidance: level 1

:: ::

The _____ is an agency of the United States Department of Labor. Congress established the agency under the Occupational Safety and Health Act , which President Richard M. Nixon signed into law on December 29, 1970. OSHA's mission is to "assure safe and healthy working conditions for working men and women by setting and enforcing standards and by providing training, outreach, education and assistance". The agency is also charged with enforcing a variety of whistleblower statutes and regulations. OSHA is currently headed by Acting Assistant Secretary of Labor Loren Sweatt. OSHA's workplace safety inspections have been shown to reduce injury rates and injury costs without adverse effects to employment, sales, credit ratings, or firm survival.

Exam Probability: **Low**

58. *Answer choices:*

(see index for correct answer)

- a. functional perspective
- b. co-culture
- c. surface-level diversity
- d. Occupational Safety and Health Administration

Guidance: level 1

:: Types of marketing ::

_____ is an advertisement strategy in which a company uses surprise and/or unconventional interactions in order to promote a product or service. It is a type of publicity. The term was popularized by Jay Conrad Levinson`s 1984 book _____ .

Exam Probability: **High**

59. *Answer choices:*

(see index for correct answer)

- a. Guerrilla Marketing
- b. Influencer marketing
- c. Vertical integration
- d. Community marketing

Guidance: level 1

Accounting

Accounting or accountancy is the measurement, processing, and communication of financial information about economic entities such as businesses and corporations. The modern field was established by the Italian mathematician Luca Pacioli in 1494. Accounting, which has been called the "language of business", measures the results of an organization's economic activities and conveys this information to a variety of users, including investors, creditors, management, and regulators.

:: Project management ::

In economics, _____ is the assignment of available resources to various uses. In the context of an entire economy, resources can be allocated by various means, such as markets or central planning.

Exam Probability: **High**

1. *Answer choices:*

(see index for correct answer)

- a. Critical path drag
- b. Expected commercial value
- c. Resource allocation
- d. Extreme project management

Guidance: level 1

:: Management ::

The _____ is a strategy performance management tool – a semi-standard structured report, that can be used by managers to keep track of the execution of activities by the staff within their control and to monitor the consequences arising from these actions.

Exam Probability: **Medium**

2. *Answer choices:*

(see index for correct answer)

- a. Total Worker Health
- b. Balanced scorecard
- c. Bed management
- d. Work breakdown structure

Guidance: level 1

:: Legal terms ::

An _____ is an action which is inaccurate or incorrect. In some usages, an _____ is synonymous with a mistake. In statistics, " _____ " refers to the difference between the value which has been computed and the correct value. An _____ could result in failure or in a deviation from the intended performance or behaviour.

Exam Probability: **Medium**

3. *Answer choices:*

(see index for correct answer)

- a. Perjury
- b. Letter rogatory
- c. Adjustment
- d. Crime against nature

Guidance: level 1

:: Inventory ::

_____ is the maximum amount of goods, or inventory, that a company can possibly sell during this fiscal year. It has the formula.

Exam Probability: **High**

4. *Answer choices:*

(see index for correct answer)

- • a. Cost of goods available for sale
- • b. Order picking
- • c. Consignment stock
- • d. Reorder point

Guidance: level 1

:: Commercial crimes ::

_____ is the act of withholding assets for the purpose of conversion of such assets, by one or more persons to whom the assets were entrusted, either to be held or to be used for specific purposes. _____ is a type of financial fraud. For example, a lawyer might embezzle funds from the trust accounts of their clients; a financial advisor might embezzle the funds of investors; and a husband or a wife might embezzle funds from a bank account jointly held with the spouse.

Exam Probability: **Low**

5. *Answer choices:*

(see index for correct answer)

- a. Embezzlement
- b. Commercial bribery
- c. The Informant
- d. Global Forum on Transparency and Exchange of Information for Tax Purposes

Guidance: level 1

:: Generally Accepted Accounting Principles ::

_____ , or non-current liabilities, are liabilities that are due beyond a year or the normal operation period of the company. The normal operation period is the amount of time it takes for a company to turn inventory into cash. On a classified balance sheet, liabilities are separated between current and _____ to help users assess the company's financial standing in short-term and long-term periods. _____ give users more information about the long-term prosperity of the company, while current liabilities inform the user of debt that the company owes in the current period. On a balance sheet, accounts are listed in order of liquidity, so _____ come after current liabilities. In addition, the specific long-term liability accounts are listed on the balance sheet in order of liquidity. Therefore, an account due within eighteen months would be listed before an account due within twenty-four months. Examples of _____ are bonds payable, long-term loans, capital leases, pension liabilities, post-retirement healthcare liabilities, deferred compensation, deferred revenues, deferred income taxes, and derivative liabilities.

6. *Answer choices:*

(see index for correct answer)

- a. Paid in capital
- b. Long-term liabilities
- c. Income statement
- d. Net income

Guidance: level 1

:: Valuation (finance) ::

_____ refers to an assessment of the viability, stability, and profitability of a business, sub-business or project.

Exam Probability: **High**

7. *Answer choices:*

(see index for correct answer)

- a. Sum of perpetuities method
- b. Period of financial distress
- c. Financial analysis
- d. The Appraisal Foundation

:: Accounting terminology ::

In accounting/accountancy, _____ are journal entries usually made at the end of an accounting period to allocate income and expenditure to the period in which they actually occurred. The revenue recognition principle is the basis of making _____ that pertain to unearned and accrued revenues under accrual-basis accounting. They are sometimes called Balance Day adjustments because they are made on balance day.

Exam Probability: **Low**

8. *Answer choices:*

(see index for correct answer)

- a. Accounts payable
- b. Adjusting entries
- c. Capital appreciation
- d. Share premium

:: Free accounting software ::

A _____ is the principal book or computer file for recording and totaling economic transactions measured in terms of a monetary unit of account by account type, with debits and credits in separate columns and a beginning monetary balance and ending monetary balance for each account.

Exam Probability: **Low**

9. *Answer choices:*

(see index for correct answer)

- a. SQL-Ledger
- b. Ledger
- c. Frontaccounting
- d. Grisbi

Guidance: level 1

:: Marketing ::

_____ or stock control can be broadly defined as "the activity of checking a shop's stock." However, a more focused definition takes into account the more science-based, methodical practice of not only verifying a business' inventory but also focusing on the many related facets of inventory management "within an organisation to meet the demand placed upon that business economically." Other facets of _____ include supply chain management, production control, financial flexibility, and customer satisfaction. At the root of _____ , however, is the _____ problem, which involves determining when to order, how much to order, and the logistics of those decisions.

10. *Answer choices:*

(see index for correct answer)

- a. Joseph E. Grosberg
- b. Impulse purchase
- c. Adobe Social
- d. Editorial calendar

Guidance: level 1

:: ::

An _____ is a comprehensive report on a company's activities throughout the preceding year. _____ s are intended to give shareholders and other interested people information about the company's activities and financial performance. They may be considered as grey literature. Most jurisdictions require companies to prepare and disclose _____ s, and many require the _____ to be filed at the company's registry. Companies listed on a stock exchange are also required to report at more frequent intervals .

11. *Answer choices:*

(see index for correct answer)

- a. functional perspective

- b. empathy
- c. Annual report
- d. imperative

Guidance: level 1

:: ::

An _____ , for United States federal income tax, is a closely held corporation that makes a valid election to be taxed under Subchapter S of Chapter 1 of the Internal Revenue Code. In general, _____ s do not pay any income taxes. Instead, the corporation's income or losses are divided among and passed through to its shareholders. The shareholders must then report the income or loss on their own individual income tax returns.

Exam Probability: **High**

12. *Answer choices:*
(see index for correct answer)

- a. similarity-attraction theory
- b. cultural
- c. deep-level diversity
- d. hierarchical

Guidance: level 1

:: Financial regulatory authorities of the United States ::

The _____ is the revenue service of the United States federal government. The government agency is a bureau of the Department of the Treasury, and is under the immediate direction of the Commissioner of Internal Revenue, who is appointed to a five-year term by the President of the United States. The IRS is responsible for collecting taxes and administering the Internal Revenue Code, the main body of federal statutory tax law of the United States. The duties of the IRS include providing tax assistance to taxpayers and pursuing and resolving instances of erroneous or fraudulent tax filings. The IRS has also overseen various benefits programs, and enforces portions of the Affordable Care Act.

Exam Probability: **Low**

13. *Answer choices:*

(see index for correct answer)

- a. Federal Deposit Insurance Corporation
- b. Municipal Securities Rulemaking Board
- c. Securities Investor Protection Corporation
- d. U.S. Securities and Exchange Commission

Guidance: level 1

:: Management accounting ::

In business, a _____ is a division that gains revenue from product sales or service provided. The manager in _____ is accountable for revenue only.

Exam Probability: **Low**

14. *Answer choices:*

(see index for correct answer)

- a. Institute of Cost and Management Accountants of Bangladesh
- b. Management accounting in supply chains
- c. Revenue center
- d. Cost accounting

Guidance: level 1

:: ::

A _____ is an entity that owes a debt to another entity. The entity may be an individual, a firm, a government, a company or other legal person. The counterparty is called a creditor. When the counterpart of this debt arrangement is a bank, the _____ is more often referred to as a borrower.

Exam Probability: **Medium**

15. *Answer choices:*

(see index for correct answer)

- a. functional perspective
- b. surface-level diversity
- c. Character
- d. Debtor

Guidance: level 1

:: Management ::

_____ is a style of business management that focuses on identifying and handling cases that deviate from the norm, recommended as best practice by the project management method PRINCE2.

Exam Probability: **High**

16. *Answer choices:*

(see index for correct answer)

- a. Critical management studies
- b. Management by exception
- c. Marketing plan
- d. The Toyota Way

Guidance: level 1

:: ::

The _____ is an American stock exchange located at 11 Wall Street, Lower Manhattan, New York City, New York. It is by far the world's largest stock exchange by market capitalization of its listed companies at US$30.1 trillion as of February 2018. The average daily trading value was approximately US$169 billion in 2013. The NYSE trading floor is located at 11 Wall Street and is composed of 21 rooms used for the facilitation of trading. A fifth trading room, located at 30 Broad Street, was closed in February 2007. The main building and the 11 Wall Street building were designated National Historic Landmarks in 1978.

Exam Probability: **Low**

17. *Answer choices:*

(see index for correct answer)

- a. Sarbanes-Oxley act of 2002
- b. co-culture
- c. imperative
- d. Character

Guidance: level 1

:: Land value taxation ::

_____ , sometimes referred to as dry _____ , is the solid surface of Earth that is not permanently covered by water. The vast majority of human activity throughout history has occurred in _____ areas that support agriculture, habitat, and various natural resources. Some life forms have developed from predecessor species that lived in bodies of water.

Exam Probability: **Medium**

18. *Answer choices:*

(see index for correct answer)

- a. Henry George
- b. Physiocracy
- c. Land value tax
- d. Prosper Australia

Guidance: level 1

:: ::

A _____ is an individual or institution that legally owns one or more shares of stock in a public or private corporation. _____ s may be referred to as members of a corporation. Legally, a person is not a _____ in a corporation until their name and other details are entered in the corporation's register of _____ s or members.

Exam Probability: **High**

19. *Answer choices:*

(see index for correct answer)

- a. similarity-attraction theory
- b. corporate values
- c. Shareholder
- d. deep-level diversity

Guidance: level 1

:: Cash flow ::

_____ s are narrowly interconnected with the concepts of value, interest rate and liquidity. A _____ that shall happen on a future day tN can be transformed into a _____ of the same value in t0.

Exam Probability: **Medium**

20. *Answer choices:*

(see index for correct answer)

- a. Valuation using discounted cash flows
- b. First Chicago Method
- c. Cash carrier
- d. Cash flow

Guidance: level 1

_____ is the collection of mechanisms, processes and relations by which corporations are controlled and operated. Governance structures and principles identify the distribution of rights and responsibilities among different participants in the corporation and include the rules and procedures for making decisions in corporate affairs. _____ is necessary because of the possibility of conflicts of interests between stakeholders, primarily between shareholders and upper management or among shareholders.

Exam Probability: **High**

21. *Answer choices:*

(see index for correct answer)

- a. Character
- b. similarity-attraction theory
- c. process perspective
- d. corporate values

Guidance: level 1

:: Accounting source documents ::

A _____ is a commercial document and first official offer issued by a buyer to a seller indicating types, quantities, and agreed prices for products or services. It is used to control the purchasing of products and services from external suppliers. _____ s can be an essential part of enterprise resource planning system orders.

Exam Probability: **Low**

22. *Answer choices:*

(see index for correct answer)

- a. Purchase order
- b. Parcel audit
- c. Invoice
- d. Air waybill

Guidance: level 1

:: Generally Accepted Accounting Principles ::

_____ is the accounting classification of an account. It is part of double-entry book-keeping technique.

Exam Probability: **Medium**

23. *Answer choices:*

(see index for correct answer)

- a. deferred revenue
- b. Normal balance
- c. Cost principle
- d. Generally Accepted Accounting Practice

Guidance: level 1

:: Corporate governance ::

The _____ is the officer of a company that has primary responsibility for managing the company's finances, including financial planning, management of financial risks, record-keeping, and financial reporting. In some sectors, the CFO is also responsible for analysis of data. Some CFOs have the title CFOO for chief financial and operating officer. In the United Kingdom, the typical term for a CFO is finance director . The CFO typically reports to the chief executive officer and the board of directors and may additionally have a seat on the board.The CFO supervises the finance unit and is the chief financial spokesperson for the organization. The CFO directly assists the chief operating officer on all strategic and tactical matters relating to budget management, cost–benefit analysis, forecasting needs, and securing of new funding.

Exam Probability: **Low**

24. *Answer choices:*

(see index for correct answer)

- a. Chief learning officer

- b. Proxy firm
- c. Chief financial officer
- d. King II

Guidance: level 1

:: United States federal income tax ::

Under United States tax law, the _____ is a dollar amount that non-itemizers may subtract from their income before income tax is applied. Taxpayers may choose either itemized deductions or the _____ , but usually choose whichever results in the lesser amount of tax payable. The _____ is available to US citizens and aliens who are resident for tax purposes and who are individuals, married persons, and heads of household. The _____ is based on filing status and typically increases each year. It is not available to nonresident aliens residing in the United States . Additional amounts are available for persons who are blind and/or are at least 65 years of age.

Exam Probability: **Medium**

25. *Answer choices:*

(see index for correct answer)

- a. 988 transaction
- b. Rate schedule
- c. Physical presence test
- d. Filing status

Guidance: level 1

:: Accounting software ::

_____ describes a type of application software that records and processes accounting transactions within functional modules such as accounts payable, accounts receivable, journal, general ledger, payroll, and trial balance. It functions as an accounting information system. It may be developed in-house by the organization using it, may be purchased from a third party, or may be a combination of a third-party application software package with local modifications. _____ may be on-line based, accessed anywhere at any time with any device which is Internet enabled, or may be desktop based. It varies greatly in its complexity and cost.

Exam Probability: **High**

26. *Answer choices:*
(see index for correct answer)

- a. Accounting software
- b. DHPOS
- c. Passport Software
- d. Tolerance group

Guidance: level 1

:: Accounting software ::

_____ is an accounting software package developed and marketed by Intuit. _____ products are geared mainly toward small and medium-sized businesses and offer on-premises accounting applications as well as cloud-based versions that accept business payments, manage and pay bills, and payroll functions.

Exam Probability: **High**

27. *Answer choices:*

(see index for correct answer)

- a. Invoiceit
- b. Boeing Calc
- c. Passport Software
- d. BIG4books

Guidance: level 1

:: Income ::

_____ is a ratio between the net profit and cost of investment resulting from an investment of some resources. A high ROI means the investment's gains favorably to its cost. As a performance measure, ROI is used to evaluate the efficiency of an investment or to compare the efficiencies of several different investments. In purely economic terms, it is one way of relating profits to capital invested. _____ is a performance measure used by businesses to identify the efficiency of an investment or number of different investments.

28. *Answer choices:*

(see index for correct answer)

- a. Return on investment
- b. Salary inversion
- c. Per capita income
- d. Property investment calculator

Guidance: level 1

:: Management accounting ::

_____ is an approach to determine a product's life-cycle cost which should be sufficient to develop specified functionality and quality, while ensuring its desired profit. It involves setting a target cost by subtracting a desired profit margin from a competitive market price. A target cost is the maximum amount of cost that can be incurred on a product, however, the firm can still earn the required profit margin from that product at a particular selling price. _____ decomposes the target cost from product level to component level. Through this decomposition, _____ spreads the competitive pressure faced by the company to product's designers and suppliers. _____ consists of cost planning in the design phase of production as well as cost control throughout the resulting product life cycle. The cardinal rule of _____ is to never exceed the target cost. However, the focus of _____ is not to minimize costs, but to achieve a desired level of cost reduction determined by the _____ process.

29. *Answer choices:*

(see index for correct answer)

- a. Target costing
- b. Hedge accounting
- c. Cost driver
- d. Overhead

Guidance: level 1

:: Generally Accepted Accounting Principles ::

_____ is all a person's receipts and gains from all sources, before any deductions. The adjective "gross", as opposed to "net", generally qualifies a word referring to an amount, value, weight, number, or the like, specifying that necessary deductions have not been taken into account.

Exam Probability: **High**

30. *Answer choices:*

(see index for correct answer)

- a. Fixed investment
- b. Engagement letter
- c. Financial position of the United States
- d. Gross income

:: Financial ratios ::

_____ is a measure of how revenue growth translates into growth in operating income. It is a measure of leverage, and of how risky, or volatile, a company's operating income is.

Exam Probability: **Low**

31. *Answer choices:*
(see index for correct answer)

- a. Envy ratio
- b. Implied multiple
- c. Operating leverage
- d. Dividend yield

:: ::

_____ is the field of accounting concerned with the summary, analysis and reporting of financial transactions related to a business. This involves the preparation of financial statements available for public use. Stockholders, suppliers, banks, employees, government agencies, business owners, and other stakeholders are examples of people interested in receiving such information for decision making purposes.

Exam Probability: **Medium**

32. *Answer choices:*

(see index for correct answer)

- a. Financial accounting
- b. imperative
- c. levels of analysis
- d. surface-level diversity

Guidance: level 1

:: Management accounting ::

_____ is a method of identifying and evaluating activities that a business performs, using activity-based costing to carry out a value chain analysis or a re-engineering initiative to improve strategic and operational decisions in an organization.

Exam Probability: **Medium**

33. *Answer choices:*

(see index for correct answer)

- a. Institute of Cost and Management Accountants of Bangladesh
- b. Direct material total variance
- c. Owner earnings
- d. Overhead

Guidance: level 1

:: Management accounting ::

The _____ is a professional membership organization headquartered in Montvale, New Jersey, United States, operating in four global regions: The Americas, Asia/Pacific, Europe, and Middle East/India.

Exam Probability: **Medium**

34. *Answer choices:*

(see index for correct answer)

- a. Accounting management
- b. Institute of Management Accountants
- c. Construction accounting
- d. Corporate travel management

Guidance: level 1

:: Accounting systems ::

In accounting, the controlling account is an account in the general ledger for which a corresponding subsidiary ledger has been created. The subsidiary ledger allows for tracking transactions within the controlling account in more detail. Individual transactions are posted both to the controlling account and the corresponding subsidiary ledger, and the totals for both are compared when preparing a trial balance to ensure accuracy.

Exam Probability: **High**

35. *Answer choices:*

(see index for correct answer)

- a. Substance over form
- b. Control account
- c. Accounting practice
- d. Single-entry bookkeeping

Guidance: level 1

:: Marketing ::

_____ or stock is the goods and materials that a business holds for the ultimate goal of resale .

36. *Answer choices:*

(see index for correct answer)

- a. Mass-market theory
- b. Inventory
- c. Field marketing
- d. Buy one, get one free

Guidance: level 1

:: Management accounting ::

In _____ or managerial accounting, managers use the provisions of accounting information in order to better inform themselves before they decide matters within their organizations, which aids their management and performance of control functions.

Exam Probability: **Medium**

37. *Answer choices:*

(see index for correct answer)

- a. Customer profitability
- b. Management accounting
- c. Invested capital

- d. Bridge life-cycle cost analysis

Guidance: level 1

:: Tax reform ::

_____ is the process of changing the way taxes are collected or managed by the government and is usually undertaken to improve tax administration or to provide economic or social benefits. _____ can include reducing the level of taxation of all people by the government, making the tax system more progressive or less progressive, or simplifying the tax system and making the system more understandable or more accountable.

Exam Probability: **Low**

38. *Answer choices:*

(see index for correct answer)

- a. 2006 Puerto Rico budget crisis
- b. Single tax
- c. Equity of condition
- d. Tax reform

Guidance: level 1

:: Management ::

Business _____ is a discipline in operations management in which people use various methods to discover, model, analyze, measure, improve, optimize, and automate business processes. BPM focuses on improving corporate performance by managing business processes. Any combination of methods used to manage a company's business processes is BPM. Processes can be structured and repeatable or unstructured and variable. Though not required, enabling technologies are often used with BPM.

Exam Probability: **Low**

39. *Answer choices:*
(see index for correct answer)

- a. Supply management
- b. Preparation
- c. Shamrock Organization
- d. Libertarian management

Guidance: level 1

:: Negotiable instrument law ::

_____ of a financial instrument, such as a cheque, is only a signature, not indicating the payee. The effect of this is that it is payable only to the bearer – legally, it transforms an order instrument into a bearer instrument . It is one of the types of endorsement of a negotiable instrument.

Exam Probability: **Low**

40. *Answer choices:*

(see index for correct answer)

- a. Holder in due course
- b. Blank endorsement
- c. Regulation CC
- d. Negotiable Instruments Act, 1881

Guidance: level 1

:: Management accounting ::

An _____ allows a company to provide a monetary value for items that make up their inventory. Inventories are usually the largest current asset of a business, and proper measurement of them is necessary to assure accurate financial statements. If inventory is not properly measured, expenses and revenues cannot be properly matched and a company could make poor business decisions.

Exam Probability: **High**

41. *Answer choices:*

(see index for correct answer)

- a. Investment center
- b. Fixed cost
- c. Inventory valuation
- d. Management accounting in supply chains

:: Budgets ::

A _____ is a financial plan for a defined period, often one year. It may also include planned sales volumes and revenues, resource quantities, costs and expenses, assets, liabilities and cash flows. Companies, governments, families and other organizations use it to express strategic plans of activities or events in measurable terms.

Exam Probability: **Low**

42. *Answer choices:*

(see index for correct answer)

- a. Zero-based budgeting
- b. Budget
- c. Zero deficit budget
- d. Performance-based budgeting

:: Accounting in the United States ::

Established in 1988, the _____ is a professional organization of fraud examiners. Its activities include producing fraud information, tools and training. The ACFE grants the professional designation of Certified Fraud Examiner. The ACFE is the world's largest anti-fraud organization and is a provider of anti-fraud training and education, with more than 85,000 members.

Exam Probability: **High**

43. *Answer choices:*

(see index for correct answer)

- a. Accounting Research Bulletins
- b. International Qualification Examination
- c. Association of Certified Fraud Examiners
- d. National Association of State Boards of Accountancy

Guidance: level 1

:: Financial accounting ::

A _____ is an ownership interest in a corporation with enough voting stock shares to prevail in any stockholders' motion. A majority of voting shares is always a _____ . When a party holds less than the majority of the voting shares, other present circumstances can be considered to determine whether that party is still considered to hold a controlling ownership interest.

Exam Probability: **High**

44. *Answer choices:*

(see index for correct answer)

- a. Holding gains
- b. Money measurement concept
- c. Controlling interest
- d. Accelerated depreciation

Guidance: level 1

:: ::

Accounts _____ is a legally enforceable claim for payment held by a business for goods supplied and/or services rendered that customers/clients have ordered but not paid for. These are generally in the form of invoices raised by a business and delivered to the customer for payment within an agreed time frame. Accounts _____ is shown in a balance sheet as an asset. It is one of a series of accounting transactions dealing with the billing of a customer for goods and services that the customer has ordered. These may be distinguished from notes _____ , which are debts created through formal legal instruments called promissory notes.

Exam Probability: **Low**

45. *Answer choices:*

(see index for correct answer)

- a. Receivable
- b. imperative

- c. cultural
- d. interpersonal communication

Guidance: level 1

:: Tax credits ::

A _____ is a tax incentive which allows certain taxpayers to subtract the amount of the credit they have accrued from the total they owe the state. It may also be a credit granted in recognition of taxes already paid or, as in the United Kingdom, a form of state support.

Exam Probability: **Medium**

46. *Answer choices:*

(see index for correct answer)

- a. Nonbusiness Energy Property Tax Credit
- b. Paradigm Partners
- c. Hope credit
- d. Tax credit

Guidance: level 1

:: Retail financial services ::

A _____ is a prepaid stored-value money card, usually issued by a retailer or bank, to be used as an alternative to cash for purchases within a particular store or related businesses. _____ s are also given out by employers or organizations as rewards or gifts. They may also be distributed by retailers and marketers as part of a promotion strategy, to entice the recipient to come in or return to the store, and at times such cards are called cash cards. _____ s are generally redeemable only for purchases at the relevant retail premises and cannot be cashed out, and in some situations may be subject to an expiry date or fees. American Express, MasterCard, and Visa offer generic _____ s which need not be redeemed at particular stores, and which are widely used for cashback marketing strategies. A feature of these cards is that they are generally anonymous and are disposed of when the stored value on a card is exhausted.

Exam Probability: **High**

47. *Answer choices:*

(see index for correct answer)

- a. Metropolitan Educational Enterprises
- b. Payments Council
- c. Merchant services
- d. Financial planner

Guidance: level 1

:: Generally Accepted Accounting Principles ::

In accounting, _____ , gross margin, sales profit, or credit sales is the difference between revenue and the cost of making a product or providing a service, before deducting overheads, payroll, taxation, and interest payments. This is different from operating profit . Gross margin is the term normally used in the U.S., while _____ is the more common usage in the UK and Australia.

Exam Probability: **High**

48. *Answer choices:*

(see index for correct answer)

- a. Gross profit
- b. Long-term liabilities
- c. Vendor-specific objective evidence
- d. Liability

Guidance: level 1

:: International trade ::

In finance, an _____ is the rate at which one currency will be exchanged for another. It is also regarded as the value of one country's currency in relation to another currency. For example, an interbank _____ of 114 Japanese yen to the United States dollar means that ¥114 will be exchanged for each US$1 or that US$1 will be exchanged for each ¥114. In this case it is said that the price of a dollar in relation to yen is ¥114, or equivalently that the price of a yen in relation to dollars is $1/114.

49. *Answer choices:*

(see index for correct answer)

- a. Exchange rate
- b. Portuguese India Armadas
- c. Trans-Atlantic trade
- d. Terms of trade

Guidance: level 1

:: ::

_____ is the process of making predictions of the future based on past and present data and most commonly by analysis of trends. A commonplace example might be estimation of some variable of interest at some specified future date. Prediction is a similar, but more general term. Both might refer to formal statistical methods employing time series, cross-sectional or longitudinal data, or alternatively to less formal judgmental methods. Usage can differ between areas of application: for example, in hydrology the terms "forecast" and "_____" are sometimes reserved for estimates of values at certain specific future times, while the term "prediction" is used for more general estimates, such as the number of times floods will occur over a long period.

Exam Probability: **Low**

50. *Answer choices:*

(see index for correct answer)

- a. Forecasting
- b. process perspective
- c. Character
- d. hierarchical

Guidance: level 1

:: Television terminology ::

A nonprofit organization , also known as a non-business entity, _____ organization, or nonprofit institution, is dedicated to furthering a particular social cause or advocating for a shared point of view. In economic terms, it is an organization that uses its surplus of the revenues to further achieve its ultimate objective, rather than distributing its income to the organization's shareholders, leaders, or members. Nonprofits are tax exempt or charitable, meaning they do not pay income tax on the money that they receive for their organization. They can operate in religious, scientific, research, or educational settings.

Exam Probability: **Low**

51. *Answer choices:*

(see index for correct answer)

- a. nonprofit
- b. multiplexing
- c. Not-for-profit
- d. Satellite television

:: ::

_____ is the income that is gained by governments through taxation. Taxation is the primary source of income for a state. Revenue may be extracted from sources such as individuals, public enterprises, trade, royalties on natural resources and/or foreign aid. An inefficient collection of taxes is greater in countries characterized by poverty, a large agricultural sector and large amounts of foreign aid.

Exam Probability: **High**

52. *Answer choices:*

(see index for correct answer)

- a. similarity-attraction theory
- b. deep-level diversity
- c. Character
- d. Sarbanes-Oxley act of 2002

:: Financial accounting ::

_____ in accounting is the process of treating investments in associate companies. Equity accounting is usually applied where an investor entity holds 20–50% of the voting stock of the associate company. The investor records such investments as an asset on its balance sheet. The investor's proportional share of the associate company's net income increases the investment , and proportional payments of dividends decrease it. In the investor's income statement, the proportional share of the investor's net income or net loss is reported as a single-line item.

Exam Probability: **Low**

53. *Answer choices:*

(see index for correct answer)

- a. Intellectual capital
- b. Hidden asset
- c. Fixed asset register
- d. Working capital

Guidance: level 1

:: Labor terms ::

_____ , often called DI or disability income insurance, or income protection, is a form of insurance that insures the beneficiary's earned income against the risk that a disability creates a barrier for a worker to complete the core functions of their work. For example, the worker may suffer from an inability to maintain composure in the case of psychological disorders or an injury, illness or condition that causes physical impairment or incapacity to work. It encompasses paid sick leave, short-term disability benefits , and long-term disability benefits . Statistics show that in the US a disabling accident occurs, on average, once every second. In fact, nearly 18.5% of Americans are currently living with a disability, and 1 out of every 4 persons in the US workforce will suffer a disabling injury before retirement.

Exam Probability: **Low**

54. *Answer choices:*

(see index for correct answer)

- a. Base period
- b. Indexation of contracts
- c. Disability insurance
- d. Absence rate

Guidance: level 1

:: Project management ::

_____ is the widespread practice of collecting information and attempting to spot a pattern. In some fields of study, the term " _____ " has more formally defined meanings.

55. *Answer choices:*

(see index for correct answer)

- a. Costab
- b. RationalPlan
- c. Scrumedge
- d. Front-end loading

Guidance: level 1

:: Value theory ::

Within philosophy, it can be known as ethics or axiology. Early philosophical investigations sought to understand good and evil and the concept of "the good". Today, much of _____ aspires to the scientifically empirical, recording what people do value and attempting to understand why they value it in the context of psychology, sociology, and economics.

Exam Probability: **Medium**

56. *Answer choices:*

(see index for correct answer)

- a. Subjective theory of value
- b. Law of value

- c. economic value
- d. Scarcity

Guidance: level 1

:: Financial ratios ::

Earnings per share is the monetary value of earnings per outstanding share of common stock for a company.

Exam Probability: **Medium**

57. *Answer choices:*
(see index for correct answer)

- a. Total revenue share
- b. Diluted earnings per share
- c. Return on capital
- d. Net interest spread

Guidance: level 1

:: Basic financial concepts ::

_____ is a sustained increase in the general price level of goods and services in an economy over a period of time. When the general price level rises, each unit of currency buys fewer goods and services; consequently, _____ reflects a reduction in the purchasing power per unit of money a loss of real value in the medium of exchange and unit of account within the economy. The measure of _____ is the _____ rate, the annualized percentage change in a general price index, usually the consumer price index, over time. The opposite of _____ is deflation.

Exam Probability: **Low**

58. *Answer choices:*

(see index for correct answer)

- a. Inflation
- b. Present value of benefits
- c. Base effect
- d. balloon payment

Guidance: level 1

:: Corporations law ::

_____ , also referred to as the certificate of incorporation or the corporate charter, are a document or charter that establishes the existence of a corporation in the United States and Canada. They generally are filed with the Secretary of State or other company registrar.

59. *Answer choices:*

(see index for correct answer)

- a. Articles of incorporation
- b. Quasi-foreign corporation
- c. Piercing the corporate veil
- d. Articles of Organization

Guidance: level 1

INDEX: Correct Answers

Foundations of Business

1. : Social responsibility

2. d: Six Sigma

3. b: Document

4. a: Net income

5. c: Firm

6. a: Comparative advantage

7. b: Brand

8. : Availability

9. a: Sustainability

10. : Balance sheet

11. d: Strategic planning

12. : Mission statement

13. b: Alliance

14. a: SWOT analysis

15. : Inventory

16. : Currency

17. : Corporate governance

18. c: Business plan

19. : Management system

20. d: Exchange rate

21. b: Procurement

22. a: Sales

23. d: Quality control

24. a: Meeting

25. : Analysis

26. a: Description

27. c: Interest

28. c: Board of directors

29. : Return on investment

30. a: Fixed cost

31. c: Reputation

32. c: Target market

33. d: Property

34. : E-commerce

35. a: Scheduling

36. c: Buyer

37. b: Arthur Andersen

38. c: Working capital

39. b: Office

40. c: Information

41. : Technology

42. a: Affirmative action

43. c: Industry

44. b: Stock exchange

45. d: Insurance

46. c: Corporation

47. c: American Express

48. a: Resource

49. c: Interest rate

50. a: Trade

51. c: Publicity

52. a: Authority

53. b: Career

54. b: Health

55. c: Marketing mix

56. d: Variable cost

57. a: Direct investment

58. a: Economic Development

59. : Advertising

Management

1. d: Resource

2. : Management process

3. b: Pension

4. : European Union

5. c: Gantt chart

6. c: Purchasing

7. a: Employee stock

8. c: Stereotype

9. a: Project management

10. : Management by objectives

11. : Ambiguity

12. b: Performance

13. : Ratio

14. d: American Express

15. a: Change management

16. : Brand

17. d: Size

18. a: Knowledge management

19. c: Job description

20. d: Certification

21. a: Reason

22. a: Free trade

23. c: Total quality management

24. a: Industry

25. b: Crisis

26. a: Market research

27. d: Workforce

28. : Variable cost

29. b: Brainstorming

30. : Organizational culture

31. b: Proactive

32. b: Grievance

33. a: Committee

34. : Labor force

35. b: Dilemma

36. c: Business plan

37. c: Business model

38. a: Autonomy

39. a: Specification

40. d: Interaction

41. b: Job satisfaction

42. b: Chief executive

43. : Entrepreneur

44. a: Expert

45. a: E-commerce

46. d: Logistics

47. b: Balanced scorecard

48. c: SWOT analysis

49. c: Virtual team

50. c: Overtime

51. d: Performance measurement

52. d: Incentive

53. d: Vertical integration

54. d: Sharing

55. a: Business process

56. c: Social loafing

57. a: Interview

58. d: Inspection

59. d: Joint venture

Business law

1. c: Administrative law

2. : Manufacturing

3. a: Affirmative action

4. b: Complaint

5. : Guarantee

6. d: Dividend

7. c: Stock

8. a: Berne Convention

9. c: Consumer Good

10. : Federal Arbitration Act

11. c: Requirements contract

12. a: Misrepresentation

13. : Credit

14. c: Uniform Electronic Transactions Act

15. a: Implied authority

16. c: Offeree

17. a: Merchant

18. b: Technology

19. a: Breach of contract

20. : Punitive

21. d: Rescind

22. d: Damages

23. d: Ratification

24. b: Option contract

25. : Consideration

26. d: Merger

27. a: Service mark

28. a: Marketing

29. b: Res ipsa

30. a: Arbitration

31. b: Reasonable person

32. a: Prohibition

33. c: Tangible

34. c: Wage

35. a: Warranty

36. : Partnership

37. c: First Amendment

38. c: Apparent authority

39. : Management

40. b: Contract law

41. a: Duty of care

42. a: Criminal procedure

43. : Petition

44. a: Industry

45. a: Assignee

46. a: Operation of law

47. d: Surety

48. d: Charter

49. a: Resource

50. c: Operating agreement

51. d: Bad faith

52. c: Mens rea

53. a: Subsidiary

54. d: Creditor

55. c: Contract Clause

56. c: Insurable interest

57. a: Trial

58. : Puffery

59. c: Lien

Finance

1. d: Wall Street

2. c: Cost of goods sold

3. a: Capital lease

4. d: Accounting method

5. c: Forward contract

6. b: Financial risk

7. : Present value

8. : Finance

9. a: Hedge

10. b: Trade

11. d: Risk premium

12. a: Consideration

13. a: Preference

14. a: Manufacturing

15. c: Volume

16. d: Periodic inventory

17. : Fiscal year

18. : Utility

19. c: Stock

20. c: Operating leverage

21. c: Adjusting entries

22. d: Expected return

23. : Contract

24. c: Asset

25. : Interest rate risk

26. a: Copyright

27. c: Managerial accounting

28. : Partnership

29. b: Schedule

30. : Rate of return

31. a: Free cash flow

32. b: Issuer

33. : Public company

34. d: Forecasting

35. b: Dividend yield

36. d: Good

37. : Inventory turnover

38. a: Fixed cost

39. c: Long-term liabilities

40. c: Return on investment

41. c: Ending inventory

42. b: Bank account

43. c: Net asset

44. : Yield to maturity

45. : Stock market

46. c: Face

47. b: Risk management

48. a: Pro forma

49. : WorldCom

50. c: Cash equivalent

51. b: Sinking fund

52. c: Variable Costing

53. b: Contribution margin

54. b: Petty cash

55. b: Investment

56. : Advertising

57. b: Debenture

58. a: Stock split

59. : Return on assets

Human resource management

1. b: Faragher v. City of Boca Raton

2. d: Training and development

3. a: Social media

4. : Recruitment advertising

5. a: Nearshoring

6. : Outplacement

7. : Organizational justice

8. c: Exit interview

9. a: Flexible spending account

10. c: Asset

11. : Asbestos

12. a: Best practice

13. d: Compensation and benefits

14. c: Meeting

15. a: Scientific management

16. c: Worker Adjustment and Retraining Notification Act

17. a: McDonnell Douglas Corp. v. Green

18. c: Job enlargement

19. : Profit sharing

20. d: Needs analysis

21. d: Onboarding

22. a: Six Sigma

23. d: Paid time off

24. a: Resignation

25. : Reinforcement

26. d: Independent contractor

27. a: Construct validity

28. b: Management

29. d: Career management

30. d: Culture shock

31. c: Trade union

32. b: Employee retention

33. b: Self-assessment

34. b: Industrial relations

35. a: Sexual orientation

36. b: Distance learning

37. : Recession

38. c: Overtime

39. c: Cost leadership

40. c: Drug test

41. b: Love contract

42. : Hostile work environment

43. b: Succession planning

44. c: Featherbedding

45. a: Strategic planning

46. d: Union shop

47. b: Pay grade

48. b: Meritor Savings Bank v. Vinson

49. a: Goal setting

50. d: Expert power

51. c: Executive search

52. c: Outsourcing

53. a: Local union

54. c: Delayering

55. : Coaching

56. b: Content validity

57. a: Ownership

58. a: Seniority

59. d: Expatriate

Information systems

1. b: Computer fraud

2. a: Privacy

3. a: Census

4. a: Supply chain management

5. c: Virtual reality

6. d: Strategic information system

7. a: First mover advantage

8. : COBIT

9. c: Extensible Markup Language

10. b: Network interface card

11. b: Data dictionary

12. d: System software

13. c: Statistics

14. b: Flash memory

15. d: Information governance

16. : Freemium

17. c: Government-to-government

18. c: Interview

19. d: E-commerce

20. a: Internet

21. c: Encryption

22. b: Drill down

23. a: Enterprise systems

24. c: Open source

25. d: Consumer-to-business

26. c: Information privacy

27. : Disintermediation

28. : Interactivity

29. c: Positioning system

30. d: Cybersquatting

31. c: Information

32. d: Business process

33. a: Outsourcing

34. d: Dimension

35. : Total cost

36. b: QR code

37. a: Decision support system

38. b: Diagram

39. b: Virtual world

40. b: Vulnerability

41. : Common Criteria

42. d: Innovation

43. b: Random access

44. d: Government-to-business

45. c: Automated teller machine

46. b: Second Life

47. c: Telnet

48. d: Data integrity

49. a: Mobile commerce

50. c: Data cleansing

51. b: Input device

52. a: Authentication protocol

53. b: Security management

54. a: Business model

55. d: Non-repudiation

56. b: Structured query language

57. d: Data visualization

58. : Keystroke dynamics

59. d: Query by Example

Marketing

1. d: Problem Solving

2. d: Loyalty program

3. d: Reinforcement

4. a: Social networking

5. : Information system

6. a: Personal selling

7. : Small business

8. d: Qualitative research

9. d: Leadership

10. a: Business-to-business

11. d: Health

12. a: Empowerment

13. a: Cooperative

14. c: Pricing

15. b: Brand equity

16. a: Billboard

17. c: Complaint

18. a: Marketing research

19. c: Infomercial

20. a: Relationship marketing

21. b: Sponsorship

22. c: Tangible

23. : Research and development

24. a: Mass marketing

25. c: Federal Trade Commission

26. : Advertising

27. b: Industry

28. d: Shares

29. b: Raw material

30. b: Trade association

31. b: Clayton Act

32. a: Convenience

33. c: Trial

34. a: Life

35. a: Need

36. d: Statistic

37. d: Target market

38. a: Customer experience

39. d: Comparative advertising

40. d: Perception

41. a: Committee

42. a: Gross domestic product

43. b: Security

44. : Property

45. b: Image

46. c: Bottom line

47. d: North American Free Trade Agreement

48. c: Exploratory research

49. d: Quantitative research

50. c: Partnership

51. c: Business marketing

52. c: Penetration pricing

53. b: Household

54. : Secondary data

55. b: Psychographic

56. c: Mass media

57. b: Fixed cost

58. b: Product manager

59. c: Product line

Manufacturing

1. b: Gantt chart

2. : Risk management

3. b: Ball

4. d: Certification

5. b: Quality costs

6. d: Value engineering

7. : Kaizen

8. b: Coating

9. a: Change control

10. : E-commerce

11. a: Aggregate planning

12. : Project management

13. c: Rolling Wave planning

14. a: Consensus

15. b: Cost estimate

16. a: Manufacturing

17. b: Heat exchanger

18. d: Quality by Design

19. : Waste

20. c: Histogram

21. : Sharing

22. c: Sensitivity analysis

23. : Supply chain management

24. c: Economic order quantity

25. c: Economies of scope

26. c: DMAIC

27. c: METRIC

28. a: Furnace

29. d: Electronic data interchange

30. b: Pattern

31. d: Flowchart

32. : Volume

33. d: Purchasing manager

34. a: Supply chain risk management

35. d: Quality management

36. : Quality assurance

37. b: Sony

38. d: Third-party logistics

39. b: Kanban

40. d: Water

41. a: Lead

42. b: Root cause

43. : Quality control

44. a: Credit

45. : Retail

46. : Process management

47. : Control chart

48. d: New product development

49. d: HEAT

50. : Materials management

51. d: Consortium

52. a: Malcolm Baldrige National Quality Award

53. : Stakeholder management

54. d: Supply chain

55. c: Assembly line

56. b: Resource allocation

57. d: Bill of materials

58. c: Quality policy

59. d: Cost reduction

Commerce

1. d: Market research

2. c: Property

3. c: Compromise

4. c: Productivity

5. d: Purchase order

6. c: Microsoft

7. : Stock

8. b: Authority

9. b: Competitor

10. d: Information technology

11. c: Quality control

12. c: Statutory law

13. c: Auction

14. b: Encryption

15. c: Commodity

16. a: Good

17. b: Household

18. d: Initiative

19. : Wall Street Journal

20. b: Return on investment

21. : Sexual harassment

22. : Value-added network

23. c: Appeal

24. c: GeoCities

25. : Direct marketing

26. : Welfare

27. : Trade

28. a: Control system

29. a: DigiCash

30. c: Liquidation

31. d: Evaluation

32. c: Total cost

33. b: Shareholder

34. : Competitive advantage

35. : Economics

36. b: Phishing

37. c: Wage

38. c: Minimum wage

39. b: Marketing mix

40. a: Tariff

41. b: Tourism

42. a: Short run

43. : Quality management

44. : Authorize.Net

45. d: Aid

46. : Automated Clearing House

47. a: Corporation

48. b: Market share

49. d: Advertisement

50. c: Case study

51. c: Inflation

52. d: Reverse auction

53. d: Product mix

54. : Market structure

55. a: Bill of lading

56. : Project

57. a: Financial services

58. b: Negotiation

59. b: Pizza Hut

Business ethics

1. a: Clayton Act

2. c: Global Fund

3. : Interlocking directorate

4. a: Copyright

5. d: Ethical leadership

6. b: Labor relations

7. : Pure Food and Drug Act

8. : Medicaid

9. a: Feedback

10. b: Insider trading

11. d: Whistleblower

12. b: Oil spill

13. c: Fraud

14. d: Social networking

15. b: Environmental audit

16. a: Real estate

17. c: Socialism

18. d: Criminal law

19. b: Risk assessment

20. b: Volcker Rule

21. d: Greenwashing

22. b: Chamber of Commerce

23. d: Exxon Valdez

24. d: Cultural relativism

25. c: New Deal

26. : Supply Chain

27. c: Arthur Andersen

28. : Fannie Mae

29. b: Right to work

30. b: Utopian socialism

31. b: Dual relationship

32. c: Executive compensation

33. : ExxonMobil

34. c: Medicare fraud

35. : Coal

36. b: Community development financial institution

37. b: Cause-related marketing

38. a: Federal Trade Commission

39. : Stanford International Bank

40. d: Solar power

41. d: Global reach

42. c: Corporate social responsibility

43. : Layoff

44. a: Constitutional law

45. a: Transformational leadership

46. d: Consumer Protection

47. b: Workplace bullying

48. : Employee Polygraph Protection Act

49. c: Forest Stewardship Council

50. a: Lead

51. b: Organizational ethics

52. b: Risk management

53. d: Great Depression

54. b: European Commission

55. c: Dress code

56. d: Catholicism

57. c: Planet

58. d: Occupational Safety and Health Administration

59. a: Guerrilla Marketing

Accounting

1. c: Resource allocation

2. b: Balanced scorecard

3. : Error

4. a: Cost of goods available for sale

5. a: Embezzlement

6. b: Long-term liabilities

7. c: Financial analysis

8. b: Adjusting entries

9. b: Ledger

10. : Inventory control

11. c: Annual report

12. : S corporation

13. : Internal Revenue Service

14. c: Revenue center

15. d: Debtor

16. b: Management by exception

17. : New York Stock Exchange

18. : Land

19. c: Shareholder

20. d: Cash flow

21. : Corporate governance

22. a: Purchase order

23. b: Normal balance

24. c: Chief financial officer

25. : Standard deduction

26. a: Accounting software

27. : QuickBooks

28. a: Return on investment

29. a: Target costing

30. d: Gross income

31. c: Operating leverage

32. a: Financial accounting

33. : Activity-based management

34. b: Institute of Management Accountants

35. b: Control account

36. b: Inventory

37. b: Management accounting

38. d: Tax reform

39. : Process Management

40. b: Blank endorsement

41. c: Inventory valuation

42. b: Budget

43. c: Association of Certified Fraud Examiners

44. c: Controlling interest

45. a: Receivable

46. d: Tax credit

47. : Gift card

48. a: Gross profit

49. a: Exchange rate

50. a: Forecasting

51. c: Not-for-profit

52. : Tax revenue

53. : Equity method

54. c: Disability insurance

55. : Trend analysis

56. : Value theory

57. b: Diluted earnings per share

58. a: Inflation

59. a: Articles of incorporation

CPSIA information can be obtained
at www.ICGtesting.com
Printed in the USA
LVHW101057301019
635717LV00003B/248/P